# PLAYBOY'S GOURMET
## BY THOMAS MARIO

Everything you need to know to prepare perfect meals·

A PLAYBOY PRESS BOOK

# Contents

PREFACE     5

HAPPY HORS D'OEUVRES!     6

BEAUTIFUL SOUP     18

A GOOD EGG     31

LET 'EM EAT PANCAKES     45

FISHING FOR COMPLIMENTS     52

LONG LIVE THE LOBSTER     65

CONSIDER THE CRAB     74

SHRIMPS SUPREME     79

HAPPY AS A CLAM     87

THE OPULENT OYSTER     94

THE WORTHY ROAST     102

CHOP TALK     115

THE STALWART STEAK     122

VARIATIONS ON VEAL     140

THE HEARTY HAM     149

BURGERMASTERY     159

LET'S STEW IT     168

THE GOURMET GOBBLER     176

FAIR GAME     182

THE SECRETS OF SAUCERY     193

THE LIFE OF SPICE 203

THE VEGETABLE KINGDOM 210

SALAD DAYS 218

SATURNALIAN SWEETS 232

CREME DE LA CREME 242

CAFE OLE! 249

INDEX 257

# Preface

What's your pleasure? Charcoal steaks blushing pink inside . . . mouth-watering supreme of chicken with béarnaise sauce . . . beef-and-kidney pie as robust as Henry VIII? Or the "wild" taste of wild game done to a turn? Perhaps such succulent delicacies from the sea as the kingly oyster, lobster handsomely dressed in a sumptuous sauce or Alaskan crab, cold and cracked?

Whatever manly fare suits your fancy, PLAYBOY's Food and Drink Editor and celebrated *chef de cuisine* Thomas Mario has prepared a book that makes it all as easy as whipping up a drink. And *Playboy's Gourmet* is designed especially for the man who likes to take over—whether at hearth or hibachi. Hearty and masculine from cover to cover, it banishes the curlicue carrot, the dainty delectables and soggy salads and brings back the lusty life!

You'll find helpful hints for preparing an impressive repast—from hors d'oeuvres through soup, fish, meat and salad to dessert and coffee—plus a vast number of toothsome recipes calculated to make you the host supreme. Try them and see if you don't enjoy the satisfaction of having your appetite whetted by well-deserved compliments.

—the editors of PLAYBOY

# Happy Hors d'Oeuvres!

Dictionarily, an hors d'oeuvre is "a relish or appetizer, served usually at the beginning of a meal." When owners of public eating places talk about hors d'oeuvres, they may mean anything from an anchovy to the Continental hors d'oeuvre wagon or even smorgasbord. In popular parlance, however, the phrase has come to mean simply something that people eat while they drink. Assembling the hors d'oeuvre platter is one of the nation's most active indoor sports. It's impossible to imagine a properly arranged office shindig, fraternity affair, New Year's Eve party or just a crowd around a punch bowl without a display of canapés, dips and dunks. What follows, therefore, is a table of tips to help you make sure *your* hors d'oeuvres turn out to be chefs d'oeuvre.

Eye appeal is, of course, of immediate importance, but—and *nota bene*—it should be the appeal that comes from the natural sight of good food, freshly unpacked, cooked or sliced. Just to see a pound of Nova Scotia salmon, for instance, sliced thin, dripping its copper-tinted fat on the platter on which it's placed, will tease many appetites into instant awakening.

There are a number of classical delicacies that men have always regarded as perfect hors d'oeuvres, and the bachelor chef could hardly do better than to employ these great old standbys. The first that comes to mind is oysters on the half shell. The secret of their cold, tangy goodness? Simple freshness. Oysters must be alive when they're opened, and they must be kept ice-cold or they won't stay alive. At large blowouts,

6

oysters aren't too practical, since they must be opened to order. If, however, you learn how to use an oyster knife or if you own a mechanical oyster opener, you can serve the plump bivalves to a large company and they'll complement any drink.

Certainly it would be hard to top pâté de foie gras as an appetizer. Anybody who's eaten it fresh in France or imported in terrines recognizes the real foie gras for a certain seraphic richness. Finally, there's the aristocrat of them all, fresh beluga caviar. The genuine beluga contains no added salt, and yet it has a deep-sea saltiness along with a curious kind of mildness. When you taste the pearl-gray eggs, soft and crisp at the same time, you wonder how something so mild could so strongly stir the taste buds. Unfortunately, the price of fresh beluga caviar, about three times the price of the best Scotch, has always had a slightly deterrent effect on holiday purse strings. But there are hundreds of other wonderful hors d'oeuvres, including a wide variety of slightly salted caviars, and when carefully chosen and set up, they make the martini martinier and turn the champagne into nectar.

A good hors d'oeuvre should harmonize with the type of drinks served. For example, if you offer your friends a tray of rum cocktails or tequila, the Mexican avocado puree called guacamole would be naturally felicitous. Thin slices of Genoa salami, in other circumstances a fine hors d'oeuvre, would be out of place. But no strict ukase need govern your choice. A mixture of Cheddar cheese and brandy goes well with almost any kind of bar offering from aquavit to vermouth. Drinkers of dry potables such as gin and vodka are always happily disposed toward herring fillets and sundry other salty snacks. So, unless you're serving every concoction in *The Official Mixer's Manual,* don't offer the conventional indiscriminate tray of hors d'oeuvres. Make the variety fit the drinks.

Be sure that the canapé carriers are oven-fresh and crisp. If necessary to restore their freshness, place them in a very slow oven, 250 degrees, 20 to 30 minutes. For dipping into cocktail spreads, you want small vehicles that won't break and that are delicately neutral in flavor. Be sure the butter used is the best, 93 score, unsalted and freshly unwrapped.

At many parties the overdressed platter of canapés is being replaced more and more frequently with the compartmental hors d'oeuvre dish or lazy Susan for self-service. It's child's play to take care of such an assortment, but the display shouldn't remain untended too long when the whoop-de-do is at its height. Dishes should be refilled as often as necessary, and the edges should be kept neat. Table livery such as linen, silver, cocktail spears, cocktail napkins, etc., should be thoughtfully chosen and arranged with taste.

Perhaps the easiest and most impressive of all hors d'oeuvres for intimate parties is the whole article of food, such as a large, well-aged Gouda cheese, a smoked turkey or a smoked ham; you can buy the latter completely cooked and glazed. Such centers of attention should be placed on a large carving board flanked with appropriate carving knife, meat fork or cheese scoop, as well as a large basket filled with thin slices of French bread, salt rye bread or cocktail-size pumpernickel rounds.

When, in his *Canterbury Tales,* Chaucer speaks of "the hors that hadde winges for to flee," he refers, of course, to "The Pegasee." But try the following hors and see if they don't have the wings it takes to get your drinking off the ground.

## LOBSTER PATE
### (About 1¼ cups)

*1  boiled fresh lobster, about 1½ lbs. raw*
*½  cup celery cut into small dice*
*3  tablespoons butter at room temperature*
*2  tablespoons mayonnaise*
*½  teaspoon lemon juice*
*¼  teaspoon onion salt*
*⅛  teaspoon Worcestershire sauce*
*2  tablespoons dry sherry*
*1  dash white pepper*

Remove all meat from lobster, discarding sac in back of head. Cut the meat into cubes about ¼ inch thick, but don't discard the green liver or coral roe, if any. Put lobster and celery through an electric meat grinder, using the finest blade. Add all other ingredients and mix well. Chill in the refrigerator.

## BRANDIED CHEDDAR SPREAD
(About 2 cups)

1 lb. sharp Cheddar cheese
⅓ cup brandy
3 tablespoons butter at room temperature
2 tablespoons heavy cream
1 dash nutmeg
1 dash cayenne pepper

Put the cheese through a meat grinder, using the finest blade. Combine in a mixing bowl with all other ingredients and mix well. Chill in the refrigerator and remove about a half hour before serving so the cheese may be spread easily. A good bourbon may be substituted for brandy with excellent results.

## GUACAMOLE WITH BACON
(About 2 cups)

2 cups mashed avocado
2 tablespoons lime juice
1 teaspoon grated onion
2 teaspoons olive oil
8 drops Tabasco sauce
½ teaspoon salt
¼ teaspoon monosodium glutamate
4 slices bacon

Buy two large, ripe avocados. Cut them in half, remove seed and scoop out meat with a spoon. Puree the avocado meat in a blender or meat grinder or force it through a large fine wire strainer. (When ripe, avocados are easy to puree by hand.) As soon as the 2 cups are mashed, combine with the lime juice, onion, olive oil, Tabasco sauce, salt and monosodium glutamate. Put the bacon into a cold frying pan and heat over a moderate flame, turning frequently, until bacon is crisp. Drain, cut or crumble into very small pieces and add to the avocado mixture. Chill thoroughly. This is an excellent dip for scooping with shrimp chips.

## SOUR CREAM AND ANCHOVY DIP
(About 2 cups)

*1 2-oz. can rolled anchovies with capers*
*¼ medium-size green pepper*
*1 cup sour cream*
*½ lb. cream cheese at room temperature*
*2 tablespoons finely chopped scallions or chives*
*4 drops Tabasco sauce*

Drain oil off anchovies and chop very fine with green pepper. In a mixing bowl, combine all ingredients and stir thoroughly until well blended. No lumps of cream cheese should appear. Chill well.

## SHRIMP CANAPES, CURRY BUTTER
(About 30)

*1 lb. (approximately 30) shrimps*
*Juice of ¼ lemon*
*½ cup sweet butter at room temperature*
*2 teaspoons curry powder*
*½ teaspoon ground coriander*
*Melba-toast rounds*
*Salt and white pepper*
*2 tablespoons finely chopped chives*

Peel the raw shrimps, removing vein in back. (This will cause them to curl into a compact round shape, best for this type of canapé.) In a heavy pot, bring 1 cup water to a rapid boil. Add ½ teaspoon salt, the lemon juice and the shrimps. Cook covered about 5 minutes. Drain and chill thoroughly. Combine the butter, curry powder and coriander; blend well. Spread thickly on the toast and place a shrimp on each round. Sprinkle lightly with salt, white pepper and chopped chives.

## HAM AND MUSHROOM CANAPES
(About 30)

*¼ lb. fresh mushrooms*
*½ cup red-wine vinegar*
*⅓ cup olive oil*

*1 medium-size onion, sliced*
*¼ teaspoon salt*
*½ cup sweet butter at room temperature*
*3 tablespoons mild prepared mustard*
*Cocktail crackers, square-shaped*
*½ lb. sliced boiled ham*
*3 tablespoons finely chopped parsley*

The mushrooms should be firm and white, with tight-fitting caps. Wash them; cut vertically into thin slices, none larger than the canapé base used. Place in a salad bowl with the vinegar, olive oil, onion and salt and marinate overnight. Combine the butter and mustard, mixing well, and spread on the canapé crackers. Cut the ham into small pieces carefully, to fit each canapé with no ragged edges, and place on the buttered canapé crackers. Drain the mushrooms, arrange on the ham and sprinkle with the chopped parsley.

## SCALLOP CANAPES, HORSERADISH BUTTER
(About 30)

*1 lb. fresh sea scallops*
*½ cup lime juice*
*½ cup sweet butter at room temperature*
*3 tablespoons prepared horseradish*
*Round cocktail crackers or melba toast*
*Salt and white pepper*
*2 tablespoons chopped chives or scallions*

Wash the scallops well and slice each one crosswise to make round pieces for fitting on the cocktail crackers; there should be approximately 30 pieces. Marinate in the lime juice overnight. During this time the scallops will become "cooked," or pickled, by the acid juice. Combine the butter and horseradish, mixing well, and spread on the cocktail crackers. Drain the scallops. Place one on each round and sprinkle lightly with salt, white pepper and chopped chives or scallions.

## HOT CHICKEN TARTLETS
### (24 pieces)

*1 cup finely diced boiled chicken*
*¼ cup condensed cream of chicken soup, undiluted*
*2 tablespoons mayonnaise*
*1 tablespoon bourbon*
*1 tablespoon sherry*
*¼ teaspoon freshly ground black pepper*
*⅛ teaspoon salt*
*24 small tartlet shells, holding about 1 tablespoon each*
*Paprika*

Be sure the chicken is free of all fat, skin or bones before dicing. In a mixing bowl, combine the chicken, cream of chicken soup, mayonnaise, bourbon, sherry, pepper and salt. (Be sure the pepper is freshly ground, since it's the ingredient that gives this appetizer its zip.) Mix well and fill the tartlet shells with the mixture. Sprinkle lightly with paprika. Place the filled shells in a shallow pan or pie plate and bake in a preheated oven at 375° about 10 minutes or until tops are browned.

Shrimp, lobster or crab meat, cooked, freed of all bones or shell and finely diced, may be used in place of chicken, in which case use condensed shrimp bisque instead of chicken soup.

## GARLIC OLIVES

*1 4¾-oz. jar extra-large or stuffed green olives*
*¼ cup olive oil*
*2 large cloves garlic, smashed*

Drain olives and put into a bowl with olive oil and garlic. (To smash garlic, place it on a cutting board, rest the flat side of a heavy knife against the garlic and hit the knife sharply. Remove the skin before placing garlic in bowl.) Cover. Place in the refrigerator and marinate at least 4 hours before serving. If the olives are marinated overnight, the flavor will be even more zestful. Remove the garlic before serving. (Increase ingredients proportionately according to the number of guests expected.)

## STUFFED DEVILED EGGS
### (About 12)

*6 eggs*
*¼ cup butter at room temperature*
*2 tablespoons mayonnaise*
*1 teaspoon prepared mustard*
*½ teaspoon dry mustard*
*¼ teaspoon onion salt*
*⅛ teaspoon pepper*
*1 tablespoon prepared anchovy paste*
*¼ teaspoon lemon juice*

Boil eggs 8 to 10 minutes; then chill. Remove shells from eggs and cut the eggs in half lengthwise. Carefully remove the yolks from the whites. Force the yolks through a fine wire sieve into a mixing bowl. Add the butter, mayonnaise, prepared and dry mustard, onion salt, pepper, prepared anchovy paste and lemon juice. Mix until very well blended. Refill whites with yolk mixture, using a pastry tube if one is handy, otherwise a spoon or small spatula. Chill thoroughly before serving.

## HERB BUTTER
### (½ cup)

*¼ lb. unsalted butter*
*2 teaspoons finely minced fresh chives*
*¼ teaspoon dried chervil*
*¼ teaspoon ground coriander*

Let butter stand at room temperature until soft enough to spread easily. Add the chives, chervil and coriander and mix thoroughly with rubber spatula. Place in refrigerator, tightly covered, and let stand for at least 2 hours for the flavors to ripen. Spread generously on canapé wafers, thin-sliced rye bread or toast. Top with sliced canned ham or with small cornucopias of prosciutto ham; then cut into small sections and serve at the martini hour.

## SHRIMP AND FENNEL SPREAD
### (About 2¼ cups)

*1 lb. fresh shrimps, boiled*
*2 cups fennel (anise) cut into ½-inch squares*
*¼ cup butter at room temperature*
*⅓ cup mayonnaise*
*4 teaspoons lemon juice*
*1 teaspoon salt*
*½ teaspoon monosodium glutamate*
*4 drops Tabasco sauce*
*½ teaspoon Worcestershire sauce*

Remove shells and veins from shrimps. Put the shrimps and fennel through a meat grinder, using the medium blade. Combine with all other ingredients in a mixing bowl. Mix well and chill in the refrigerator.

## OYSTER PATE
### (About 1 cup)

*12 medium-size oysters, opened*
*¼ lb. cream cheese at room temperature*
*¼ teaspoon celery salt*
*¼ teaspoon Worcestershire sauce*
*¼ teaspoon onion salt*
*1 tablespoon dry sherry*

Examine oysters and remove any pieces of shell. Pat them with a paper towel to remove as much moisture as possible. Put the oysters, cream cheese and all other ingredients into a blending machine and mix at high speed until a smooth mixture is formed, stopping the machine, if necessary, to force the unchopped pieces of oyster toward the blending knives, using a rubber spatula. (The mixture will be quite soft when removed from the blending machine.) Chill, covered, at least a half day in the refrigerator and it will be firm enough to spread easily. This savory is especially tasteful when served with thin rye crackers or thin whole-wheat crackers.

## DEVILED HAM AND EGG SPREAD
### (About 1¼ cups)

*2 hard-boiled eggs*
*2 tablespoons prepared deviled Smithfield ham*

2 tablespoons butter at room temperature
2 tablespoons mayonnaise
1 teaspoon mild prepared mustard
1 teaspoon minced chives or scallions
½ teaspoon tarragon vinegar
⅛ teaspoon freshly ground black pepper

Cut the eggs lengthwise into eighths. Put the eggs and all other ingredients into a blending machine and mix at high speed until a smooth mixture is formed. If necessary, stop the machine and with a rubber spatula force the unmixed portions into the bottom of the well. Chill in the refrigerator.

## LIEDERKRANZ SPREAD
(About 1 cup)

1 4-oz. pkg. Liederkranz cheese
½ 3½-oz. bottle pickled cocktail onions
8 medium-size pimiento-stuffed olives
2 teaspoons vinegar from pickled onions

Put the cocktail onions and olives into an onion chopper; chop coarsely. Combine Liederkranz with chopped onion, chopped olives and vinegar from pickled onions. Mix thoroughly with a rubber spatula. Chill in the refrigerator 1 day before using.

## SWISS CHEESE AND KIRSCH SPREAD
(About 2 cups)

1 lb. natural Swiss cheese
¼ cup kirschwasser
¼ cup heavy sweet cream
¼ cup butter at room temperature
4 dashes Tabasco sauce
⅛ teaspoon white pepper
⅛ teaspoon garlic powder

Put the cheese through a meat grinder, using the fine blade. In a mixing bowl, combine the cheese with all other ingredients and mix well with a rubber spatula until well blended. Chill in the refrigerator. Remove from refrigerator about a half hour before serving so that the cheese may spread easily. The flavor will be better at room temperature.

## HOT SHRIMPS, MUSTARD BUTTER
### (Approximately 30 shrimps)

*1½ lbs. medium-size shrimps, cooked*
*¼ cup butter*
*1 tablespoon Bahamian mustard (other sharp mustard may be substituted)*
*1 tablespoon dry white wine*
*2 teaspoons finely chopped chives*
*¼ teaspoon salt*
*¼ teaspoon garlic powder*
*¼ teaspoon sugar*

Remove shells and veins from shrimps. Melt butter in a chafing dish over a low flame or in an electric skillet heated to 250°. Add mustard and mix well until mustard is thoroughly blended with butter. Add all other ingredients and heat slowly until shrimps are heated through and well coated with sauce. Keep warm over simmering water in bottom of chafing dish.

## BROILED OYSTERS WITH HAM
### (24 oysters)

*24 medium-size oysters, opened*
*Nutmeg*
*Celery salt*
*Bread crumbs*
*12 very thin medium-size slices prosciutto or Westphalian ham*

Examine oysters carefully and remove any loose pieces of shell. Drain on paper towels to remove excess liquid. Sprinkle lightly with nutmeg and celery salt and dip into bread crumbs. Cut each slice of ham in half and wrap a piece around each oyster, fastening with two toothpicks. Place the oysters in a shallow metal pan and broil under a preheated broiler flame about 2 minutes on each side. Remove toothpicks and insert clean ones before serving.

## HAM BEIGNETS, CHIVE DIP
### (12 to 15 pieces)

*1 cup water*
*2 tablespoons butter*
*½ teaspoon salt*

⅛ teaspoon nutmeg
½ cup cornmeal
½ cup all-purpose flour
4 eggs
1 cup ground cooked ham
Vegetable fat
1 cup mayonnaise
¼ cup sour cream
3 tablespoons minced chives or scallions

In a heavy saucepan, bring water to a boil. Add butter, salt and nutmeg. Stir until butter dissolves. Add cornmeal and flour. Stir vigorously until blended and remove from flame; the mixture will be very thick. Gradually stir in the unbeaten eggs one at a time, then the ham. Mix well and place in the refrigerator until cold. Melt fat to a depth of ¼ inch in an electric skillet set at 370°. Drop in cold batter by level teaspoonfuls. Fry, turning once, until brown on both sides and drain on absorbent paper. Mix mayonnaise with sour cream and chives and serve in a separate bowl.

## GRILLED SARDINES, WHITE-WINE BUTTER
(12 hot canapés)

1 3¼-oz. can boneless and skinless sardines
1 envelope instant minced onions
½ cup dry white wine
¼ cup butter at room temperature
3 slices white bread
Paprika

Carefully remove sardines from tin without breaking and split each lengthwise into two pieces. Soak the instant minced onions in the white wine for 5 minutes. Simmer over a slow flame until the wine is reduced to about 2 tablespoons. Let the wine mixture cool until it is nearly room temperature. Mix it thoroughly with the butter into a smooth paste. Toast the bread on one side only under a moderate broiler flame and arrange the sardines on the untoasted side, allowing four sardine halves to each piece of bread. Spread or brush the white-wine butter over the sardines. Sprinkle lightly with paprika and broil under a moderate broiler flame until edges of bread begin to brown.

# Beautiful Soup

When Alice in Wonderland requests a song of the Mock Turtle, that personage chooses to sing of:

> *"Beautiful soup! Who cares for fish,*
> *Game or any other dish? . . .*
> *Soup of the evening,*
> *    Beautiful soup!"*

There is a large body of men who share the Mock Turtle's enthusiasm. For what is so fine on a cold November day as a big bowl of piping-hot minestrone, fortified with pasta and vegetables, fragrant with the pungent aroma of freshly grated Romano cheese? Don't bother to answer.

Pity the poor soul who has not yet discovered soup. He is always searching for hors d'oeuvres, entrees, savories and Escoffier knows what else to pique his appetite. But your true soup man—ah! Let his nostrils tell him that an oversize pot of shrimp gumbo is simmering in the pantry and he will be bothered by no other fiddle-faddle.

These days, every soup maker must be prepared to defend his art against the challenge of thousands of canned, jarred, frozen and dehydrated potages that are stocked on shelves everywhere. The average man, in his kitchenless kitchen, is not likely to turn out such exotica as kangaroo soup or cream of snail soup with curry, but these, and others equally extraordinary, are now obtainable in gourmet shops. And even the proudest *chef de potage* will probably concede that several brands of cream of tomato soup, as well as some of the canned clear soups such as beef bouillon or clam madrilene, couldn't easily be improved upon. But for some reason, those soups that are neither cream soups nor clear bouillons, such as Philadelphia pepper pot or mulligatawny or *petite marmite*—the main-dish soups—don't seem to take kindly to the can; and it so happens that these hearty soups are the very ones that turn out to be the real attractions at today's informal buffet tables.

Beethoven once said, "Only the pure in heart can make a good soup." Whether you're cardiacally pristine or not, though, you can become a competent soup maker.

New cooks who are puzzled by the term *stock* should learn that it's merely the liquid which is produced when a food is cooked in water. To oversimplify perhaps a bit, if you boiled a turnip, the cooking liquid would be turnip stock. When you steam clams open, the juice that squirts out of the shells, as well as the water used in steaming, becomes clam broth or clam stock. Fresh stock is automatically created every time you boil poultry or meat. Thus, the stock for the most exquisite French soup, *petite marmite,* is the result of boiling chicken and beef in the same pot. When you cook a smoked beef tongue, the cooking liquid may later be used for a rich puree of split peas or lentil soup. Not all boiled meats produce a useful stock, however. When you simmer corned beef, the stock that's left is not useful in soup making—it's too salty.

All of these natural stocks will usually be enhanced by the addition of a few bouillon cubes or packets of powdered instant bouillon. Instant stocks, however, vary considerably in quality and strength. Some chicken cubes have a genuine chicken flavor; others are spurious. It's a good idea to experiment until you find a brand that suits you. Normally, you need four instant cubes or packets of powder to each quart of water to produce a good stock. When you use all bouillon cubes and water instead of a fresh stock, a few tablespoons of butter melted in the soup just before it's served will provide a certain meatlike mellowness.

A tip for those who would become soup men supreme: Don't drop chunks of vegetables into a pot. First of all, keep a steady eye on your French knife, and if you're cutting vegetables into half-inch dice, aim for the half-inch mark each time. Don't have some pieces of the same vegetable large and others small. In many recipes, the vegetables will be sautéed before the stock is added to the pot. This takes time, of course, but a sautéed onion has a richer flavor than a boiled onion, and this perceptible difference is later conveyed to the soup.

One or two marrowbones, sawed in half-inch pieces and added to any soup that is simmered for an hour or longer, will provide a hearty beef flavor.

In many of the recipes, a very small amount of flour will be added to the sautéed vegetables. The reason for this is not merely to make a thick soup thicker but to give the stock a certain body that would otherwise be missing. Also, in puree soups such as black bean, the small amount of added flour keeps the liquid part of the soup from separating from the heavier puree on the bottom of the pot or soup bowl.

Many a soup is impressively transformed simply by making a few last-minute additions before it's ladled into the tureen. Besides the butter added at the last moment, to which you've already been tipped, try such pepper-uppers as Worcestershire sauce, Tabasco sauce, cayenne pepper and monosodium glutamate, sprinkled in judiciously, to taste.

The following recipes, as indicated, are sufficient for four man-sized appetites—or eight of the other kind.

## PETITE MARMITE
### (Serves 4)

2 lbs. chuck of beef (in one piece)
1 small fowl
1 marrowbone
2 peeled whole onions
2 large fresh tomatoes
½ small white turnip
½ small parsnip
2 pieces celery
2 large carrots

1 teaspoon bouquet garni
2 teaspoons salt
1 wedge cabbage (enough for 1 pint
   when diced)
1 cup fresh or frozen peas
Bouillon cubes (optional)
Toasted French bread
Grated Parmesan cheese
Fresh chopped chives and chervil (optional)

(We're using the term *fowl* in the accepted poultry-buff sense, meaning a very tough old chicken. Unappetizing? Not at all. With long, slow cooking, it imparts that pronounced chicken flavor you need for a *marmite*.)

At a buffet table, the marmite (or pot) may be quite a large one, not petite at all. For individual service, however, the small earthenware crock is normally used. The fowl and boiled beef contribute their fine flavor to the soup but are not usually served in large quantity. Customarily, most of the fowl and beef is put aside after cooking and enlisted into service for a later meal—in a salad, hash or casserole.

Have the butcher split a marrowbone, removing marrow intact if possible. Into a large soup pot, put chuck, fowl, the marrowbone, onions, tomatoes, turnip, parsnip, celery, carrots and bouquet garni. Cover with cold water and add salt. Bring to a boil. Skim well. Reduce flame and simmer slowly until meat and fowl are almost done, about 2 hours. Add cabbage and cook until done. In a separate small pot, cook peas until done; then strain. Strain the soup. Cut carrots into crosswise sections. Cut cabbage into dice. Set carrots and cabbage aside. Discard the other whole vegetables cooked in the soup pot. Correct seasoning of strained broth, adding bouillon cubes if necessary. Cut the desired amounts of chicken breast and beef into small diamond-shaped pieces. Cut marrow into ½-inch pieces and cover with boiling water; then drain well. Among four marmites, divide the marrow, carrots, cabbage, peas and cut-up fowl and beef. Pour strained broth, scalding hot, into marmites. Pass toasted French bread and grated Parmesan cheese at the table. Fresh chopped chives and chervil may be sprinkled on.

## BLACK-BEAN SOUP
(Serves 4)

*1 cup black beans*
*3 tablespoons butter or bacon fat*
*1 onion, diced*
*1 piece celery, diced*
*1 small green pepper, diced*
*1 clove garlic, minced*
*2 tablespoons flour*
*1 large potato, diced*
*1½ quarts soup stock*
*1 cup tomato juice*
*1 teaspoon bouquet garni*
*¼ cup dry sherry or 3 tablespoons bourbon*
*1 hard-boiled egg*
*Thin slices of lemon*
*4 frankfurters, sliced (optional)*

Wash beans in cold water. Cover with 1 pint cold water and soak overnight. (Or simply boil beans and liquid for 2 minutes and let stand 1 hour; then cook as follows.) In a heavy soup pot, melt butter or fat. Add onion, celery, green pepper and garlic and sauté until the onion turns yellow. Stir in flour. Add the beans (together with the water in which they were soaked), potato, soup stock, tomato juice and bouquet garni and bring to a boil. Skim well. Reduce flame very low and simmer until beans are tender, about 2 to 2½ hours. Stir occasionally to keep beans from sticking. Cool. Puree in an electric blender. Add sherry or bourbon. Season. If soup is too thick, thin with additional stock. Reheat. Chop egg fine. Pour soup into bowl and sprinkle with egg. On each portion float a thin slice of lemon. (Frankfurters may be added to the soup in place of the chopped egg.)

## MANHATTAN CLAM CHOWDER
(Serves 4)

*12 large chowder clams*
*2 ozs. salt pork*
*2 cloves garlic, minced*
*1 green pepper, diced*

*1 leek, diced*
*2 medium-size onions, diced*
*2 pieces celery, diced*
*2 tablespoons flour*
*1 cup canned tomatoes, chopped fine*
*1 teaspoon leaf thyme*
*½ teaspoon marjoram*
*3 cups diced potatoes*
*2 tablespoons minced parsley*
*1 tablespoon catsup*
*1 tablespoon chili sauce*
*Salt and pepper*

With a vegetable brush, scrub clams under cold running water. In a soup pot, cover clams with cold water. Bring water to a boil and remove pot from flame as soon as shells are just beginning to open; overcooking will toughen clams. Remove from pot and set aside. Strain and reserve the broth, avoiding any sediment in bottom of pot. When clams are cool enough to handle, remove meat from shell. Chop the tough skirt of each clam extremely fine; cut the remainder of the meat into small dice. Set aside. Chop salt pork very fine. Sauté in a large soup pot. (Bacon fat, vegetable fat or butter may be substituted for the salt pork.) When fat is melted, add garlic, green pepper, leek, onions and celery. Sauté until onion turns yellow, not brown. Stir in flour. Add the strained clam broth, tomatoes, thyme and marjoram and bring to a boil. Skim well. Reduce flame and simmer very slowly about 1 hour. Add potatoes and parsley and simmer slowly until potatoes are tender. Add catsup, chili sauce and salt and pepper to taste. If clam flavor seems weak, add 1 bottle of prepared clam broth or bouillon powder to taste, or both. Just before the soup is ready to serve, add the chopped clam meat.

## NEW ENGLAND CLAM CHOWDER
### (Serves 4)

Follow the Manhattan-chowder recipe, omitting tomatoes, thyme, marjoram, catsup and chili sauce. When soup is removed from fire, add 1 pint scalded half-and-half (milk and cream in equal amounts).

# POLPETTI IN BRODO (ITALIAN BROTH WITH MEATBALLS)
### (Serves 4)

> 2  *slices long Italian bread, ½ inch thick*
> 2  *egg yolks, beaten*
> 2  *teaspoons minced parsley*
> ½  *lb. ground beef*
> ½  *teaspoon salt*
> 1  *dash nutmeg*
> 1  *dash pepper*
> 2  *tablespoons grated Parmesan cheese*
> 2  *quarts chicken broth, fresh or canned*
> 1  *cup very small size, fine Italian pasta*
> ¼  *cup minced parsley*

Soak the bread in cold water 15 minutes. Squeeze gently to remove excess water. Tear into very small pieces. In a mixing bowl, combine the bread with egg yolks, parsley, beef, salt, nutmeg, pepper and Parmesan cheese. Mix very well until no pieces of bread are visible; the mixture should feel quite moist. If necessary, add several tablespoons cold water. Shape into tiny balls the size of marbles, no more than ½ inch in diameter, and set aside.

In a wide soup pot, bring chicken broth to a boil. Add meatballs and pasta, cover the pot and again bring to a boil. Simmer slowly until done, about 10 minutes. Add parsley and correct seasoning. Serve with grated cheese.

# ONION SOUP
### (Serves 4)

It has become fashionable these days to list onion soup on restaurant menus as French onion soup. The French do love the soup and have loved it for centuries, but it is equally enjoyed by the Italians and Spaniards. As a matter of fact, Italian chefs are greater purists than the French as far as onion soup is concerned. It's the simplest soup in the world, consisting of browned onions and stock. Many French cooks, however, are guilty of adding flour to the onions after the onions are pan-fried. The soup then turns a cloudy dark brown, like the color of a chestnut. Italian chefs of the better sort do not add flour, and the soup remains transparent gold.

Most Italian chefs also want their onion soup to be boiling hot when it is brought to the table, and they spike it liberally with crushed whole pepper. They know that a good onion soup should almost shock you with its distinctive flavor. The soup should not be offensively strong, but it must be peppery, alive and brimming with energetic goodness.

> 4 Spanish onions
> 2 cloves garlic
> 4 tablespoons butter
> 6 cups chicken broth
> ½ teaspoon crushed whole peppercorns
> ¼ teaspoon Worcestershire sauce
> 8 slices French or Italian bread
> Grated Parmesan or Romano cheese
> Paprika
> Salad oil

Peel Spanish onions and cut into rings or long, thin strips. Chop garlic extremely fine. Put onions and garlic into a soup pot with the butter. Place over a moderate flame and sauté until the onions are a deep yellow—not brown. Stir frequently to prevent browning.

Add chicken broth (or 6 cups of boiling water and 6 bouillon cubes). Add crushed peppercorns and Worcestershire. Simmer slowly 20 minutes.

While the soup is simmering, toast slices of French or Italian bread, using the broiler flame as a toaster. Sprinkle the untoasted side generously with grated Parmesan or Romano cheese. Sprinkle lightly with salad oil. Dust lightly with paprika. Place the cheese side of the bread under the broiler flame and broil until the cheese browns lightly.

Season the soup to taste. The cheese croutons may be passed with the soup at the table together with additional grated cheese. The soup may also be poured into an earthen casserole, an armada of five or six croutons floated on top, and then placed in the oven and baked until croutons form a complete crust over the bubbling pool of onions.

# CHICKEN MULLIGATAWNY SOUP
(Serves 4)

2 lbs. chicken backs and necks
1 bay leaf
½ teaspoon rosemary
4 sprigs fresh dill
4 sprigs parsley
1 teaspoon salt
1 peeled onion
1 piece celery
2 tablespoons butter
1 medium-size onion, diced
1 leek, diced
1 piece celery, diced
1 small green pepper, diced
1 medium-size clove garlic, minced
2 tablespoons flour
2 tablespoons curry powder
¼ teaspoon ground coriander
1 cup diced eggplant
½ cup diced peeled apple
¼ teaspoon salt
½ cup quick-cooking rice
½ cup sweet cream

Cover chicken backs and necks with cold water. Bring to a boil, discard water and again cover with cold water, 2 quarts this time. Add bay leaf, rosemary, dill, parsley, 1 teaspoon salt, the whole onion and piece of celery. Bring to a boil. Reduce flame and simmer until chicken is very tender, about 1 hour. Taste broth; if it needs additional strength, add instant chicken cubes or powder. Skim off fat and strain broth. Separate chicken meat from bones and skin. Cut meat into small dice and set aside for later use.

Melt butter in a soup pot. Add the diced vegetables and garlic and sauté until the onion turns yellow. Add flour, curry powder and coriander and mix well. Add the strained chicken broth. Simmer slowly 1 hour, skimming when necessary. Add eggplant and apple and simmer, keeping the pot covered, until the eggplant is tender.

√

In a separate saucepan, combine ½ cup boiling water, ¼ teaspoon salt and the rice. Remove from flame, cover and let the rice stand in the water 5 minutes. Add the rice to the soup pot. Add sweet cream and the diced chicken. Slowly bring to a boil just before serving. Correct seasoning.

## CORN VICHYSSOISE SOUP
(Serves 4)

The smoothest and most satisfying of cold summer soups is here welcomed into the corn belt. To remove *raw* corn pulp from the cob, cut each row of corn on the cob through the center of the kernels, splitting them in half. Then, using the back of the knife, scrape until the pulp oozes out.

> 2 tablespoons butter
> 1 medium-size onion, sliced
> 2 leeks, white part only, sliced
> 1 cup raw corn pulp
> 1½ cups sliced raw potatoes
> 3 cups water
> 3 chicken-bouillon cubes
> ½ cup milk
> ½ cup light cream
> Salt and white pepper
> 2 teaspoons minced chives or scallions

In a soup pot, melt the butter. Add the onion and leeks and sauté slowly until the onion barely turns yellow. Add the corn pulp, sliced potatoes, water and bouillon cubes. Simmer slowly for about 30 minutes, until the potatoes and other ingredients are very soft. Strain the soup by forcing it through a food mill or wire strainer. Let it cool to room temperature; then chill in the refrigerator until very cold. Add the milk and cream just before serving, seasoning to taste with salt and white pepper. If soup seems too thick, it may be thinned by adding more milk. Serve in prechilled soup cups and sprinkle with minced chives just before delivering to the table.

## PHILADELPHIA PEPPER POT
(Serves 4)

> 2  small leeks, diced
> 1  onion, diced
> 2  pieces celery, diced
> 1  green pepper, diced
> 2  tablespoons butter
> 2  tablespoons flour
> 2½  quarts stock
> 1  teaspoon bouquet garni
> ¾  lb. honeycomb tripe, diced
> 2  large potatoes, diced
> ½  cup fine-size egg noodles
> ¼  teaspoon freshly ground black pepper
> ¼  cup finely minced parsley
> 1  4-oz. jar pimientos, diced

Sauté the diced vegetables in butter until the onion turns yellow. Add flour and mix well. Add stock and bouquet garni. Bring to a boil. Add honeycomb tripe and again bring to a boil. Skim well. Reduce flame and simmer until tripe is tender, about 2 hours. Add potatoes, noodles broken into small pieces, pepper, parsley and pimientos. Simmer slowly until noodles and potatoes are tender. Thin soup with additional stock if necessary. Season to taste.

## PUREE OF PEA SOUP WITH MUSHROOMS
(Serves 4)

This is the kind of thick old-world soup that is always enhanced by the addition of a ham bone. If you happen to have one left over from a baked ham or if you can inveigle your butcher into letting you have one, by all means use it. Diced mushrooms and small ham croutons make this soup a meal in itself.

> 2  tablespoons bacon fat or vegetable fat
> 1  onion, minced
> 1  clove garlic, minced
> 1  carrot, minced
> 1  small bay leaf
> ⅛  teaspoon sage

*1 cup quick-cooking dried split peas*
*1½ quarts soup stock*
*1 ham bone*
*¼ lb. fresh mushrooms*
*2 tablespoons butter*
*2 ozs. sliced cooked ham*
*½ teaspoon sugar*
*2 dashes Tabasco sauce*
*Salt and pepper*

Put the bacon fat, onion, garlic, carrot, bay leaf and sage into a soup pot. Place over a moderate flame and sauté until the onion turns yellow—not brown. Add the peas and soup stock. (If no soup stock such as chicken broth or beef broth is available, use 1½ quarts of boiling water and 6 bouillon cubes instead.) Add the ham bone and bring soup to a boil. Reduce flame and simmer slowly until the peas are very soft, from 1½ to 2 hours. While the soup is simmering, wash the mushrooms and cut them into ¼-inch cubes. Put the mushrooms and butter into a separate saucepan or pot. Cook covered, stirring frequently, until the mushrooms are tender. Set aside. When the peas are tender, remove the ham bone from the soup. Force the soup through a strainer or food mill. Cut the ham into ¼-inch squares and combine with the strained soup and mushrooms. Simmer 5 minutes. Add sugar and Tabasco sauce and salt and pepper to taste.

## FLORENTINE MINESTRONE
### (Serves 4)

*1 cup white pea beans*
*1 teaspoon salt*
*2 tablespoons olive oil*
*1 clove garlic, minced*
*1 onion, diced*
*1 piece celery, diced*
*2 quarts soup stock*
*2 tablespoons tomato paste*
*1 carrot, diced*
*1 very small zucchini, diced, peeled or unpeeled*
*1 medium-size potato, diced*
*1 tablespoon minced parsley*

1  teaspoon rosemary
½  teaspoon oregano
2  whole cloves
2  ozs. small Italian pasta (macaroni rings)
½  head cabbage (small), diced
Grated cheese

Soak pea beans in a quart of cold water overnight.
In the morning, add salt to the water. Bring to a boil
and simmer slowly until beans are tender. Add more
water, if necessary, to keep beans covered during
cooking.

In another pot, heat olive oil. Add garlic, onion and
celery. When the onion turns yellow, add soup stock,
tomato paste, carrot, zucchini, potato, parsley, rosemary, oregano and cloves. Simmer slowly until vegetables are very tender. Add pasta and cabbage to the
pot and cook until pasta and cabbage are tender.

Divide the cooked beans in half. Mash one-half of
them in an electric blender or by forcing them through
a food mill or colander. Add the mashed beans and
the whole beans, together with their cooking liquid, to
the soup pot. Bring to a boil. Simmer 5 minutes and
season to taste. If the finished soup is too thick, add
stock to bring it to the desired consistency. Serve with
grated cheese.

# A Good Egg

Squid lay them. Auks lay them. Titmice, tinamous and teal lay them. Even Broadway shows on Boston tryouts, all too often, lay them. But mainly chickens, by the millions, lay them. Since the first pecking order was established in the jungles of prehistoric India, the lowly chicken egg—unborn progeny of the most ridiculous of barnyard creatures—has become man's most prodigal delicacy: from the three-minute egg of early morning to the century egg of a late-evening snack in Chinatown, from the cold egg stuffed with artichoke puree on the hors d'oeuvre tray to the *Salzburger nockerl* on the dessert plate (a weightless cloud of beaten egg floating atop a sea of brandied vanilla sauce).

For the bachelor chef who treats it with respect and understanding, the pristine egg can become a vessel of many such gustatorial delights. His first prerequisite, of course, is discrimination. Even the archaeologist on a trek for fossils insists on a contemporary breakfast egg. Thanks to modern refrigeration, freshness isn't usually a problem, but even today in an occasional supermarket carton you'll run across a no-goodnik—a sorry specimen with watery white and sagging yolk. The magnanimous cook preparing omelets or scrambled eggs can afford to overlook such symptoms, but if poaching or frying is his wont, then swift but decent burial is strongly advised. The best safeguard is to give each egg the once-over in a small dish before committing it to pan or poacher.

Ancient Egyptians were said to have whirled their eggs in slings at such speeds that internal friction finally boiled them in their own shells. Though we don't recommend that you try this technique yourself, there are a few modern improvements that might be suggested. First is the iron frying pan—the classic utensil of *eggmeisters* the world over—a seasoned skillet that has known only the velvety touch of omelet and wiping cloth. Its mellow surface is eternally innocent of meat or vegetable, soap or water. Those less fastidious or more gluttonous, of course, may prefer the trusty and commodious electric griddle, which can take on six or eight eggs at a time without making a cruel yolk of the proceedings. For shirring, earthenware and porcelain dishes are the thing; for poaching, the standard inset pan for those who favor gentle steaming. Whether you boil or bake, shirr or coddle, fry or scramble, you'll want a long, pliable spatula that's wide enough to convey finished product to serving dish without loss of dignity.

But before you venture forth with whisk and chafing dish at the ready and tantalizing visions of crab-meat foo yong or *stracciatella à la Romana* dancing mistily before your eyes, pause long enough to devour a few morsels of basic information on egg cookery. An egg taken directly from the refrigerator, for instance, will require more cooking time than one that's been nesting on the pantry shelf for an hour or so. A strapping Leghorn egg must likewise spend longer on the fire than a pullet pellet. Another time consumer is the small boiling pan with six or eight eggs in it—a crowd that reduces the water temperature so radically that you may have to wait ten minutes for three-minute eggs.

To a self-respecting hen, overcooking would be the most disgraceful destiny for her unsprung offspring. If you leave your shirred eggs in the oven a moment too long, they will come forth looking, and perhaps even tasting, like an albino innertube. On the top of the stove, eggs must always be cooked *below* the boiling point, with the water barely drawing its breath around the edge of the pan. At this genteel temperature, soft-boiled eggs should simmer 3 to 5 minutes, medium eggs 6 to 8 minutes, hard-boiled eggs no less than 15 to 18 minutes. But remember—they should be firm, not stony. As soon as they are plucked from the deep, they must be plunged into cold water.

Otherwise, internal heat will go right on cooking them, producing a baleful green-rimmed yolk that will stare reproachfully at the thoughtless chef. Edward Lear had another sobering thought:

*"There was an old man from Thermopylae*
*Who never did anything properly,*
*But they said, 'If you choose*
*To boil eggs in your shoes,*
*You shall never remain in Thermopylae.' "*

For young men who wish to remain in Thermopylae —and in the good graces of their feminine dinner guests—we commend the following delicacies:

## POACHED EGGS BENEDICT
### (Serves 2)

> 1 6-oz. jar hollandaise sauce
> 1 tablespoon vinegar
> ½ teaspoon salt
> 4 eggs
> 4 slices ready-to-eat ham
> 2 English muffins, split, toasted
> 1 small truffle, sliced

Warm the hollandaise sauce, following directions on the jar. In a wide, shallow saucepan, bring 1 quart of water to a boil, adding the vinegar and salt. Open each egg into a small dish, and then, stirring the boiling water with a spoon, slip each egg into the vortex. Reduce flame and let simmer 3 to 4 minutes, spooning water over each yolk several times during cooking. Lift eggs from water with a slotted spoon and trim off any ragged edges of white. Place in a bowl of warm water until ready to serve. Broil or sauté ham slices 3 or 4 minutes. On each serving dish, place a split, toasted muffin. Place a ham slice on each muffin half. Lift each egg from the water with a slotted spoon and rest on towel to drain all excess water. Then place on ham. Spoon hollandaise on top of eggs and top with a slice of truffle. Serve at once. The purists who recoil from prefab sauces will find recipes for hollandaise on page 201.

## CRAB-MEAT FOO YONG
(Serves 4)

*1 6-oz. pkg. frozen king-crab meat*
*8 eggs*
*½ teaspoon salt*
*¼ teaspoon monosodium glutamate*
*⅛ teaspoon pepper*
*3 tablespoons cold water*
*½ cup celery cut into small dice*
*2 tablespoons thin-sliced scallions*
*¼ cup thin-sliced water chestnuts*
*½ cup well-drained bean sprouts*
*Salad oil*

Foo yong is a dish of flat omelets served with a hot, clear Chinese sauce. To serve it as hot as possible, prepare the sauce (listed next) before the omelets are cooked. First thaw crab meat. Then drain, squeeze dry and break into small pieces. In a deep bowl, beat eggs until whites are no longer visible. Add salt, monosodium glutamate, pepper, cold water, crab meat, celery, scallions, water chestnuts and bean sprouts. Mix well. In two omelet pans, pour salad oil to a depth of ¼ inch. When fat is hot, add one-eighth of the egg mixture to each pan. When egg is browned on bottom, turn it with a wide spatula and brown on other side. Make eight flat omelets in this manner. Place two on each serving plate and cover them with the following hot sauce.

## SAUCE FOR EGG FOO YONG
(Serves 4)

*1 cup chicken broth*
*½ teaspoon soy sauce*
*¼ teaspoon brown gravy color*
*½ teaspoon sugar*
*¼ teaspoon monosodium glutamate*
*4 teaspoons cornstarch*
*⅛ teaspoon pepper*

Mix all ingredients in an electric blender at high speed for 15 to 20 seconds. Pour into saucepan and cook, stirring often, until thick.

# SHIRRED EGGS WITH SHAD ROE
(Serves 4)

> 1 pair fresh or canned shad roe
> Salad oil
> Salt and white pepper
> Juice of ¼ lemon
> 4 tablespoons melted butter
> 8 eggs
> 4 tablespoons butter (not melted)
> 2 tablespoons vinegar
> ¼ cup drained capers
> 2 tablespoons minced parsley

Preheat broiler 10 minutes. Place roe in broiler pan. Brush them lightly with salad oil and sprinkle with salt and pepper. If fresh, broil them 8 to 10 minutes, turning once; if canned, only until light brown. Sprinkle roe with lemon juice. Cut them diagonally into slices about ½ inch thick and divide into four portions. Pour 1 tablespoon melted butter into each shirred-egg dish. Add 2 eggs, duly salted and peppered, and place roe slices on top of the eggs. Bake in 350° oven for 10 to 12 minutes or until whites of eggs are set; avoid overcooking. Meanwhile, brown the unmelted butter in a small frying pan and add vinegar and capers. Then remove from fire. When the eggs are cooked, pour the buttered capers over them. Garnish with parsley and serve at once.

# SCRAMBLED EGGS WITH CHILI AND TOMATOES
(Serves 4)

> 8 slices fresh tomato, ½ inch thick
> Salt, pepper and paprika
> Flour
> Salad oil
> 8 eggs
> 6 tablespoons sweet butter
> ⅓ cup canned green chili peppers, diced small

Sprinkle tomato slices with salt, pepper and paprika. Dip into flour, patting off excess. Heat oil to a depth of ⅛ inch in skillet and, as soon as it sends up the first wisp of smoke, sauté the tomato slices until lightly browned on both sides and set aside in a warm place. Beat eggs until whites are no longer visible and sprinkle generously with salt. Melt 4 tablespoons butter in a large skillet or electric griddle set at 300°. Add eggs and chili peppers and cook, stirring constantly and scraping pan bottom frequently, until half-done. Add balance of butter and continue cooking and stirring until eggs are neither dry nor soupy. Spoon into serving dishes or platter and surround with slices of fried tomato.

## SCRAMBLED EGGS WITH ANCHOVY TOAST
### (Serves 4)

6 ozs. sweet butter
2 teaspoons anchovy paste
2 teaspoons minced chives
¼ teaspoon lemon juice
8 eggs
Salt and white pepper
8 slices white bread

Let 3 ozs. butter stand at room temperature until it is soft enough to spread easily. Mix with the anchovy paste, chives and lemon juice. Place in the refrigerator until needed. Preheat the broiler in order to toast the bread when needed. Beat the eggs thoroughly. Season them generously with salt and pepper. In a large skillet over a low flame, melt half the remaining butter. Add the eggs, stirring frequently until they begin to set; then add the remainder of the butter, bit by bit, and continue to cook the eggs until done. Toast the bread and spread each piece with anchovy butter. Cut the toast diagonally and stack it or overlap it around eggs on platter or serving dishes.

## SCRAMBLED EGGS WITH ROQUEFORT CHEESE
### (Serves 4)

¼ lb. Roquefort cheese
8 eggs
Salt, pepper and paprika

*⅛ teaspoon Tabasco sauce*
*6 tablespoons sweet butter*

Crumble the Roquefort by hand or with a fork into small pieces and set aside. Beat eggs until whites are no longer visible and sprinkle lightly with salt, pepper and paprika. Add Tabasco sauce and mix well. Melt 4 tablespoons butter in a skillet over a slow flame or in an electric griddle set at 300°. Add eggs and cook, stirring constantly and scraping pan bottom frequently, until half-done. Add Roquefort and balance of butter and continue cooking and stirring until eggs are neither dry nor soupy. Spoon onto serving dishes or platter and serve with buttered toast triangles.

## SCRAMBLED EGGS WITH SMOKED OYSTERS
### (Serves 4)

Follow preceding recipe, but instead of Roquefort, add one 3⅔-oz. can smoked cocktail oysters, drained of oil. Cook until eggs are done and serve with buttered toast triangles. Not a dish for squares.

## SCRAMBLED EGGS INDIENNE
### (Serves 4)

*½ cup butter*
*¼ lb. fresh mushrooms, sliced*
*1 green pepper, minced*
*1 canned pimiento, diced*
*1 teaspoon ground turmeric*
*½ teaspoon ground cumin*
*¼ teaspoon finely minced hot chili pepper*
*8 eggs, beaten*
*Salt*
*4 slices toast*

Melt the butter in a chafing dish over a direct flame. Add mushrooms, green pepper, pimiento, turmeric, cumin and chili pepper and sauté slowly until mushrooms and green pepper are tender. Place chafing dish over hot water in bottom section of dish. Add eggs and cook, stirring frequently, until soft-scrambled. Add salt to taste and spoon over hot toast.

## THE OMELET

But our experiments with eggspertise are only half-done; the elegant omelet remains unsavored—an egg dish with a golden heart—and a purple past. When Leopold II of Belgium arrived at Mont St.-Michel and demanded that an omelet be brought to him and served right where he stood on the pavement, the nearby restaurant owner, Madame Poulard, quite properly and proudly refused to serve him. "Tell him he must come inside and eat with the others, or he'll get none of my omelets," she said. The king yielded.

To be really effective, then, an omelet chef must be something of a show-off. The Poulard omelets owe their magnificent reputation not to any secret formula but, in large part, to the theatricality with which they are served. Guests are seated beside granite walls. The eggs are beaten with a fine wire whisk in deep bowls and then are poured into an oven pan with a handle almost five feet long. They are cooked in an open fireplace. Then the plump golden oval is turned onto a large platter and rushed to the table.

This doesn't mean that in order to call attention to your efforts you should try to emulate Blondin, the French acrobat who once balanced himself on a wire 160 feet above Niagara Falls while he ate an omelet he had previously cooked. But you should make the presentation on the best oval platter or dinner plates you can commandeer, and you should be familiar with some of the supporting cast used to make an omelet colorful—the occasional small ribbon of tomato sauce poured around the omelet, the green sprigs of watercress for a color garnish, the extra dollop of filling peeping from an open end or the glossy sheen imparted by brushing with a lump of butter just before serving.

Alexandre Dumas, *père,* novelist and chef, was correct as far as he went when he said, *"Une omelette est à la cuisine ce que le sonnet est à la poésie."* The omelet is, indeed, as brief and beautiful as a sonnet, but unlike the sonnet, it's extremely mortal. You must eat it while it's still hot. Once allowed to cool, its magnificent blond beauty vanishes into deep wrinkles.

An omelet should be light, but it can't be too much like chiffon or it becomes an airy bit of nonsense. The so-called puffy omelet, for example, in which the egg whites are beaten separately and folded into the yolks, is tediously dull and dry. The straight French omelet, on the other hand, in which the eggs are only slightly beaten, is as luscious as a Renoir nude. It's pale gold rather than dark brown on the outside and semisoft—almost frothy—inside.

Eggs for an omelet should be large, fresh, Grade A and (extremely important) should *not* be cold. To the expert omelet maker, a cold egg is as distressing as a cold woman. Take the eggs out of the refrigerator and store them at room temperature at least an hour before making the omelet. Use only the best lightly salted butter. You'll find omelet recipes that advise you to add milk or cream to the eggs; snub them. Actual tests show that milk and cream tend to make the omelet tough. A small amount of water added to the eggs, however, makes the omelet more tender than it would be otherwise, since the water retards the coagulation of the egg yolks. Besides salt and pepper, you'll get excellent results by using a small amount of monosodium glutamate crystals.

Make your omelet neither too small nor too big. If it's too small, there will be an excessive amount of crust. Three omelets of one egg each, for instance, bear only a slight resemblance to a single omelet of three eggs. Don't make your omelet too big or the long cooking period will toughen it and will cause it to crack when it is folded. A three- or four-egg omelet is the ideal size. Therefore, when making an omelet for two, use two pans.

Be gentle with your eggs—beat them, yes, but not to death. Be gentle when it comes to fire, too; there's a knack to knowing just how much heat will firm the eggs without searing them. And have the stage set with the necessary props beforehand—pan, bowl, beater, spatula, butter, eggs and seasoning all within easy reach.

Most important, the pan must be big enough so that the liquid egg can spread sufficiently. For a three-egg omelet, a normal man's portion, the pan should be about 8½ inches from rim to rim. For a four-egg omelet the pan should be 10 inches from rim to rim. Should you be so underprivileged as to have no well-seasoned, "cured" omelet pan, remedy the situation by purchasing the best you can find—at once. Most new pans come coated with a protective film and with manufacturer's directions for its removal. The proper seasoning of the pan—once the coating's been removed —usually includes thorough greasing and then baking in a hot oven for a half hour, which seals the pores. Those handsome, provincial baked-enamel pans don't have pores, so merely need a good initial wash and wipe.

Stuffed omelets are fine for any time of day, from the noonday session in the conference room to the impromptu after-opera supper. Light Bordeaux wines or a rosé, crisp French or garlic bread and crumbly aristocratic cheeses of the blue family, such as Stilton, Gorgonzola or Roquefort, are old friends of the omelet.

Here, now, is our how-to for the basic French omelet and variations:

## FRENCH OMELET
### (Serves 1)

Into a deep mixing bowl, open 3 eggs. Add 1 table-spoon cold water, ¼ teaspoon salt, ⅛ teaspoon monosodium glutamate crystals and a dash of ground white pepper. Beat with a fork at medium speed for 30 seconds. Put a tablespoon of butter into the omelet pan. Turn on a slow to medium flame, heating the butter until it just melts but has not turned brown. Tilt the pan so that the bottom and sides become covered with butter. Quickly beat the eggs a few more strokes and then pour them into the pan just as the butter begins to sputter. Reduce the flame slightly. Wait about 10 seconds. A thin, solid layer of egg will have formed on the pan bottom. With your fork or spatula, lift the bottom layer slightly upward and tilt the pan, permitting the liquid egg to flow beneath. Repeat this step several times until the egg on top does not flow to the bottom. There will still be a slight residue of liquid egg on top. Spread this with a fork so that there is no pool collected on one spot. Continue to cook until the top is merely moist and frothy. The heat of the omelet will complete the cooking after the omelet is folded. You can, if you wish, lift the omelet slightly to peer beneath and see whether it is turning the proper golden hue. If necessary, step up the heat or lower it. (Restaurant chefs sometimes place the omelet under a broiler flame to complete the top cooking. If you do this—and it isn't particularly recommended—your broiler must be preheated and you must take the greatest care not to overcook the omelet and make it dry and tough.)

If a filling is to be used in the omelet, add the filling down the center and fold the omelet. Slide the omelet to the edge of the pan and, with your spatula, fold the outer edges inward, just as you would fold a letter for mailing. The omelet may resist folding. Simply hold your spatula in place until the omelet submits.

Even if the omelet is not to be filled, it should be folded as described. Then, holding the serving plate in the left hand, place the rim of the omelet pan so that the edge rests on the plate. Quickly invert the pan so that the omelet rests bottom side up on the plate. Tuck in the bottom of the omelet on each side to make it as plump as possible. Use paper toweling if it's uncomfortable to handle. Brush the top with a lump of butter. Add more filling at an open end.

If, after a certain number of tries, you still find it awkward to turn the omelet from the pan onto the plate, you can simply lift it with a spatula onto the plate and turn it bottom side up with your hands, using the paper toweling.

Once mastered, the omelet can be an almost unlimited source of inventive pleasure. It can vary all the way from the hearty western omelet with ham and onions to the classic French omelet Celestina (actually an omelet within an omelet), the flat Genoese *frittata* packed with greens and herbs, the Burmese pork-filled omelet and the Chinese egg foo yong studded with almost any meat, fish or seafood in the world. The omelet trainee should be warned when inventing recipes not to use any old tired scraps of food. For these, use the nearest disposal unit, not the noble omelet.

Consider the cheese theme for omelet diversification. The simplest cheese omelet is one in which grated Parmesan cheese is added to the eggs before pouring them into the pan. If you want a slightly sharper flavor, you might add grated Romano cheese and a dash of cayenne pepper. If you prefer a more subtle blend of flavors, you could combine grated Parmesan cheese with shredded Swiss cheese. If a sturdier flavor appeals to you, you will use diced sharp old Cheddar cheese scattered into the pan right after the liquid has set on the bottom. If you like cheese and bacon, cheese and ham, cheese and pimientos, cheese and asparagus or cheese and crab meat, any of these embellishments can be most delicious. In the same manner, any other food of your choice can be developed into omelet fillings.

Foods in sauce, such as seafood Newburg or creamed chicken hash or kidney stew, are spooned onto the omelet just before it is folded. Foods without sauce, cut into small pieces, such as diced ham, chopped peppers, diced potatoes, etc., are merely scattered into the pan after the eggs have set on the bottom but are uncooked on top.

Straight from our own omelet pan, we now cite five offerings toward which we eggophiles are particularly partial.


## OMELET WITH CURRIED CHICKEN LIVERS
### (Serves 2)

Wash 2 ozs. fresh chicken livers and cut into slices about ½ inch thick. Cover with cold water. Bring to a boil. Drain off the water and set the livers aside. Chop 1 small onion and 1 medium-size clove of garlic extremely fine. In a small saucepan, melt 1 tablespoon butter. Add the onion and garlic. Sauté until the onion just turns yellow. Add 1 tablespoon curry powder and ⅛ teaspoon chopped dried basil. Mix well. Open an 8-oz. can tomatoes and strain the juice into the saucepan. Chop the tomato meat coarsely and add it to the pan. Cook slowly until the mixture reduces to a thick sauce. Add the livers and cook 2 minutes more. Season to taste. Prepare two omelets in the usual way, adding a few tablespoons chicken-liver filling before the omelets are folded. Spoon additional liver filling onto the plates.

# OMELET WITH SHERRIED LOBSTER
(Serves 2)

Boil a 1¼-lb. fresh lobster 20 minutes. Cool. Remove the lobster meat from the shell. (Or buy a freshly cooked lobster from your seafood dealer.) Cut the lobster into slices about ¼ inch thick. In the top part of a double boiler, over simmering water, melt 2 tablespoons butter. Add the sliced lobster meat and 3 tablespoons dry sherry. Sprinkle with salt, pepper and celery salt. Let the mixture simmer 5 minutes or until the lobster is heated through. Add ¼ cup light cream and 2 tablespoons chopped chives or scallions. When the cream becomes hot, beat 1 egg yolk well. Slowly stir the egg yolk into the cream and cook, stirring constantly, until the sauce is thickened. Remove the double boiler from the flame. Season the lobster to taste. Prepare two omelets in the usual way, adding a few tablespoons lobster filling to each omelet before it is folded. (Reheat the lobster filling before adding it to the eggs, if necessary.) Spoon additional lobster filling onto the plates.

# OMELET WITH MUSHROOMS IN
# SOUR CREAM
(Serves 2)

Wash ¼ lb. fresh mushrooms. Separate mushroom caps from stems. Cut mushroom caps and stems into slices about ⅛ inch thick. Melt 2 tablespoons butter in a saucepan. Sauté mushrooms until tender. Add 2 tablespoons dry white wine, ½ teaspoon grated onion and a dash of nutmeg. Add ½ cup sour cream. Mix very well. Cook slowly up to the boiling point, but do not boil. Add salt and pepper to taste. Prepare two omelets in the usual way. Spoon a few tablespoons mushroom filling onto each omelet before folding. Add balance of filling to plates.

# SPINACH OMELET PARMESAN
(Serves 2)

Cook a 10-oz. package of spinach, following the printed directions, and drain very well—squeezing out excess juice by hand if necessary. Melt 2 tablespoons butter in a saucepan or skillet and sauté 1 Spanish onion, cut into thin strips, until light yellow, not brown. In a bowl, combine spinach, onion and 4 tablespoons grated Parmesan. Season with salt and pepper to taste and set aside. For each omelet, beat 3 eggs. Add 1 tablespoon cold water, ¼ teaspoon salt, a dash of monosodium glutamate and pepper. Melt 1 tablespoon butter in a pan. As soon as it sputters, pour in the eggs and half the spinach mixture, stirring at once. Wait a few seconds until the omelet begins to set on the bottom; then lift it with a spatula and tilt pan to permit uncooked egg to flow to the pan bottom, repeating several times if necessary. Keep flame low to permit omelet to cook through but not burn. When it has become soft yet cohesive on top, slide the omelet to the far edge of the pan, fold it once or twice and turn onto serving dish. Repeat process.

## OMELET WITH PROVOLONE
### (Serves 2)

Chop 1 small onion very fine. Heat 1 tablespoon olive oil in a small saucepan. Before the oil smokes, add the onion. Sauté until onion turns yellow. Add an 8-oz. can tomato sauce, ⅛ teaspoon garlic salt and ⅛ teaspoon leaf thyme. Simmer slowly 5 minutes. Cut 6 anchovy fillets into small dice and add to pan. Cut 2 ozs. sliced provolone cheese into ½-inch squares. Add the cheese to the pan. Continue to cook only until the cheese softens. Avoid overcooking. Add salt and pepper to taste. Prepare two omelets in the usual way, adding a few tablespoons provolone filling to each omelet before it is folded. Spoon additional filling onto serving plates. No fair licking the spoon.

\* \* \*

(For a spirited omelet dessert—*Mandarin Omelet with Curaçao*—turn to page 239.)

# Let 'Em Eat Pancakes

Evidences of America's ascending culinary tastes abound everywhere, but few with the ubiquity or sophistication of the once-plebeian pancake. Just a few generations ago, this now-princely provender was but a stolid staple munched mostly by lumberjacks and grubstakers. And even as recently as the Thirties, the now-familiar crepe suzette was still an exotic and rather wicked delicacy seldom savored save surreptitiously, along with cognac and curaçao, behind the bolted doors of sumptuous speakeasies. Today, however, after four decades of marination in worldwide gourmandise, our multiplying army of homegrown epicures can circle-tour the entire kingdom of cuisine simply by taxiing from one city neighborhood to another, sampling the local pancake specialties. You may embark on a sensuous sojourn from fragrant Chinese egg rolls to tender Russian blini with caviar and sour cream, from feather-light French crepes to plump Italian cannelloni stuffed with crab meat, from lusty Polish *nalésniki* to Danish pancake balls as light as a Scandinavian summer breeze, from German apple *Pfannkuchen* as big as the wheel of a Mercedes to tiny Swedish *plattar,* darkly resplendent with lingonberry jam. For pancake fanciers still America-oriented, of course, old-fashioned griddlecakes are the hearty and perennial favorite. A robust repast for fast breaking or snack taking, the griddlecake is nevertheless the most temperamental member of the pancake family. Pleasingly plump but velvety light when properly prepared, it will turn as rubbery as a gum eraser in contact

with a too hot pan. And even in its traditional griddle
of cast iron, this peevish pancake may emerge looking
and tasting like a discarded discus if the flame is either
too high or too low. But fortunately for modern
chefs, the antique griddle has been supplanted by the
electric skillet, happily regulated by a thermostat. Once
on the fire, the griddlecake should be cooked to a
medium-light brown and turned only once. Then—
framed by a rasher of bacon or a quartet of link
sausages—it should be rushed to the table for the
homage of hot maple syrup and sweet butter and
wolfed down while it's still at its peak of tender succulence. Prized by more Continental palates, the "true"
pancake—though delicate as chiffon—is a far sturdier
specimen, less fastidious about its preparation, yet still
marvelously comestible hours afterward. It can be
chilled, frozen, folded, rolled, stuffed, baked, fried,
sautéed, flambéed or gratinéed—but it stays appetizingly
mottled brown and tender as the lightest soufflé. Cooked
ahead of time and set aside, it can be served at a
moment's notice with just one or two final flourishes.
For the inventive and adventurous chefs, this versatile
victual offers a realm of infinite pleasure and dis-
covery; once the basic batter is mastered, he can woo
the pancake-smitten with a cornucopian variety of
fillings. The classic crepe, for instance—a thin pancake
spread with preserves and then flambéed—takes on a
thousand different personalities with each new combination of liqueur and preserves, or even such tantalizing
alternatives as sliced brandied peaches, Nesselrode
sauce, cherries jubilee, fried bananas, chestnuts in
vanilla sauce and pineapple spears in rum. In concoct-
ing one of these light delights, it will be well to remember that the French crepe is far closer to lace than
burlap. This delicate texture is best attained by
abandoning whisk and egg beater in favor of an
electric blender, which will produce in 20 seconds a
lightness of batter that no expenditure of manual labor
could achieve. No batter will be worth the beating,
however, unless it goes to its reward in the right recep-
tacle. A black iron omelet pan seven to eight inches in
diameter is the perfect choice, but almost any good
frying pan of these dimensions will serve just as well—
provided it's light enough to be wielded effortlessly but

heavy enough to keep the batter safe from burning. For the sake of discouraging an overheated liaison between pan and batter, they must be separated by a chaste film of shortening. The most efficient technique is to rub the pan until it shines with a small cube of larding pork; the easiest, to cover the pan bottom with salad oil and pour off the excess; the tastiest, to anoint the pan evenly with a modest measure of drawn butter. To prepare, melt table butter slowly, skim off the foamy surface and, shunning the white sediment at the bottom, pour off the golden balance. Thus clarified, it will never overtan in the pan.

As a holiday from the routine of five-course dinners, pancakes make a light and informal tiffin that is neither immobilizingly heavy nor rigidly relegated to formal meal hours. Their nutlike aroma, their seductive sizzle in the skillet are guaranteed to lure hungry hordes kitchenward in deep of night, at crack of dawn or blaze of curaçao.

## CREPES, BASIC BATTER
### (Serves 4)

*3 eggs*
*½ cup milk*
*¼ cup cold water*
*⅛ teaspoon salt*
*½ cup sifted flour*
*¼ cup clarified butter or salad oil*

Place eggs, milk, water and salt into the well of an electric blender. Add flour. Blend at high speed for 20 seconds and turn off machine. With a rubber spatula, scrape the sides clean of any adhering flour. Resume blending at the same speed for another 20 seconds. Heat a teaspoon of clarified butter in a 7½-inch frying pan over a moderate flame. Drain off any excess. Pour in 3 tablespoons batter and tilt the pan so that the mixture covers the bottom completely. Adjust flame to prevent overrapid browning. When done, turn with a spatula and brown other side. Remove from pan, set aside and continue in this manner until all batter is used.

## CREPES WITH CURAÇAO
### (Serves 4)

*Crepes, basic batter*
*½ cup orange marmalade*
*¼ cup sweet butter*
*Grated rind of ½ medium-size orange*
*2 tablespoons sugar*
*2 dashes orange bitters*
*2 tablespoons cognac*
*4 tablespoons curaçao*

Spread each crepe with 2 teaspoons orange marmalade, roll up and set aside. Melt butter in a saucepan or chafing dish (large enough to accommodate all the crepes side by side). Add orange rind, sugar and orange bitters. Stir well. Arrange crepes in pan. Turn them to coat each side completely with butter. When hot, add the cognac and curaçao. When liqueurs are hot, set them ablaze for a minute or two and spoon crepes onto serving dishes.

## CREPES WITH ROQUEFORT
### (6 appetizer portions)

*Crepes, basic batter*
*3 ozs. Roquefort cheese, finely crumbled*
*¼ cup bread crumbs*
*½ cup light cream*
*1 dash white pepper*
*1 dash cayenne pepper*
*½ cup heavy cream*
*3 ozs. Swiss Gruyère process cheese*
*Paprika*

Cook crepes in 4½- to 5-inch pan. In small mixing bowl, combine Roquefort, bread crumbs, light cream, white and cayenne peppers and mix well. Spread each crepe with 2 teaspoons of this mixture, roll up and set aside. Heat heavy cream to boiling point, but do not boil, and pour over crepes. Shred Gruyère, using the large-holed side of a metal grater, and spread evenly over the crepes. Sprinkle lightly with paprika. Place under preheated broiler until cheese browns and serve at once.

## CANNELLONI WITH CRAB MEAT
(Serves 4)

*Crepes, basic batter*
*1 6½-oz. can crab meat*
*¼ cup mayonnaise*
*2 tablespoons minced green pepper*
*1 tablespoon minced parsley*
*2 tablespoons minced scallions*
*1 teaspoon French mustard*
*¼ teaspoon lemon juice*
*Salt and pepper*
*1 8-oz. can tomato sauce*
*½ teaspoon oregano*
*Grated Parmesan cheese*
*Salad oil*
*Paprika*

Carefully remove any cartilage or shell from crab meat and break meat into small pieces. Combine in a mixing bowl with mayonnaise, green pepper, parsley, scallions, mustard, lemon juice, salt and pepper. Spread each crepe with this mixture, roll up and place in a shallow casserole. In a small saucepan, heat tomato sauce and oregano to boiling point and pour over crepes, sprinkling generously with grated Parmesan cheese, lightly with salad oil and paprika. In oven preheated to 375°, bake about 20 minutes or until cheese browns and serve bubbling hot.

## GRIDDLECAKES, MAPLE PECAN SYRUP
(Serves 2)

*1 egg, well beaten*
*1 tablespoon sugar*
*⅔ cup milk*
*¼ cup salad oil*
*1 teaspoon grated lemon rind*
*1 cup sifted self-rising cake flour*
*¼ cup maple syrup*
*3 tablespoons coarsely chopped pecans*
*2 tablespoons butter*

Set griddle or the electric skillet at 390°. If you don't have a thermostatically controlled griddle, you should preheat the griddle iron and then test it for temperature before pouring the batter. The iron will be hot enough when a few drops of cold water sprinkled on it bounce around for a second or two and then disappear. Don't overgrease the griddle. Use a crumpled piece of paper towel to spread the fat in a light film on the griddle or use a piece of larding pork.

In a mixing bowl, combine the beaten egg and sugar. Mix well. Add the milk, salad oil and lemon rind, mixing well again. Gradually add the self-rising cake flour. Beat with a rotary eggbeater or wire whisk until the batter is smooth. Pour the batter onto the preheated griddle iron, using a pitcher or ladle. Pour enough to make cakes about 4 inches in diameter. Turn to brown on both sides, but don't turn them until they are dull around the edge and bubbly in the center. Once turned, don't turn them again. In a small saucepan, combine the maple syrup, pecans and butter. Heat over a slow flame until the butter melts. Reheat just before serving. Stack the griddlecakes on warm serving plates. Pour the hot syrup over the cakes.

## BLUEBERRY GRIDDLECAKES
### (Serves 4)

*1 12-oz. pkg. frozen cultivated blueberries*
*½ cup white table syrup*
*3 tablespoons butter*
*2 eggs, beaten*
*1 cup buttermilk*
*¼ cup light cream*
*2 tablespoons salad oil*
*1½ cups sifted flour*
*1 teaspoon baking soda*
*½ teaspoon salt*
*2 tablespoons sugar*

Let the blueberries stand at room temperature until half-thawed and drain off liquid, adding it to the white table syrup and butter in a small saucepan. Heat until butter melts and keep warm until serving time. In a mixing bowl, combine beaten eggs, buttermilk, light cream and salad oil. Sift together the flour, baking soda, salt and sugar and add to mixture, stirring until dry flour is no longer visible. To this batter (which should be somewhat lumpy), add the drained blueberries. Preheat an electric griddle to 390°, grease lightly and pour in batter, allowing ¼ cup for each pancake. When medium brown on bottom and dull beige on top, turn and brown other side. Borne swiftly to serving plate, crowned with melting butter and bathed in hot blueberry syrup, this steaming savory— though rustically American as hominy—is regal provender for the most pampered palate.

Once lured, *Pfannkuchen* fan and buckwheat buff, crepicure and *nalésniknik* can easily be persuaded to expedite affairs by laying silverware, slicing butter and warming brandy for the chef and then, enjoyably, to do a round of griddling for themselves—following the advice in the Middle English couplet:

> *And every man and maide doe take*
> *    their turne,*
> *And tosse their pancakes up for feare*
> *    they burne.*

# Fishing for Compliments

In fish cookery there are more branches of learning than there are schools in the sea. For fish enthusiasts hanging around your apartment, you can serve anything from raw carp, featured in native Japanese restaurants and sometimes delivered alive on a silver platter, to the French version of stuffed shad, which is kept warm in a baker's oven for 15 hours, until every last little bone disintegrates into the pillowy, sweet white flesh. You can make a saffron-scented, garlic-tinged, tomato-laden bouillabaisse containing 20 different kinds of fish and seafood (and a fine kettle of fish it is, indeed) or you can sauté a mountain trout that takes six minutes' sizzling in the frying pan.

To enjoy this kind of largess, you needn't go spearfishing by torchlight or take rod and line and go hunting for tiger shark in tropical waters. Merely walk to the nearest fish stall, dip into the deep moat of cracked ice and shanghai the freshest specimens you can find. A fish is fresh when its eyes are bulging and brightly arrogant, when the flesh is firm and your fingers leave no imprint, when the scales hug the body tightly and the fragrance is sweet and clean. If there's too pungent an odor, don't buy. It's been held in storage too long and it will develop an off-flavor when cooked. Of course, fish smoked or dried will have a characteristic aroma, not to be confused with staleness.

Fortunately, fish such as king salmon, from far-away places, now travel refrigerated by plane to all parts of the country. Fresh-water fish are carried in tank trucks with freshly pumped water and are delivered alive to big-city markets. A few years ago all frozen fish were watery and stale-tasting, but recent advances in freezing are remarkable. Now you can buy frozen rainbow trout, some imported from Denmark, delightfully rich and subtle in flavor. Even pound blocks of quick-frozen fillet of sole or haddock have been improved to the point where they can seriously challenge the flavor of the same fish freshly caught.

Lemon and fish form a fine finny affinity. No expert fish chef will start cooking his fish unless he has on hand a generous supply of lemons. It doesn't matter whether the fish is a fat butterfish or a lean bluefish— lemon picks up and slicks up its natural deep-sea flavor. You use lemon juice to anoint all baked fish before it goes into the oven and after it's placed on the serving platter. When you poach a piece of fish, the juice, together with the squeezed lemon itself, must go into the poaching water. And when the fish is carried to the table, it must be accompanied by generous wedges of lemon.

Butter also—fresh, sweet, 93-score butter—should be brushed on fish before it is broiled and just before it is served. When you sauté a fine piece of fish, you may use butter, but the butter in this case should be clarified, that is, slowly melted and then freed of all foam on top and solids on the bottom. Clarified butter, sometimes called drawn butter, will not turn a bitterish black when the fish is sautéed, as untreated butter will. If clarifying butter is a nuisance, you should use a clean, clear vegetable oil.

Parsley also has an old and honorable kinship with fish. Serve sprigs of parsley as a garnish on the fish plate. Chop it as fine as powder and, along with the lemon juice, add it to the butter which is brushed on the cooked fish. Dry the fresh, curly parsley and fry big handfuls of it in deep fat to go along with your fish fry.

When raw, fish, unlike meat, is tender. You cook it to change its flavor and to "firm" it rather than to tenderize it. Whenever a thin slice or fillet of fish is baked or fried too long, it will become wizened and sterile in flavor. The same drying out will occur with a large whole fish baked at too high a temperature;

so keep the flame low. For cooking quickly under or over a strong flame, keep the fish on the fire for as brief a cooking period as possible. To protect small fish from the ravages of the heat, dip the fish on all sides into flour. When you broil a thick fish steak, such as salmon, sprinkle the side of the fish exposed to the flame with bread crumbs and brush with butter or coat the raw fish with flour and then brush it with oil. Both the bread-crumb treatment and the flour coating will form a delicious insulation.

Because of its natural tenderness, a fish should be handled very gingerly when it's on the fire. When you're broiling a fish, don't turn it; broil it on one side only. Then, if the fish is thick, transfer it to the oven section, still unturned, where the heat will cook the unbroiled side. Thirty years ago, Andrew Pagani, fish chef of the old Waldorf-Astoria, was known for his hollering, "Never turn the fish!" Actually, the idea is much older than that. Louis Diat, famous chef of the Ritz-Carlton, handled fish in precisely this same manner.

If you turn a piece of fish in the frying pan, lift it carefully with tongs, turn it with a large, long spatula or use two spatulas or a spatula and a long meat fork.

The fact that many fish recipes recommend a short cooking period is undoubtedly the clue to the present popularity of fish among those who like ease in their daily living. The amateur chef can, in 10 or 20 minutes, assemble a sizzling platter of shad roe, a planked salmon steak, an eel stew or a delightful plate of sole *bonne femme*.

For those who enjoy eating under the sign of Pisces, we offer the following easy formulas:

## BROILED DEVILED MACKEREL
(Serves 4)

Buy 2 mackerel, 1¼ lbs. each. Have the fish dealer clean and split the fish for broiling, removing the backbone. Let ¼ cup of butter stand at room temperature until it is soft enough to spread easily. Combine the butter with 1 tablespoon prepared mustard, ½ teaspoon dry mustard, ¼ teaspoon Worcestershire sauce and a dash Tabasco sauce. Mix well until very smooth. Dry the inside of the fish with paper towels. Spread the butter mixture on the inside of the fish. Sprinkle the inside with bread crumbs. Place fish skin side down on a greased shallow broiling pan. Place the pan under a preheated broiler flame. Broil about 8 to 10 minutes or until fish is golden brown. Do not turn fish. Transfer to serving plates with large spatula.

## RAINBOW TROUT WITH ALMONDS
### (Serves 4)

Thaw 4 frozen rainbow trout, or 8 for heavyweight appetites. Pour boiling water over 3 ozs. shelled almonds and let steep in the water 2 or 3 minutes. Drain water off the almonds and slip the skin off each one. Cut the almonds lengthwise into thin slivers. Place them in a shallow pan with 2 tablespoons melted butter. Bake in a preheated oven at 375°, stirring frequently, until almonds are brown, usually about 15 minutes. Avoid charring almonds. Wash trout well in cold water. Dry with paper towels. Sprinkle generously with salt, pepper and paprika. Dip the fish into flour, coating each piece completely. In an electric skillet, heat ¼ inch oil to 370°. Sauté the fish until well browned on both sides. Sprinkle almonds over fish on serving plates or platter.

## SCOTCH SALMON
### (Serves 4)

In a mixing bowl or casserole, place 2 sliced onions, 2 smashed cloves garlic, 2 sliced pieces celery, 2 bay leaves, 1 cup red-wine vinegar and ¼ cup salad oil. Place 4 salmon steaks, 6 to 8 ozs. each, in the vinegar mixture and marinate for ¾ hour to 1 hour. Remove salmon from the vinegar mixture. Place it on a greased shallow broiler pan. Brush salmon lightly with butter. Sprinkle with salt, celery salt and paprika. Sprinkle lightly with bread crumbs. Place under a preheated broiler flame, 550°, for 5 minutes. Remove pan to oven section of range and bake 5 minutes longer.

## COLD SALMON, TARTAR SAUCE
### (Serves 4)

    1 medium-size onion, sliced
    1 piece celery, sliced
    1 bay leaf
    Juice of ½ lemon
    Salt and pepper
    4 fresh salmon steaks, 6 ozs. each
    ½ cup mayonnaise
    ½ teaspoon grated onion
    ½ teaspoon white-wine vinegar
    2 dashes Tabasco
    1 tablespoon finely chopped sour pickle
    1 teaspoon finely minced parsley

Pour 2 cups water into a wide saucepan. Add the onion, celery, bay leaf and lemon juice, ½ teaspoon salt and ⅛ teaspoon pepper. Bring to a boil, reduce flame and simmer very slowly 10 minutes. Add salmon steaks to the liquid, carefully placing each on the bottom of the pan; they should not overlap. Cover and simmer for 10 to 12 minutes. Then chill the steaks in their own liquid in the refrigerator. Combine mayonnaise with remaining ingredients. Remove steaks carefully from their liquid, using a wide spatula to keep them intact, and with a small paring knife, remove skin and center bone. Serve sauce separately at the table. This lordly dish fairly cries for a glass of chilled Rhine wine or Rhine wine and seltzer. Don't let the cry go unheeded.

## SALMON HASH-BROWNED WITH EGG
### (Serves 4)

    4 medium-size potatoes
    1½ lbs. fresh salmon steak
    ¼ cup butter
    ¼ cup minced onion
    ¼ cup minced green pepper
    ⅛ teaspoon garlic powder
    Juice of ¼ lemon
    ½ teaspoon sugar
    ½ teaspoon Worcestershire sauce

*Salt and pepper*
*Salad oil*
*4 eggs*

Peel and slice potatoes about ½ inch thick. There should be about 3 cups. Boil potatoes in salted water until tender and then drain. Cover salmon with water in a saucepan. Add 1 teaspoon salt. Bring to a boil and simmer until salmon is very tender (about 12 to 15 minutes); then drain. When fish is cool enough to handle, carefully remove all bones and skin and flake the meat into small pieces by hand. Chop the potatoes fine with a French knife. Melt butter in a saucepan. Add onion and green pepper and sauté until onion is tender, not brown. In a deep mixing bowl, combine chopped potatoes, salmon, sautéed vegetables, garlic powder, lemon juice, sugar and Worcestershire sauce. Mix very well until salmon and potatoes cohere. Add salt and pepper to taste. Chill the mixture in the refrigerator. Preheat an electric skillet to 350° and grease very lightly with salad oil. Shape the salmon mixture into four large or eight small oval cakes about ¾ inch thick. Sauté until golden brown. Prepare 4 poached or fried eggs and place atop cakes on warm serving plates. Pass chili sauce in a sauceboat.

## FRIED FILLET OF SOLE
(Serves 4)

For years, gourmets have monotonously pointed out that there is no true sole in American waters, only flounder. This may be literally true, but the fish we buy in this country as gray sole is so tenderly pleasing and succulent that nobody now stops to argue whether it's flounder or sole. The fillets of any of the flat fish are ideal for frying. There are no special mysteries in frying fillets; simply dip them into flour, eggs, then bread crumbs and drop them into deep fat. But we would like to pass on some of the artful steps used by professional chefs that transform the ordinary fried fish into a really rare repast. First of all, don't use the usual prepared toasted bread crumbs. Make your own moist white-bread crumbs as follows: Cut a loaf of long Italian or French bread into ½-inch-thick slices. Let the slices be exposed to the air for 1 day. Then cut them into small cubes. Drop them into an electric blender, a small quantity at a time. Run at high speed until crumbs are fine. Remove crumbs from blender and repeat the process until all the bread has been made into crumbs. Store in the refrigerator until needed.

Wash in cold water 1 lb. fillet of sole. Combine ¼ cup milk and ¼ cup light cream and steep the fillets in this mixture for 15 minutes. Drain the fillets. Sprinkle with salt, celery salt, white pepper and paprika. Dip into flour, patting off any excess. Beat 2 eggs with 2 teaspoons salad oil until well blended. Dip the fillets into the egg mixture, then into bread crumbs. Pat crumbs firmly onto each fillet. Chill the fillets, if possible, about ½ hour before frying. This chilling tends to make the coating more firm and dry. Heat fresh, clean oil in a deep fryer set at 370°. Or heat ½ inch oil in an electric skillet set at 370°. Fry fillets until medium brown on each side. Drain on absorbent paper. Serve with prepared tartar sauce, catsup, Russian dressing or aïoli sauce (recipe follows).

## AIOLI WITH HORSERADISH
(Serves 4)

Aïoli is a garlic-flavored cold sauce resembling mayonnaise in consistency and delightful when served with fried, boiled or broiled fish. It should be served in a sauceboat. Into an electric mixer, not a blender, put 2 egg yolks. Beat slightly. Gradually add, almost drop by drop at first, 1 cup olive oil. As the sauce thickens, the oil may be added in a very thin trickle. Avoid adding too much oil at one time or the eggs and oil will not blend. Add 1 teaspoon sugar, ½ teaspoon salt, ¼ teaspoon pepper, 1 tablespoon wine vinegar and 3 tablespoons horseradish. Over the sauce, crush 3 cloves garlic in a garlic press. Mix well. Chill the sauce thoroughly before serving.

## STUFFED SOLE WITH MUSSELS
(Serves 4)

Prepare sole for frying as in previous sole recipe.

Mince 2 tablespoons parsley and 1 small onion. Sauté the onion in 3 tablespoons butter until tender but not brown. Drain a 4-oz. tin of smoked mussels. Chop mussels coarsely. In a mixing bowl, combine the mussels, parsley, onion, ½ cup bread crumbs and the juice of ¼ lemon. On each piece of breaded sole, place about 2 tablespoons of the mussel mixture. Roll up sole. Fasten each piece with two toothpicks. Flatten each piece of rolled stuffed sole slightly on two sides. Heat ½ inch salad oil in an electric skillet set at 370°. Fry sole until brown, turning once. Remove toothpicks.

## POACHED HALIBUT FONDUE
(Serves 4)

Place 4 halibut steaks, about 6 ozs. each, in a wide, shallow saucepan. Add just enough water to cover the fish. Add the juice of 1 lemon. Drop the squeezed lemon into the water. Add 1 teaspoon salt and ½ teaspoon onion salt. Bring to a boil. Reduce flame and simmer slowly 10 minutes. Remove halibut from saucepan, draining well, and arrange fish on a greased shallow baking pan or shallow ovenware. Into the top part of a double boiler over barely simmering water, put ½ cup heavy cream, 8 one-ounce pieces Gruyère cheese diced small and ¼ teaspoon salt. Heat slowly, stirring with wire whip, until cheese melts and mixture is smooth. Beat 2 egg yolks slightly and slowly add to cheese mixture. Remove from fire. Pour melted cheese over halibut steaks. Sprinkle with paprika. Preheat broiler to 550°. Place the halibut under the broiler flame for a few minutes or until the cheese turns a light golden brown.

## SHAD ROE WITH ALMONDS
(Serves 4)

Spring is the shad season, but you can always get canned roe. Though shad is a luscious fish, it is quite bony; in large city markets you can buy it boned. Shad roe, not unnaturally, are the eggs of the female shad; they are always sold in pairs, which should be separated before cooking and served with crisp shoe-string potatoes, grilled tomatoes and a watercress salad.

> ½ cup shelled almonds
> 2 tablespoons salad oil
> 2 pairs fresh shad roe
> ¼ cup melted butter
> Salt, celery salt and pepper
> 1 lemon
> 4 sprigs parsley

Pour boiling water over the almonds. Let remain 5 minutes. Drain and remove skins. Place on a small shallow pan or pie plate. Sprinkle with salad oil. Place in preheated oven at 350° for about 10 minutes, stirring frequently. Remove as soon as they are toasted brown and sprinkle with salt.

Preheat the broiler to 450°. Separate each pair of shad roe into two portions. Wash well, taking care not to break the membrane. Place on a shallow pan or metal pie plate. Brush with melted butter. Sprinkle with salt, celery salt and pepper. Place under the broiler flame and broil about 5 or 6 minutes on each side or until brown. Beware of sputtering fat. Transfer roe to a platter. Again brush with melted butter. Sprinkle with the juice of ½ lemon; cut the remaining ½ lemon into wedges as a garnish, with parsley. Sprinkle the browned almonds over the roe and dig in.

## FINNAN HADDIE WITH EGG
### (Serves 4)

> 1 lb. finnan haddie
> 2 tablespoons butter
> 2 tablespoons flour
> 1 cup hot milk
> ½ cup hot cream
> Salt and pepper
> 4 slices toast
> 4 poached eggs

Wash finnan haddie, cover with cold water and bring to a boil. Reduce flame and simmer 15 minutes or until fish flakes easily when pressed with a fork. Drain. When cool enough to handle, remove any skin and bones from the fish and break it into large flakes. In a heavy saucepan, melt the butter. Remove from flame and stir in the flour. Then—gradually—add hot milk and cream, continuing to stir constantly. Return to a moderate flame and simmer sauce about 10 minutes or until all starchy taste disappears. Combine sauce and finnan haddie. Simmer 5 minutes. Season with salt and pepper. Spoon finnan haddie over toast and place a poached egg atop each portion.

## BLUEFISH WITH TOMATOES AU GRATIN
### (Serves 4)

> 2 fresh bluefish, 1½ lbs. each
> 2 medium-size firm, ripe tomatoes
> Salt and pepper
> Ground coriander
> 1 8-oz. can tomato sauce
> 2 tablespoons dry white wine
> ¼ teaspoon oregano
> ¼ cup grated Parmesan cheese
> Paprika
> Olive oil

Have the fish dealer slit the bluefish in half, removing head and backbone. Wash fish well in cold water. Dry with paper toweling. Place skin side down in a shallow pan or casserole brushed with olive oil. Cut out stem end of tomatoes and slice each tomato crosswise into six slices. Sprinke fish with salt, pepper and coriander and arrange the sliced tomatoes atop fish. Combine tomato sauce, white wine and oregano in a small saucepan. Slowly bring to a boil and pour over fish. Sprinkle Parmesan cheese, paprika and olive oil over sauce. Bake in preheated 425° oven for 25 to 30 minutes or until cheese is browned. Transfer fish from pan to serving dishes or platter with a long, wide spatula in order to keep long pieces intact.

## FLOUNDER, MANDARIN STYLE
### (Serves 4)

1 lb. fillet of flounder
¾ cup cold water
2 egg yolks
1 cup sifted all-purpose flour

*1 teaspoon salt*
*1 2-oz. can mushrooms, pieces and stems*
*¾ cup fresh or canned chicken broth*
*1 teaspoon bottled Chinese oyster sauce or soy sauce*
*1 tablespoon minced fresh ginger*
*2 tablespoons sugar*
*2 tablespoons vinegar*
*1 tablespoon cornstarch*
*2 tablespoons cold water*
*1 11-oz. can mandarin-orange sections*
*Salad oil*

Wash flounder in cold water and dry well on paper toweling. Cut each fillet through the long seam running through the center, separating each one in half. Cut each of these halves lengthwise again, then into finger-size strips about 3 inches long. Pour the ¾ cup cold water into the well of an electric blender. Add egg yolks, flour and salt. Blend at high speed for 30 seconds. With a rubber spatula, scrape sides of blender and again blend at high speed for 15 seconds. Pour this batter into a wide mixing bowl. Add fish strips and set aside. Drain mushrooms and place in saucepan with the chicken broth, oyster sauce, ginger, sugar and vinegar. Slowly bring to a boil. Dissolve the cornstarch in 2 tablespoons cold water and, when chicken broth boils, slowly pour cornstarch mixture into it, stirring constantly. Cook until sauce is no longer cloudy, 1 or 2 minutes, and remove from fire. Drain mandarin-orange sections and add to sauce. Keep warm over a very low flame, or in the top section of a double boiler, until serving time. In an electric skillet preheated to 350°, pour salad oil to a depth of ½ inch. Lift fish strips from batter, permitting excess to drain off, and fry in skillet until light brown on both sides. Pour hot sauce onto warm serving plates. Arrange fish strips on top. Serve with fluffy white rice, green peas and green tea.

## NORWEGIAN FISH BALLS
### (Serves 4)

*1 lb. fresh halibut*
*1 medium-size onion*

2 egg yolks
Salt
½ teaspoon monosodium glutamate
¼ teaspoon white pepper
1 dash freshly grated nutmeg
¼ cup heavy sweet cream
¼ cup bread crumbs

Have the fish dealer grind the halibut twice through the fine blade of a food chopper, making sure there is no skin or bone on fish before chopping. Put the ground halibut into a deep mixing bowl. Grate the onion into bowl. Add beaten egg yolks, 1 teaspoon salt, monosodium glutamate, pepper, nutmeg, cream and bread crumbs and mix very well. Shape into balls of uniform size no larger than 1¼ inches in diameter. In a shallow saucepan or Dutch oven fitted with lid, bring 1 quart water to a boil. Add 1 teaspoon salt and lift fish balls carefully into pan. They will sink to the bottom at first, then rise as they cook. Simmer over a low flame 10 to 12 minutes, keeping the pan covered. Reserve ¾ cup of the cooking liquid with which to prepare the dill-sauce recipe that follows. (Or you may prefer to serve these tasty nuggets on cocktail toothpicks as a chilled appetizer dipped into horse-radish sauce.)

### DILL SAUCE FOR FISH BALLS
(About 1¼ cups)

2 tablespoons sweet butter
2 tablespoons flour
¾ cup hot fish stock
½ cup light cream
1 teaspoon instant bouillon powder
½ teaspoon dried dill
3 teaspoons horseradish
Salt and pepper

Melt butter in a saucepan over a low flame, but don't let it brown. Remove pan from fire and stir in flour until well blended. Slowly add hot fish stock to pan, stirring constantly with a wire whip. Then stir in cream and return to a moderate flame. Bring sauce to a boil, reduce flame and simmer 10 minutes, stirring frequently. Stir in bouillon powder. Remove pan from flame. Add dried dill, horseradish and salt and pepper to taste. Keep warm over a very low flame or in the top section of a double boiler until serving time.

## BOILED WHOLE STRIPED BASS
### (Serves 10 to 12)

Buffet tables as well as formal dinners are often adorned with a large, whole boiled fish such as salmon or striped bass. The best utensil for cooking such a fish is a long, oval fish boiler with removable rack. If such gear isn't available, tie up the whole fish in cheesecloth and cook it in a large pot. Use the cloth to remove the fish from the pot. A 6- to 8-lb. striped bass or salmon will provide about 10 to 12 portions. To cook it, first prepare a vegetable-flavored stock, court bouillon: Into a large pot, put 3 quarts water, ½ cup white-wine vinegar, 2 sliced onions, 2 sliced carrots, 2 sliced pieces celery, 8 sprigs parsley, 1 bay leaf, ¼ teaspoon rosemary, 4 teaspoons salt and 12 slightly crushed peppercorns. Bring to a boil. Simmer 30 minutes. Strain the liquid. Pour over whole fish. Bring to a boil. Reduce flame. Simmer about ¾ hour. To test fish for tenderness, insert a long, thin skewer into backbone. It should flake easily. Transfer fish gently onto silver platter covered with a large white cloth napkin. Remove as much skin as possible from fish. Serve with hollandaise sauce if hot or with mayonnaise if cold. When your guests taste this, they'll flip, and that's no fish story.

# Long Live the Lobster

The lobster is the playboy of the deep; he is a night person, an epicure, a traveler. During the daylight hours, he remains relatively stable on the ocean bed, but after sundown he becomes noticeably restless, moving about with vigor and dash despite his armor-plated bulk. He has the true gourmet's fondness for seafood, being partial to clams in the shell, and he has been especially equipped by nature to enjoy this delicacy: One claw is larger than the other—with this he holds the clam while with the daintier claw he extracts the tasty tidbit piece by piece. As for his traveling preferences, he finds the airplane more congenial than train or truck.

A century ago, the lobster's travels were limited. The shipping of the first live lobster from New England to Chicago back in 1842 was a major event, something like the launching of a satellite. The crustacean got as far as Cleveland (traveling by the fastest possible overland route); there canny Clevelanders, sensing it was not long for this world, boiled it with much pomp before whizzing it on to the Windy City.

Those were the days when lobsters were sold for a penny apiece on the Maine coast; not far inland, they brought fabulous sums in so-called lobster palaces. New York's Broadway, where well-fixed bachelors took their popsies for seafood dinners, became known as lobster alley.

Today, lobsters are available to everyone. The wonderful thing about them is that although they're no longer the rare romantic food of the gaslight era, they've lost none of their gustatory enchantment whatever. Even the most jaded epicure will tighten his bib at the sight of a bright-red lobster lifted from a steaming pot, hiding beneath its armor the firm white flesh, the soft green liver, or tomalley, and (if the lobster happens to be female) the crisp roe.

It's not quite fair to compare the northern lobster, with which the present thesis is concerned, with the spiny lobster taken from warm waters off California, Mexico, South Africa and Australia. The latter, sold in frozen form as rock lobster or *langouste,* is as different from a Maine lobster as veal is different from beef. Although rock lobster is easy to handle and never too costly, it lacks the moist, vivacious flavor of the cold-water titans and their incredibly sweet claw meat.

Just because two lobsters are alive doesn't by any means indicate that they're of equal quality. The very best lobster is one which is snatched right out of the "pot" (a trap of wooden lath) in which it was caught and rushed to the boiling water. If you live in South Bend or Santa Fe, this ideal state of affairs isn't practicable. Lobsters will stay alive out of their own habitat about two weeks, provided their gills are kept moist with ice, seaweed or water. If your fish dealer happens to have a tank of freshly pumped water and if he receives a daily supply of the restless thoroughbreds, you'll usually have no problem. If you have any doubt about the condition of a live lobster, simply lift it up and observe its tail movements. Collar the fellow on the top of the back with the pincers pointed forward so they'll be unable to swing around and nip you. Look at its tail. If it barely shows signs of movement, the lobster is on his way to an early demise. If the tail snaps underneath, you've got your hands on a lively, luscious specimen.

Generally, the color of a good live lobster is a deep charcoal brown tinged with green or blue and showing, here and there, speckles of red or orange. Like all creatures in the sea around us, variations of this main color theme will be found. Some lobsters are black; in rare instances, cream-colored. If, however, a barely moving lobster shows large patches of orange or red, it means that its life is ebbing, and it has no place on your bachelor board.

After you've lifted and held a number of live lobsters, you'll learn more or less automatically to select those that are heavy for their size. Lobsters that have just molted and replaced their shell will feel somewhat hollow and will show deep red at the joints. They're perfectly edible, but the meat isn't as succulent as lobsters that haven't recently thrown off their old armor plate for new. Look for lobsters with large-size claws, since the meat is so delectable. A lobster who loses a claw in battle will simply grow another one, but it takes several moltings before the new claw reaches full size again.

If you're buying a fresh-cooked lobster, a really wonderful labor-saver, again check the tail. It should be tightly curled underneath the body. Lift the tail up. If it snaps back impudently, the lobster was good before it was boiled. A cooked lobster should have a clear, salty seashore fragrance, not a dank fishy smell.

Chicken lobsters weighing from ¾ to 1 pound apiece —it takes six years to attain even this baby size—are tender and toothsome, but the amount of labor necessary to extract a fair-size portion always makes a hungry seafood man hone for something more mature. Lobsters weighing from 1¼ to 1¾ pounds are just about perfect for single portions. Real lobster lovers will demand double or triple portions. Above two pounds, the specimens tend to be tough and dry. Normally a 1¼-pound lobster when cooked will yield one cup of lobster meat for such dishes as lobster cocktail or lobster Newburg. Frozen cooked northern-lobster meat is always more or less of a frustration. It looks luscious in the can, but the moment it thaws, all of the lobster's goodness flows out in sad little rivulets. Unlike shrimps, which can take freezing well, northern lobsters are still best when they're alive and kicking.

## BOILED LOBSTERS

The best way to boil lobsters is not to boil them. Steam them. Old Maine lobstermen are forever reminding you that the lobsters prepared in a clambake are not actually baked but are steamed by the seaweeds covering the hissing hot rocks. The essential point to remember is, no matter how you cook a lobster, don't overcook it. A lobster contains sublime, sensuous broth, and it shouldn't be drawn or spilled in vain. In spite of the fact that seafood houses submerge lobsters in boiling water (a convenience for them), you'll do better to cook the lobsters with only enough water to fairly cover the bottom of the pot, about one cup to a gallon pot. Choose a pot into which your lobsters will fit comfortably. Be sure the pot has a tight-fitting lid. Bring the water to a boil. Place the lobsters in the pot on their backs. Cover the pot. Let the water come to a second boil and then cook 10 minutes for a medium-size lobster; 7 or 8 minutes will do for a chicken lobster. The small amount of water will generate enough heat to cook the lobsters without washing away too much of their own nectar.

To serve a boiled lobster, remove it from the pot with a pair of large tongs. Wait a moment or two so it isn't too hot to handle. Use pot-holder mitts if necessary. On a heavy cutting board, lay the lobster on its back, pincers forward. Insert a heavy French knife (the heavier the better) into the belly. Split the tail in two without separating the halves, if possible. Turn the head toward you. Cut toward the head and down until the lobster is divided. Remove the small sac, sometimes called the "queen," right in back of the head. It's the lobster's stomach and usually contains some gritty matter. Remove the vein running the length of the body. Don't discard the tomalley or roe, if any. Twist off the claws by hand. With the heavy knife, crack the claws for easy dissection at the table. When you crack the claws beforehand, you eliminate the use of a nut cracker at the table, a clumsy weapon if ever there was one. Serve the lobster with a sauceboat of melted butter to which a healthy squeeze of lemon juice has been added. Lobster etiquette, certainly the least dainty but the most practical in the world, is usually observed with oversize bib napkins as well as extra hand napkins, oyster forks or the smaller-tined lobster forks, larger finger bowls and a whopping salad bowl or platter for lobster shells discarded in battle.

## BROILED LOBSTERS

Preheat the broiler to 400°. To split a live lobster for broiling, place it on its back, pincers forward. Insert a knife between the tail and body sections to cut the spinal cord. Then cut the lobster in half in the same manner described above for the boiled lobster, removing the sac and intestinal vein. Leave the claws intact. Brush generously with melted butter or salad oil. Sprinkle the flesh side lightly with salt, celery salt, white pepper and paprika. Place the lobster flesh side up in a shallow baking pan. Place the pan under the broiler flame. Broil 5 minutes. Remove the lobster from the broiler section. Cover the lobster with aluminum foil. Place in the baking section of the oven and bake 8 to 10 minutes for a medium-size lobster. Allow more baking time for larger-size lobsters. Remove the claws and crack them with a heavy French knife before sending the lobster to the table. Serve with large lemon wedges and melted butter livened with lemon juice. For broiling lobster outdoors over charcoal, fasten the lobster in a wire broiler rack. Broil 6 to 8 inches above the source of heat. The flesh side will get done very quickly. Remove the claws and broil them a minute or two longer close to the charcoal.

Either boiled or broiled lobsters are always sensational lead spots at the table. Other dishes seem pale by comparison. However, a large platter of crisp, salty French-fried potatoes, some sliced beefsteak tomatoes and a bowl of coleslaw with mustard dressing are quite compatible. For the finale, a cold, billowy wedge of lemon chiffon pie, along with coffee.

Once you've mastered the basic skills of boiling and broiling, you'll want to go on to other specialties in the great lobster variety show. Here, now, is a gaggle of lobster recipes:

## COLD STUFFED LOBSTER
### (Serves 2)

*2 boiled lobsters, 1¼ lbs. each, chilled*
*1 large fresh tomato*
*⅔ cup diced ripe avocado*
*⅓ cup mayonnaise*

> *2 tablespoons chili sauce*
> *⅛ teaspoon Worcestershire sauce*
> *½ teaspoon lemon juice*
> *Salt and pepper*
> *2 teaspoons finely chopped chives*

Split the lobsters in two, removing the claws and saving the lobster shells. Remove sac and vein from each lobster. Remove meat and cut into dice ¼ inch thick. Bring a saucepan of water to a rapid boil. Lower the tomato into the water for 15 seconds; then place it under cold running water. Peel off the skin and cut out the stem end. Squeeze gently to eliminate excess juice and cut it into ¼-inch dice. Combine with lobster meat, diced avocado, mayonnaise, chili sauce, Worcestershire sauce and lemon juice. Mix thoroughly. Add salt and pepper to taste. Carefully spoon the lobster mixture into the lobster shells. Sprinkle with chopped chives and serve very cold.

## LOBSTER FRA DIAVOLO
### (Serves 2)

> *1 No. 2 can Italian-style tomatoes with tomato paste*
> *1 small onion, minced*
> *2 tablespoons olive oil*
> *1½ ozs. brandy*
> *⅛ teaspoon garlic powder*
> *1 tablespoon minced parsley*
> *½ teaspoon basil*
> *¼ teaspoon rosemary*
> *2 live lobsters, 1¼ lbs. each*
> *Salt and pepper*

Put the tomatoes with tomato paste into a blending machine. Blend until no large pieces of tomato remain. In a medium-size saucepan, sauté the onion in olive oil until it just turns yellow, not brown. Add the brandy, light it and burn for a few seconds. Add the tomatoes, garlic powder, parsley, basil and rosemary. Simmer over a very low flame, stirring occasionally. Split the lobsters, following previous directions. Remove the tomalley and set it aside for later use. In a large pot fitted with a tight lid, bring 1 cup water to a boil. Add

the split lobsters. Steam for 5 minutes, no longer.
Remove lobsters from the pot. Pour liquid in which
lobsters were steamed into the tomato mixture. Remove
lobster meat from shells. Cut into slices ½ inch thick
and add to the tomato mixture. Simmer a few minutes.
Slowly stir the tomalley into the saucepan. Simmer,
don't boil, stirring constantly, 2 minutes more. Season
to taste.

## LOBSTER NEWBURG
(Serves 2)

*2 boiled lobsters, 1¼ lbs. each*
*¼ cup butter*
*⅛ teaspoon paprika*
*⅓ cup dry sherry*
*½ cup light cream*
*½ cup milk*
*1 envelope instant chicken broth*
*2 egg yolks, beaten*
*¼ cup milk*
*Salt and white pepper*

Cut the cooked lobster meat into slices ½ inch thick.
In a heavy saucepan, melt the butter over a low flame.
Add the lobster. Sprinkle with paprika. Sauté for a
minute. Add the sherry, light cream and ½ cup milk.
Slowly bring to a boil. Add the instant broth. Combine
the beaten egg yolks with ¼ cup milk, mixing well.
Add 3 tablespoons of the hot liquid from the pan to
the egg yolks. Gradually stir the egg-yolk mixture
into the pan, stirring constantly and cooking only until
the sauce thickens. Overcooking will cause it to curdle.
As soon as the sauce begins to bubble around the
edge of the saucepan, remove from the fire. Add salt
and pepper to taste. Spoon Newburg over hot, fresh
toast.

## LOBSTER STUFFED WITH CRAB MEAT
(Serves 2)

*2 live lobsters, 1½ to 1¾ lbs. each*
*Butter*
*3 tablespoons minced onion*

2  tablespoons minced green pepper
½  cup light bread crumbs or cracker crumbs
1  tablespoon minced parsley
1  teaspoon lemon juice
1  cup fresh crab meat
Salt, pepper and paprika

Prepare the lobster as for broiling, following previous
directions. Remove the tomalley and set it aside. Melt
3 tablespoons butter in a saucepan. Add the onion and
green pepper. Sauté until onion is yellow. Combine
bread crumbs with sautéed vegetables and parsley.
Add lemon juice, crab meat and lobster tomalley. Add
salt and pepper to taste. Broil the lobster as directed.
After removing the lobster from the broiler and before
transferring it to the oven, stuff the cavities of the
lobster near the head with the crab-meat mixture.
Sprinkle lightly with paprika. Bake as directed in the
recipe for broiled lobster.

## LOBSTER ROLLS
(Serves 4)

Crepes, basic batter
1  boiled chicken lobster
¾  cup diced cooked pork or chicken
1  5¼-oz. can bamboo shoots, drained
1  medium-size piece celery, diced
2  scallions, diced
1  teaspoon soy sauce
1  teaspoon sugar
¼  teaspoon monosodium glutamate
Salt and pepper
1  egg, beaten
Frying fat

Cut both lobster and pork into tiny cubes about the
size of the bamboo shoots. In a mixing bowl, combine
lobster, pork, bamboo shoots, celery, scallions, soy
sauce, sugar, monosodium glutamate, salt and pepper.
Divide this filling among the 12 pancakes. Brush the
inside rim of each with beaten egg and roll up, folding
and pressing the ends in securely for complete sealing.
Place each roll folded side down in a shallow pan or

platter and chill thoroughly. Heat deep fat to 370° (or until the first wisp of smoke). Lower rolls slowly into fat and brown on all sides. Serve immediately with hot Chinese mustard and Chinese plum or duck sauce.

## LOBSTER STEW A LA PLAYBOY
### (Serves 2)

> 2 boiled chicken lobsters
> ⅓ cup butter
> Salt, white pepper and paprika
> 2 cups milk
> ¼ cup light cream
> ⅛ teaspoon onion salt
> ⅛ teaspoon monosodium glutamate
> Tabasco sauce

Separate the lobster tomalley and the roe, if any, from the meat. Slice the meat ½ inch thick. Force the tomalley and the roe through a coarse sieve or colander into a heavy saucepan. Add the butter. Sauté very slowly, stirring constantly, about 2 minutes. Add the lobster and sauté about 2 minutes more or until each piece of lobster has absorbed some of the butter. Sprinkle the lobster lightly with salt, white pepper and paprika. Add the milk and cream. Add the onion salt and monosodium glutamate. As slowly as possible, bring the liquid up to the boiling point, but do not boil. Remove from the fire. Add a dash of Tabasco sauce. You can eat the lobster stew at once, but to permit the flavors really to ripen and "marry," keep the lobster stew in the refrigerator overnight. Then reheat it in a double boiler only until hot, not an instant longer.

# Consider the Crab

There's something about the texture of crab meat that is indescribably perfect. It is neither as firm as meat or poultry nor as soft as fish. It has a subtlety of flavor that almost forces you to eat it slowly in order to appreciate its delicate deep-sea tang. It has a kind of luxurious aftertaste that compels you to scrape the salad bowl or casserole for fear of losing a single flake of its goodness. If a playboy knows his crab lore, he can hold his playmate spellbound as he regales her with stories about the life of the short-tailed crustacean. For instance, there are the great king crabs of the Northwest. It is in the spring that millions of female crabs start to leave their bed and board at the bottom of the North Pacific to scramble slowly toward the warm shore water for you know what.

A few weeks later the male crabs discreetly follow. At first they scout around hunting for a suitable mate. The giant six-foot, six-legged bachelors go through a rhythmic dance to catch the eyes of their chosen ones. If male and female feel that they are compatible, they hold claws. Then the conquering male carries his intended about for three to seven days for all the other deep-sea playboys to admire. This ceremony makes it legal. Thanks to this great yearly formality, we can enjoy at our tables the heavenly flavor of Alaskan crab meat all year long.

Ex-servicemen who spent some time around Australia's Great Barrier Reef will never forget the first time they saw armies of Aussie crabs lining up in mass formation, one row after the other, like companies on a parade ground. The whole group moves in unison, wheels to the right or left. Now and then you'll see a single squad in line formation marching in perfect discipline.

If a human invasion moves near, these West Pointers of the sand break into fast retreat, climbing pell-mell over one another's backs. In danger of being converted into baked deviled crabs, they forget their military etiquette and disappear by burying themselves in the sand until peace reigns over all.

Fight fans love the pugilist crabs of the British Samoa Islands. These hardy boys spar, jump, feint and then cut loose with rights and lefts that literally knock out their opponents. For boxing gloves, Samoan crabs use small anemones, one held in each of their claws. The sea anemones in this part of the world are equipped with sting cells that are discharged upon contact with an enemy. If you approach one of these crabs, he'll try to ward you off at first, but if you insist on coming closer, he'll let go with a roundhouse blow that will send you flying—easy enough for a creature who can walk forward, backward or sideways with equal skill.

The shell that a crab wears is a hard substance that cannot stretch. As the crab grows, its body tissue becomes too large for the shell to contain it. The crab then throws off its old shell and grows a new one. In the interim period, before it acquires a new suit of armor, the crab is known as a soft-shell—one of summertime's greatest seafood delicacies.

Catching, boiling and cleaning a crab is a complex and bothersome business. For this reason, almost every fish or seafood store sells crab meat freshly boiled, ready for the table. Fresh crab meat is put up in cans that are not hermetically sealed. The meat thus processed has no tinny flavor and is a wonderful food for bachelor boys or girls who love light but sophisticated fare.

When buying freshly boiled crab meat, be sure it does not have a fishy odor or sticky feel. The best quality is free of small pieces of bone, shell or cartilage. When you buy fresh crab meat, ask the clerk to open the can and dump the meat to inspect it. It's an old fisherman's custom sometimes to pack big lumps on the top and smaller flakes on the bottom.

Crab meat is a perishable food and should be kept under refrigeration at all times. It should not be held more than a day or two in your refrigerator. At seafood stores, fresh crab meat is kept packed in cracked ice until sold.

We recommend the following easy-to-prepare crab-meat dishes. Before serving them, however, be sure your refrigerator carries a cargo of dry beer or ale.

## CRAB-MEAT COCKTAIL
### (Serves 4)

In a small mixing bowl, combine ¾ cup catsup, 2 tablespoons horseradish, ½ teaspoon Worcestershire sauce, 2 dashes Tabasco sauce, juice of ¼ lemon and ⅛ teaspoon celery salt. Mix well. Chill thoroughly.

Examine 1 pint freshly cooked crab meat to remove any pieces of shell or cartilage. Line four champagne glasses or four fruit-cocktail glasses with lettuce leaves. Divide the crab meat among the four glasses. Pour the cocktail sauce on top.

## CRAB-MEAT SALAD
### (Serves 4)

Cut into ¼-inch squares enough celery to make 1 cup. Put the celery into a large mixing bowl with 1 quart freshly cooked crab meat. Add 1 tablespoon vinegar and 1 tablespoon lemon juice. Add ¾ cup mayonnaise, ¼ cup chili sauce, 1 teaspoon salt, ¼ teaspoon pepper, ¼ teaspoon celery salt and 1 tablespoon grated onion. Toss all ingredients lightly with a salad spoon.

Line four dinner plates with lettuce or romaine leaves. Spoon the salad into the center of the plates. Cut 2 hard-boiled eggs into quarters. Place 2 quarters of egg on each salad plate. Place 2 wedges of fresh tomato on each salad plate, alternating egg and tomato. Garnish each plate with extra-large ripe olives.

To make avocado-and-crab-meat salad, use 1 pint diced avocado and 1 pint freshly cooked crab meat instead of 1 quart crab meat. For those who like straight mayonnaise, omit chili sauce and add 2 table-spoons sweet cream before tossing salad. Chopped chives, if you prefer, may be used in place of the grated onion.

## CRAB-MEAT CAKES
(Serves 4)

Pick over carefully one 13-oz. can or ¾ pound freshly boiled crab meat, removing any bones, cartilage or pieces of shell. Separate yolks and whites of 3 eggs. Beat yolks well with a rotary eggbeater or wire whip. Gradually add 3 tablespoons flour to yolks, beating well. Add 1 tablespoon grated onion, ½ teaspoon salt, ⅛ teaspoon pepper and ½ teaspoon dry mustard. Add crab meat, mixing well.

Beat the 3 egg whites until stiff and fold into mixture with a U-shaped motion, bringing the mixing spoon down, over and up in order to keep egg whites light.

Melt vegetable shortening in a heavy frying pan to a depth of ¼ inch. Drop crab-meat mixture by tablespoonfuls into hot fat. Keep portions uniform. Brown lightly on both sides. Drain on absorbent paper. If cakes become cool, they may be placed in a pre-heated oven for 2 or 3 minutes just before serving. Serve with an 8-oz. can tomato sauce, heated, or with cold tartar sauce.

## BAKED CRAB WITH ALMONDS,
### SAMOAN STYLE
(Serves 4)

Remove all cartilage or pieces of shell from two 6½-oz. cans crab meat. Mix 6 tablespoons finely chopped blanched almonds with 1 tablespoon salad oil. Place in a shallow pan and bake in a 375° oven until light brown, taking care not to scorch; set aside. Put 2 table-spoons butter into a saucepan with ¼ cup each finely diced onion and celery and fry until onion is yellow. Remove from heat. Stir in 2 tablespoons flour. Very slowly add 1 cup hot light cream, stirring constantly. Return to a moderate flame. Simmer 5 minutes and remove from fire. In a mixing bowl, combine the cream sauce, crab meat, 1 teaspoon soy sauce, 2 table-spoons brandy and 2 tablespoons minced canned chili pepper. Add salt to taste, a dash of monosodium glutamate, and stir in ¼ cup bread crumbs. Pile crab-meat mixture into four coquilles or crab shells. Spread toasted almonds on top and bake 20 minutes in an oven preheated to 375°.

## BAKED DEVILED CRABS
### (Serves 4)

When you buy the crab meat, ask the fishmonger for four crab shells. If he does not have them, you may use four very large clam shells or four small casseroles. Chop 1 medium-size onion very fine. Place in a sauce-pan with 2 tablespoons butter or vegetable fat. Heat, stirring frequently, until onion turns yellow. Add 2 tablespoons flour, mixing well. Remove pan from flame. Gradually add ½ cup hot milk, stirring well. Return to a small flame. Cook, stirring frequently, for 4 minutes. Add 2 cups cooked fresh or canned crab meat. Add 1 tablespoon chopped parsley, ¾ teaspoon salt, ¼ teaspoon pepper, 1 teaspoon prepared mustard and ½ teaspoon dry mustard. Mix well.

Add 2 unbeaten egg yolks. Continue to cook, stirring constantly, until mixture is very thick. Remove pan from the fire. Chill the mixture in the refrigerator until quite cold.

Place the crab-meat mixture in the four crab shells or large clam shells. Sprinkle with fine bread crumbs. Sprinkle lightly with paprika and salad oil. Bake in a hot oven, 450°, for 15 to 20 minutes or until crumbs are brown. We guarantee you won't hear any crabbing when your guests wade into this spicy treat.

# Shrimps Supreme

In learning the art of shrimp cookery, one should know something, first of all, about the life and loves of the slender crustacean. Before birth the shrimp is part of a single egg mass that sometimes numbers three-quarters of a million potential shrimps. When hatched, the shrimp drifts around in shallow, slow-moving waters for several weeks until he grows to about a quarter of an inch in length. Then, feeling his oats, he sets out for deeper water and saltier adventures. Not long afterward he faces an adolescent problem. Although his body grows big, his shell remains inflexible, unable to expand. With a few well-timed flicks, he simply throws off his old shell and acquires a new one. His sex life is designed for the utmost variety: He is born male; as he matures, he gradually becomes female.

On the Pacific coast one may find the so-called ghost shrimps, so transparent you can see the heart beat. Blind shrimps have been taken from caves in Cuba. And in the western-American deserts, at rare intervals, small armored shrimps have been discovered coming to life when flash storms awakened dormant shrimp eggs in the sand.

The entire shrimp industry, in recent years, has experienced a magical prosperity. In 1945 someone discovered that if you trawl for shrimps at night while the shrimps are free-swimming, you'll come up with a much bigger haul than in the daytime. New shrimp beds were discovered in deeper waters. Today, shrimp is the little tail that wags the whole Gulf of Mexico, from which are taken most of the 250 million pounds of shrimps we eat annually.

For the eager young chef aching to do something different, the prime advantage of shrimps as a culinary medium is the fact that they are available in almost any conceivable form—and in sizes from baby to jumbo. You can now buy shrimps raw, dipped in butter and crumbs, cooked with the shells on, or with both shells and veins removed. If you live in a town where fresh-shrimp deliveries are not frequently made, you can buy shrimps frozen. Gourmets everywhere agree that the sweet seafood flavor and the firm texture of the frozen shrimps compare favorably with the fresh specimens.

When you buy fresh raw shrimps, you want shellfish that are completely free of any trace of off-odor or stickiness. The shells must be firm, clinging tightly to the body of the shrimps. All shrimps are sold beheaded, since the head constitutes about 40 percent of the shrimp's weight.

A few years ago the only shrimps you could buy were the gray variety. Now you will find raw shrimps that are brown, greenish brown, pink and even red. Just to make the shrimp spectrum a little more bewildering, tradesmen refer to all fresh shrimps as "green shrimps." But in spite of the varieties in color, there aren't too many differences in eating quality. Normally, the bigger the shrimps, the higher the price. The men who run the shrimp boats, however, prefer the flavor of the medium-size shrimps to the extra-large ones. The outsize shrimps will sometimes become dry after cooking. The largest-size shrimps run 15 to the pound or less. The smallest grade are 60 per pound or more.

The Chinese used to open shrimps by flaying the shells with bamboo poles. Until a few years ago, in factories where dried shrimps were being prepared, "shrimp dancers" were hired to tramp on the shells with special shoes. In your own bachelor apartment, this elaborate exorcism is hardly necessary. You can buy a shrimp cleaner that will remove both shells and veins in one operation. To clean them by hand, only a few deft movements need be learned. Simply tear the underbelly of the shell with one hand while holding the shrimp with the other. Peel off the top and biggest part of the shell. Then, holding the end of the tail in one hand, pull the tender contents free. To remove the vein, start at the fat end and, using the corner of your index finger, a very small skewer or pointed knife, peel down the length of the shrimp's body until the vein is out. You can't always see the vein as a distinct color, although you can feel it and separate it from the body. Sometimes it's black, sometimes orange, pink or white. In certain sections of the South and in some of the older hostelries, shrimps are served with the vein left intact. It won't harm you; now and then, however, it may be gritty.

When you boil shrimps, you'll sometimes detect an iodinelike odor. This is completely harmless and merely indicates that the shrimps were dieting on a variety of small marine life known as Balanoglossus. To moderate the pungent odor of boiling shrimps, add some acid such as lemon juice or vinegar to the pot. In addition, some cooks like to add herbs as well as seasoning vegetables to the water. Others like shrimps boiled in beer—a process that gives a delicate, slightly bitter tang to the shrimp flavor. Then there are fanciers who want their shrimps boiled only in plain salted water and who will tolerate no tampering with the natural flavor. Shrimps may be boiled in or out of the shell. When boiled out of the shell, they tend to curl a little more tightly than they do when boiled *au naturel*.

The one hard-and-fast rule that applies to boiled shrimps, as well as to all other seafood, is simply: Don't overcook. If you do, the shrimps will be both dry and tasteless. To boil large specimens for such dishes as shrimp cocktail or shrimp salad, plunge the shrimps into rapidly boiling water to which 1 teaspoon salt per quart of water has been added. When the water comes to a second boil, allow 5 minutes' cooking time; then remove from the water. If cooked shrimps are to be stored in the refrigerator, it's a good idea to return them to the cooking liquid after it has cooled. Keep them immersed in this liquid until serving time.

## SHRIMP MARINARA
(Serves 2)

3 tablespoons butter or olive oil
1 lb. raw shrimps, peeled and deveined
2 cloves garlic
2 cups canned Italian plum tomatoes, chopped fine
1 tablespoon parsley flakes
½ teaspoon oregano, chopped fine
2 tablespoons tomato paste
Salt and pepper

Melt the butter (or heat the oil) in a saucepan and add
the shrimps. Force the garlic through a garlic press or
mince very fine and add it to the pan. Sauté the
shrimps over a moderate flame until they turn pink.
Add the tomatoes, parsley, oregano and tomato paste
and simmer slowly 6 to 8 minutes. Season to taste.

## SHRIMP RABBIT
(Serves 2)

2 tablespoons butter
½ lb. cooked shrimps, peeled and deveined
¾ lb. sharp process American cheese
1 teaspoon prepared mustard
½ teaspoon dry mustard
¼ teaspoon paprika
½ teaspoon Worcestershire sauce
⅛ teaspoon celery salt
⅓ cup beer

Melt the butter in the top part of a double boiler over
simmering water. Add the shrimps and cook until
they are glossy with butter and heated through, about
2 to 3 minutes. Cut the cheese into cubes approximately
½ inch thick and add to shrimps with the other ingredients. Cook until the cheese is completely melted,
stirring well. Serve over toast.

## FRIED SHRIMPS
(Serves 2)

¾ lb. raw shrimps, shelled and deveined
1 egg, well beaten

½  cup cold water
¾  cup flour
½  teaspoon salt
¼  teaspoon baking powder
1  teaspoon grated onion
Deep fat for frying

Cut the shrimps, splitting them about three-quarters of their length, leaving the tail end intact. Wash well and dry on paper toweling. In a deep mixing bowl, combine the beaten egg and water. Sift the flour, salt and baking powder into the bowl. Add the grated onion. Beat with a wire whisk or rotary beater until the batter is very smooth, 2 to 3 minutes. Heat the fat to 370° or until the first wisp of smoke appears. Dip the shrimps into the batter. Place them one by one gently in the fat and fry until light brown, turning once during frying. Drain on paper toweling. Sprinkle with salt and serve with a cold sauce made by combining ¼ cup mayonnaise with 2 tablespoons sour cream and 2 teaspoons horseradish. Or simply serve with cold prepared tartar sauce.

## SHRIMP AND AVOCADO COCKTAIL
(Serves 2)

½  ripe avocado
Lettuce leaves
½  lb. cooked shrimps, peeled and deveined
½  cup chili sauce
1  teaspoon horseradish
½  teaspoon lemon juice
¼  teaspoon Worcestershire sauce
2  dashes Tabasco sauce
1  tablespoon finely chopped chives or scallions

Be sure the shrimps, avocado and chili sauce are ice-cold. Cut the avocado into dice about ½ inch thick. Place several small lettuce leaves in cocktail dishes and place the shrimps and avocado on the lettuce bed. Mix together the chili sauce, horseradish, lemon juice, Worcestershire sauce, Tabasco sauce and chives and pour over the shrimps. Serve with a small wedge of lemon. You may also substitute thawed frozen grapefruit segments for the avocado.

# SHRIMPBURGERS
## (Serves 2)

*1 lb. cooked shrimps, peeled and deveined*
*2 eggs*
*2 tablespoons flour*
*2 teaspoons grated onion*
*1 teaspoon dry mustard*
*1 teaspoon salt*
*⅛ teaspoon pepper*
*Vegetable fat*

Force the shrimps through a meat chopper, using the coarse blade. Separate the egg yolks from the whites and beat whites with rotary beater until stiff. In a mixing bowl, combine the ground shrimps, egg yolks, flour, grated onion, mustard, salt and pepper. Mix well. Fold in the egg whites. Melt the vegetable fat to a depth of ¼ inch in a large frying pan. When the fat is hot, drop the shrimp mixture by large spoonfuls into the pan. Sauté until golden brown on each side.


# BROILED MARINATED SHRIMPS
## (Serves 2)

*1 lb. raw shrimps, peeled and deveined*
*1 onion, sliced*
*1 carrot, sliced*
*1 piece celery, sliced*
*3 sprigs parsley*
*2 tablespoons salad oil*
*Juice of ½ lemon*
*Salt and pepper*
*Bread crumbs*
*Paprika*

In a deep bowl, combine the shrimps, onion, carrot, celery, parsley, salad oil and lemon juice. Mix well and store overnight in the refrigerator. When ready to use, remove the shrimps from the vegetables. Preheat broiler to 500°. Sprinkle the shrimps with salt and pepper. Dip into bread crumbs, coating thoroughly. Place in a shallow metal pan. Sprinkle lightly with salad oil and paprika and broil from 3 to 5 minutes on each side or until brown. Serve with tartar sauce, catsup or the sour-cream dressing in the fried-shrimp recipe given earlier.

## COLD SHRIMPS, MUSTARD DRESSING
### (Serves 2)

2 egg yolks
2 teaspoons prepared mustard
1 teaspoon dry mustard
¼ teaspoon turmeric
2 tablespoons vinegar
2 tablespoons sugar
¼ teaspoon onion salt
1 lb. cooked shrimps, peeled and deveined
¼ cup diced celery
2 tablespoons minced green pepper
Lettuce leaves
2 medium-size tomatoes

Beat the egg yolks well in a small bowl. (Use the egg whites to make a pink lady for your date.) Gradually add the prepared mustard, dry mustard, turmeric, vinegar, sugar and onion salt. Beat until the mixture is smooth and completely free of lumps. Place the egg-yolk mixture in the top part of a double boiler over simmering water. The water in the bottom section should not touch the top section. Beat constantly with a wire whip until the mixture just begins to thicken. This may take less than a minute. Remove immediately from the fire, turn the mixture into a bowl and chill in the refrigerator. Mix the chilled sauce with the shrimps, celery and green pepper. Line a bowl with lettuce leaves. Spoon the shrimp mixture over the lettuce and garnish with tomato wedges.

## SHRIMP PAN ROAST
### (Serves 2)

Like oyster pan roast—which is not a roast at all but a form of stew—shrimp pan roast follows the tradition of the old eastern oyster houses.

¼ cup butter
1 lb. cooked shrimps, peeled and deveined
1 teaspoon paprika
½ teaspoon celery salt
2 teaspoons horseradish
1 teaspoon Worcestershire sauce
¼ cup chili sauce
Salt and pepper
1½ cups light sweet cream
2 slices toast
Paprika

In a heavy saucepan, melt the butter. Add the shrimps and sauté over a moderate flame for 2 minutes. Add the paprika, celery salt, horseradish, Worcestershire and chili sauce and sprinkle generously with salt and pepper. Simmer 2 minutes longer. Add the cream, mixing well, and bring to the boiling point. Let the liquid merely simmer for several minutes. Place the toast in deep soup bowls. Spoon the shrimps over the toast. Pour the liquid into the bowls. Add a dash of paprika to each portion. Serve with oyster or Trenton crackers. Happy chomping.

# Happy As a Clam

To a student of seafood, a clam is impudence itself.
Remember the first time you tasted one and how, in
comparison with the subtler oyster, the clam on the
half shell seemed positively brash and roistering?
Your taste buds experienced a strange, flippant sensa-
tion, and you undoubtedly asked yourself, if you
reacted like most raw-clam eaters, whether it was good
or bad. You probably were still on the fence after
you'd finished the first half-dozen littlenecks. But
days later, for some unexplained reason, you were
overtaken by what is known as clam hunger—a sudden
irrational yearning for the bumptious, chewy morsels.

Even on the sea bottom, the clam is a self-asserting
creature who refuses to know his place. The oyster
is a cooperative fellow who fastens onto a mud flat
and proceeds to grow plump until he's dredged up and
delivered to an oyster bar. But the clam resists all
care and cultivation because he doesn't stay in one
place long enough to take orders. He patiently waits
until you get right on top of him, and then he deftly
burrows out of sight and gloats. When he wants to eat,
he raises his insolent neck up to the water and siphons
down his food. If you're on the Pacific coast and you
reach for him by hand, he just may turn out to be a
razor clam, and you'll wind up with no supper and a
mutilated mitt. Or he may be one of the geoduck
clams (pronounced *gooey-duck*) with a neck over two
feet long that he pulls down into the sand faster than
you can dig. Now and then, along the Atlantic shores,

entire colonies of clams will suddenly disappear and then, just as mysteriously, reappear in a capricious game of peekaboo.

Along the British shores, there are the notorious red-nosed clams, tough and mean enough to bore through rock so solid even power drills have a tough time making a dent. But the ultimate in audacity is displayed by the Tridacna clam of Australia's Great Barrier Reef, a monster sometimes weighing over 500 pounds—so heavy that when its shells fasten onto the anchor chain of a tugboat, the boat can't budge.

But behind the clam's rude manners, one soon discovers pure sweetness and succulence. Its snappy seafood flavor blends well with countless other foods yet never loses its identity. You may eat a piece of fish and perhaps not know whether it's halibut or cod, but there's no mistaking a clam. Whether it's an icy clam-juice cocktail in a men's bar, a gigantic clambake on the beach, bisque of clams in a cosmopolitan hotel or fried clams at a roadside stand, the distinctive clam flavor emerges—pert, salty sweet and rich.

There's no country in the world where clam dishes are created in such profusion as in the United States. The French and English eat oysters and mussels but pay relatively little attention to the clam. Even in this country, the mischievous mollusks were snubbed for a long time. Colonial New Englanders were actually starving when Ruth Aldon Bass of Duxbury, Massachusetts, watching a pig rooting in the shore sands, followed his lead and came up with the first New England clam chowder.

Of all specialty cooks, clam men are undoubtedly the most obstinate mavericks in the world. As surely as the tides rise and fall, it can be predicted that some bullnecked legislator in the coming months will introduce a law forbidding the use of tomatoes in New England clam chowder. With just as much certainty, it can be stated that when you order a clam stew in New York City, you'll automatically get hard-shell clams, and if you ask for soft clams you'll be looked upon as a bean-headed bumpkin from Maine with the straw still sticking out of your ears. Now, all of these arbitrary views over which regional cooks have locked spoons for decades have a certain piquant charm, but they don't make for interesting culinary inventions. New England clam chowder with milk, Manhattan clam chowder with tomatoes or Rhode Island clam chowder with neither tomatoes nor milk can all be found in good or bad versions, depending upon the imagination and judgment that go into their making.

Unlike fresh oysters, which are not sold in most states during the *R*-less months, you can enjoy hard- or soft-shell clams all year long even though some states limit the season during which clams may be taken. Market clams vary in size from the one-inch bean clams on the Pacific coast to the New England chowder clams, which sometimes run to six inches in diameter.

## CLAMS ON THE HALF SHELL

For cocktail parties, *intimes,* predinner frolics, late beer busts or simply for the gratification of the inner man at any time of the day or night, clams on the half shell are a smart idea. On restaurant menus, large clams on the half shell are listed as cherrystones. The smaller sizes are called littlenecks. Raw clams should be served positively glacial. The cocktail sauce served with the clams should be absolutely volcanic. You can buy raw clams already opened. These should be purchased right before eating. If they remain open several hours, they tend to shrink somewhat and lose flavor. Should this happen, some of their freshness can be restored by sprinkling them with ice-cold bottled clam juice or salt water just before serving. A teaspoon of salt to a pint of water is about right.

For the man who wants to open his own clams, there are mechanical clam openers that do a good, fast job. You can open them somewhat more neatly with an oyster knife, a short, stubby utensil with a blunt blade and a round handle. Ask or bribe your seafood dealer for a lesson in this manly art of clam opening.

For variety, place a dollop of ice-cold caviar on each freshly opened clam on the half shell. You may add chopped chives or scallions to the cocktail sauce or zip it up with horseradish, Tabasco sauce, Worcestershire sauce or cayenne pepper. The opened clams may be sprinkled with lemon or lime juice, white-wine vinegar or garlic-flavored vinegar.

## STEAMED SOFT CLAMS

Soft clams, known generally as steamers, have a milder yet somehow richer flavor than their hard-shell kin. The best are about two inches long, and you provide at least a dozen per guest. The shells of raw soft clams are normally open, with the neck protruding. A man must eat a peck or two of soft clams before he fully realizes why fingers were invented. It would be the silliest of affectations to attempt to separate the steaming-hot shells of a soft clam, pull off the brown skin covering the neck, lift the clam out of the shell, dip it into hot clam broth, bathe it in melted butter and finally pop it into the mouth by means of anything other than the thumb and index finger.

Since the steamer clam keeps its shell open in its sandy natural habitat, it's frequently full of that habitat. To remove the sand from soft clams, wash them well under cold running water, scrubbing them with a vegetable brush. Then cover them with cold water. Add 2 tablespoons salt and 2 tablespoons corn-meal or oatmeal for each gallon of water in which the clams are steeped. Let them remain in this water overnight in the refrigerator. Before steaming, throw off the water and again wash the little beggars. Place them in a steamer kettle or in a pot with a tightly fitting lid. Add 1 cup water for each quart of clams. Bring water to a boil. Reduce flame slightly and let the clams steam for 6 minutes, stirring a few times so that those on top may be in closer contact with the boiling water. When the clams are steamed wide open, remove them from the pot, place them on a platter and cover them with a cloth napkin to keep them hot. The liquid remaining in the pot is clam broth or clam juice. It may be used for clam-juice cocktails or clam soup, but ordinarily it is served at the table along with the steamers. Pour off the liquid carefully, avoiding as much as possible the sediment remaining on the bottom of the pot. Strain the broth through three thicknesses of cheesecloth. For each guest, provide a small dish of melted sweet butter, enlivened with lemon juice, as well as a cup of the strained clam broth.

Provide your guests with outsize napkins, and if they seem reluctant to tie them around their necks, set the sensible, etiquette-breaking example yourself. Soft-shell clams are flamboyantly messy eating, and though a few snobs may prefer to wear their butter stains as proudly as Heidelberg students wear dueling scars, the majority will be grateful to you for protecting their dinner jackets, shirts, ties, cummerbunds and décolletages.

## BAKED CLAMS WITH OREGANO
### (Serves 4)

*½  cup butter*
*2  medium-size cloves garlic*
*10  sprigs parsley*
*¾  teaspoon oregano*
*⅓  cup Italian-bread crumbs*
*32  cherrystone clams on the half shell*
*Salt and pepper*

Anybody who has ever tasted oregano in pizza or pasta will love this dish. Let the butter stand at room temperature until it can be spread easily. Preheat the oven to 475°. Remove garlic skin. Smash the garlic with the flat side of a heavy knife. Chop together the garlic, parsley and oregano until the parsley is almost like a powder. Add the bread crumbs and butter. Mix to a smooth paste. If you can get rock salt, spread it to a depth of ½ inch in a large, shallow baking pan or in pie plates. The salt will enable you to place the clams evenly in the pan without tilting and losing their juice. Sprinkle the clams lightly with salt and pepper. Divide the butter mixture, spreading a dab on each clam. Place the clams in the pan. Bake until the edges just begin to curl, usually about 10 to 12 minutes. Avoid overbaking.

## CLAM BALLS
### (Serves 4)

*1  tablespoon butter*
*1  egg yolk*

2 medium-size potatoes, peeled and boiled
1 7-oz. can minced clams, drained
⅓ cup bread crumbs
½ teaspoon lemon juice
1 teaspoon grated onion
1 teaspoon horseradish
1 tablespoon very finely chopped parsley
Salt and pepper
Flour
2 whole eggs, beaten
Bread crumbs

The best thing since the invention of beer and pretzels is beer and clam balls. Into a mixing bowl, put the butter and egg yolk. Force the hot potatoes through a potato ricer or food mill into the bowl. Stir well at once. Add the drained clams, ⅓ cup bread crumbs, lemon juice, grated onion, horseradish and parsley. Add ¼ teaspoon salt and ⅛ teaspoon pepper or more to taste. Stir well. Chill the mixture in the refrigerator for 2 or 3 hours. Shape into balls about 1 inch in diameter. Dip the clam balls first into the flour, then into the beaten eggs and finally into bread crumbs. Fry in a kettle of deep fat preheated to 370°. Drain on absorbent paper. Serve them furiously hot.

## CHICKEN AND CLAMS VALENCIA
(Serves 4)

3 lbs. young chicken cut for frying
Salt, pepper and paprika
Cooking oil
3 tablespoons butter
1 green pepper, diced
1 onion, finely chopped
1 clove garlic, finely chopped
1 bay leaf
¼ teaspoon saffron
¼ cup dry white wine
1 11½-oz. jar clams in juice
1 chicken-bouillon cube
1 cup rice

Sprinkle the chicken with salt, pepper and paprika.

Heat ¼ inch of oil in a large frying pan. Fry the chicken until light brown on both sides. Remove chicken from the pan and set aside. In a large, heavy pot fitted with a tight lid, melt the butter. Add the green pepper, onion, garlic and bay leaf. Sauté slowly until the onion just turns yellow. Put the browned chicken into the pot. Add the saffron and wine. Drain the juice off the clams and add enough water to make 1¾ cups liquid. Pour this liquid into the pot. Add the bouillon cube. Cover and simmer slowly for ½ hour. Add the rice to the pot, stirring well so that the rice is immersed in liquid. Again cover the pot and cook slowly until the rice is tender, from 15 to 20 minutes. Add the clams and cook a minute or two longer, just long enough to heat the clams through. Spoon the rice-and-clam mixture onto the serving platter. Place the chicken on top. Then just clam up and eat.

# The Opulent Oyster

You can't talk about oysters and leave out sex. The two subjects have been inseparable ever since Caesar and his imperial armies tramped into England and tasted the British bivalves. So exhilarated were the conquerors that they carried the oysters packed in snow, re-iced in the Alps, all the way back home. Romans tasted the sweet morsels on the half shell and hurried to cultivate them. Every saturnalia thereafter included oysters on the bill of fare.

Oysters were soon eaten all over Europe. By the time of Charles I in England, a popular breakfast combination was a plate of raw oysters and a pint of wine. Among all classes of people it was believed there was no love potion more effective than oysters. Byron, the English poet, described them as an "amatory food." The tradition that oysters are a sex stimulant has never died. To this day oyster bars abound with young blades gulping down big plates of freshly opened Cape Cods before rushing out to their dates.

Scientists in modern times have always discounted the idea that oysters are an aphrodisiac. They would no more endorse this theory than they would agree that fish is a brain food or that onions will remove warts. But a Dutch scientist pointed out that the oyster is rich in mineral elements which "contribute to its stimulating and aphrodisiac qualities." If normal good health affects our reproductive capacities, oysters can very well be a contributing factor to this health, since they are one of nature's most perfectly balanced foods from a nutritional standpoint, containing most of the important vitamins and minerals. But all this talk about fertility, in our opinion, was started by the oysters themselves. If all the female's eggs were fertilized and lived, in a few generations there would be a stack of oysters four times the size of the earth. Fortunately, their eggs are an aperitif for hungry fish —and fishermen. Only one oyster larva out of 10,000 finds a suitable home on the ocean bottom. Even then, many adult oysters are the victims of such enemies as the starfish or the drill—which can bore a hole right through an oyster shell to enjoy a fresh seafood snack.

Those who like to boast that their ancestors came over on the *Mayflower* should keep silent in the presence of these venerable creatures. During the Eocene, long before man roamed the earth, oysters were busily propagating themselves. Huge mounds of ancient oyster shells near Damariscotta, Maine, testify to the fact that oysters were a gourmet's treat enjoyed by American Indians long before the Pilgrims set foot on Plymouth Rock. Oysters even have blue blood; their large copper content gives them this distinctive status.

Generally speaking, people don't eat oysters because they're searching for vitamins, virility or even for pearls, but simply because oysters taste so delectable. They are one of the few foods that are eaten whole, organs and all. When your oyster fork spears a plump, raw bivalve, pearly gray with close folds of flesh, as cold and salty as the sea, and you dunk the shimmering morsel into a bath of cocktail sauce zesty with horseradish and Tabasco, you're not eating, you're in orbit. When you've finished the plate, you examine the ring of empty shells carefully, hoping that one more may be left. You pick up the cold cups with your fingers and drain the last drop of oyster liquor. The rest of the meal is an anticlimax—unless it happens to be more oysters.

We have often been consulted on whether they should be swallowed whole: We don't believe, frankly, that whole-oyster swallowers have a completely open-and-shut case. We're among the clique who believe in crunching the delicate mollusk between the teeth to enjoy its best sea flavor. But the issue is sometimes complicated: In Port Lincoln, Australia, oyster eaters seldom try to gulp down whole specimens; oysters there are as big as a large dinner plate—a foot in diameter.

Names of oysters in the United States indicate usually the bays or coves from which the oysters are taken. All eastern oysters are of the same variety. A Chatham oyster, a Chincoteague or a Delaware Bay are all members of the *Osterea virginica*. Oysters grown in northern waters, however, are noted for their saltiness while southern oysters are famed for their subtle sweetness. Cape Cods, lynnhavens and Chincoteagues are some of the most popular in oyster bars. Bluepoint is the name for small or medium-size oysters harvested before they are completely grown.

Cooking doesn't make an oyster tender. Every chef knows that the more you heat an oyster, the tougher it becomes. Treat the oyster at the range as though you were showing a guest to a warm fireplace. Don't set him afire.

Although chefs have devised elaborate oyster dishes such as oyster soufflé with Parmesan cheese, oysters in tartlet shells with caviar and oysters stuffed with truffles, most men prefer their seafood in the hearty styles eaten in oyster bars and homes all over the country. But plain cookery doesn't mean Simple Simon cookery, for in the preparation of oysters, every little deviation of seasoning or cooking time at once becomes noticeable. If you adhere studiously to the following formulas, however, your oysters will leave a wake of pure pleasure behind them.

## HORSERADISH AND TABASCO SAUCE
### (Serves 4)

Raw-oyster eaters sometimes yearn for a change from the conventional cocktail sauce made of catsup or chili sauce. Try this Continental concoction with your half shells: In a small jar, combine 4 tablespoons olive oil, 2 tablespoons vinegar, 1 teaspoon dry mustard, 2 teaspoons grated onion, juice of ½ lemon, 8 drops Tabasco sauce, 2 tablespoons horseradish, 1 teaspoon sugar, ¼ teaspoon salt and ¼ teaspoon freshly ground pepper. Shake well. Chill several hours before serving.

## STEAMED OYSTERS

Steamed-clam devotees will dig this one: Place oysters in a pot with 1 inch of water. Put on a tightly fitting lid. Bring the water to a boil. Reduce flame and simmer until shells open. Serve in the shells at the table. Dip into melted butter to which a small amount of lemon juice has been added.

## BARBECUED OYSTERS

In North Carolina, men have long enjoyed alfresco oysters in this style: Place oysters in the shell on an iron grating over a charcoal or wood fire and wait for the shells to open, revealing the oyster simmering in its own natural juice. Then use a pair of gloves to snatch up the hot bivalves and merely sprinkle lemon juice on top before devouring.

## FRIED OYSTERS
### (Serves 4)

Buy 24 freshly opened medium-size oysters. Pick over carefully to remove any small pieces of shell adhering. Drain off oyster liquor. Dry each oyster carefully on a clean towel or absorbent paper. Sprinkle with salt, pepper and celery salt. Beat 2 eggs slightly. Add 1 tablespoon salad oil, 2 tablespoons water and 2 tablespoons sweet cream. Beat well. Dip oysters into the egg mixture. Remove and dip into 1 cup fine cracker crumbs. Be sure each oyster is thoroughly coated with crumbs, which act as a protective coating and keep the intense heat of the frying fat from toughening the oysters.

Fry in deep vegetable fat or lard heated to 385°, or hot enough to brown a cube of day-old bread in 40 seconds. Place only one layer of oysters at a time in fry basket. Don't overfry—a light golden color will insure tenderness. Turn out on absorbent paper to dry any excess fat. Serve at once. If oysters are kept standing, the steam inside will cause the crumbs to become soggy.

On the table there should be a gravy boat of creamy, cold tartar sauce, a bottle of catsup and a plate of lemon wedges. French-fried potatoes, potato chips or shoestring potatoes are welcome. Iced beer or ale should be stationed right alongside the dinner plate. To top the meal, bring on a billowy lemon meringue pie and large cups of hot coffee.

## OYSTER STEW
### (Serves 4)

Buy 24 large or 36 medium-size, freshly opened oysters. Place oysters in a heavy saucepan with 4 tablespoons butter, 1 teaspoon salt, ¼ teaspoon celery salt, ¼ teaspoon paprika and ¼ teaspoon Worcestershire sauce. Heat together with oyster liquor only until ends of oysters begin to curl. Further heating will toughen them. Into another saucepan, put 1 quart milk and 1 cup light cream. Heat until milk begins to bubble around edge of pan, but be careful not to boil.

Put the oysters together with their juice and seasonings into four large soup bowls or tureens. Pour hot milk over oysters. Add 1 teaspoon butter to each bowl and sprinkle generously with paprika just before serving. Chopped scallions, a Louisiana fillip, may be added to the stew if desired. Keep a large mound of Trenton or oyster crackers at the table. Oyster-stew eaters will not object to a platter of assorted cheeses and plenty of coffee to complete the occasion.

## BAKED OYSTERS ROCKEFELLER
### (Serves 4)

Oysters Rockefeller are a New Orleans specialty now eaten all over the country. They are simply oysters baked on the half shell spread with a mixture of bread crumbs, butter, herbs and seasonings. If the herbs are not available, cooked chopped spinach is sometimes used as a substitute. To keep the oysters on an even keel in the baking pan, they are frequently set in a bed of coarse rock salt so that each oyster bakes evenly. Be careful that the salt does not get into the oysters.

Buy 24 freshly opened large oysters on the half shell. If you buy them opened at the fish store, use them within two or three hours. If you can open the oysters yourself with an oyster knife, do so just before baking them. An automatic oyster-opening gadget can now be purchased in many household-equipment stores. Once open, the oysters should be placed in a wide, shallow baking pan.

Into a mixing bowl, put ¼ lb. softened but not melted butter. Keep the butter at room temperature for a short while to soften it if necessary. Add a small grated onion and ½ cup grated white-bread crumbs. Add ¼ teaspoon salt, ¼ teaspoon celery salt, ⅛ teaspoon pepper and a dash of Tabasco sauce. Add the juice of ¼ lemon. Add 1 teaspoon each of the following herbs, all finely chopped: tarragon, chives, chervil and parsley. Mix all ingredients thoroughly. Spread this mixture over the oysters. Bake in a hot oven, 450°, for 10 to 12 minutes. Serve with iced dry white wine. Follow up with a huge bowl of garlic-scented tossed salad, long, crusty bread and a platter of French or Viennese pastries and coffee.

## SHERRIED OYSTERS
### (Serves 4)

If you've ever eaten the wonderful oysters from Chincoteague, Maryland, you'll understand George Washington's famous passion for this seafood. Sherried oysters are served in a delicate sauce that doesn't mask the provocative flavor of the bivalves. Serve on crisp, hot toast or on a mound of white rice with buttered fresh green peas.

Drain the oyster liquor from 36 oysters. Measure ¼ cup of the oyster liquor. Add enough milk to make 1½ cups liquid. Heat over a slow flame, but do not boil. In another saucepan, melt 3 tablespoons butter. Add the oysters and sauté only until the edges of the oysters begin to curl. Remove from the pan, using a slotted spoon. Don't overcook or they will become tough. Stir 3 tablespoons flour into the pan, blending well. Add ¼ teaspoon paprika, then gradually the 1½ cups liquid. Bring to a boil, reduce flame and simmer 5 minutes. Add ¼ cup sherry. Chop 4 scallions, using the white part and about 1 inch of the green, and add with oysters to the pan. Season to taste.

## BAKED SCALLOPED OYSTERS
### (Serves 4)

½ lb. bacon
8 shallots, minced fine
½ cup cream
1 cup light bread crumbs or cracker crumbs
¼ cup minced fresh parsley
2 teaspoons minced fresh tarragon
32 large, freshly opened oysters on half shell
Salt, celery salt and pepper
Paprika
Juice of 1 lemon
Lemon wedges

Cut the bacon into ½-inch squares. Put it and the shallots into a heavy saucepan and sauté over a low flame until bacon is almost crisp, stirring frequently. In a mixing bowl, combine well the bacon mixture, cream, bread crumbs, parsley and tarragon. Sprinkle oysters with salt, celery salt and pepper. Spread with the bread-crumb mixture and sprinkle with paprika and lemon juice. Place oysters on the half shell in a large, shallow pan (on top of a layer of rock salt, if available, to keep each shell in a flat position) and bake 20 to 25 minutes in a preheated 450° oven. Serve with lemon wedges.

## OYSTERS NEWBURG WITH TRUFFLES
### (Serves 4)

24 large, freshly opened oysters
¼ cup butter
½ lb. mushrooms, sliced thin
1 teaspoon paprika
1½ cups light cream
¼ cup dry sherry
2 tablespoons brandy
6 egg yolks, beaten
2 medium-size truffles, chopped fine
¼ teaspoon chopped chervil
Salt and pepper
4 slices toast

Examine oysters carefully and remove any pieces of shell. Drain their juice and set ½ cup aside. Melt butter in a heavy saucepan over a very low flame. Add oysters. Sauté until oysters just begin to curl around edges and remove from pan. Put mushrooms and paprika into the pan and sauté until mushrooms are just tender. Add the ½ cup oyster juice, the cream, sherry and brandy. Bring to a boil, reduce flame and simmer 5 minutes. Remove ¼ cup sauce from pan. Mix it with egg yolks, then return slowly to pan, stirring constantly and cooking only until sauce shows first sign of thickening. Overcooking will curdle the mixture. Remove from heat. Add oysters, truffles, chervil and salt and pepper to taste. Spoon over toast on serving dishes.

## OYSTERS SAUTE, CHIVE SAUCE
### (Serves 2)

12 freshly opened oysters
¾ cup light cream
Bread crumbs
1 tablespoon chopped fresh chives
Salt and pepper
1 egg, beaten
1 tablespoon cold water
Flour
2 tablespoons butter
2 tablespoons salad oil

If fresh oysters are not available, a 10½-oz. can of fancy large oysters may be substituted. Drain oysters well, reserving liquor. Add milk to liquor, if necessary, to make ½ cup. Combine liquor with light cream, ⅓ cup bread crumbs and chives. Season to taste with salt and pepper. Heat very slowly and keep warm until serving time. Combine egg and cold water. Sprinkle oysters with salt and pepper. Dip into flour, then into the beaten egg, finally into bread crumbs, making sure that each is thoroughly coated. Put butter and oil into an electric skillet preheated to 370°. Sauté oysters until light brown on both sides. Pour hot sauce into shallow casseroles and place oysters on sauce.

# The Worthy Roast

Since *Pithecanthropus erectus* charred his first loin of mastodon over a campfire, the roast has been man's most popular—and, in the opinion of many, his most prodigal—meat course. From ewe to yak, gnu to caribou, warthog to wildebeest, hardly a creature from the ark has managed to escape the oven or the roasting spit. Of this vast four-footed throng, however, no beastie has made more boards—or boarders—groan with pleasure than that sumptuous Sunday-dinner staple, the immemorial roast beef. We therefore begin our exploration of the roast realm with this venerable viand.

It must be a great satisfaction to Englishmen to realize that, although they have gone unchallenged as the world's worst cooks, their roast beef has been the envy of gourmets everywhere. For centuries the English cook, fully conscious that he couldn't tell sauce from seltzer, has treated his mighty roast beef with a kind of affectionate humility, simply placing the plain ribs carefully on the fire—unseasoned, ungarnished and unmolested. In this courtly kitchen gesture, English instincts have been perfect, for good roast beef should be manipulated as little as possible.

Logically enough, while the cooks of merrie England were doing right by their ribs, sirloins and haunches, British cattlemen were busy developing the world's best beef on the hoof. Merely the names Aberdeen Angus and Hereford show the origin of the blue-ribbon beef we eat today.

English carvers were also instrumental in establishing

THE WORTHY ROAST 103

the reputation of English roast beef. Unlike the non-interventionist cooks, these carvers were a breed of learned craftsmen who, as early as the 16th Century, were avidly reading the procedures in the *Boke of Kervynge*. At the table of Edward IV there stood four official carvers, especially trained knights of the high order known as bannerets, famed for the skill with which they lifted their mighty Sheffield blades and delivered the king's roast beef.

With good reason, then, did the poet Richard Leveridge write:

> *When mighty roast beef*
> *was the Englishman's food,*
> *It ennobled our hearts*
> *and enriched our blood;*
> *Our soldiers were brave*
> *and our courtiers were good.*
> *Oh! the roast beef of old*
> *England!*

Today, however, it's a generally accepted fact that Britishers no longer enjoy the world's best beef. American cattle are better fed and better shaped.

Fortunately, you can now buy rib roast without worrying too much about such criteria as marbling, grain, conformation, porosity of bone, hues of fat and other professional guides that frequently confuse the amateur chef. First of all, look for the U.S. Department of Agriculture (USDA) stamp, indicating the quality, which is printed on the back of the roast. If the meat is stamped *prime*, you're buying the best grade of beef available. Normally, the quantity of prime beef available for retail stores is rather small. If prime isn't obtainable, you'll want the next-best grade, which is *choice*. Now, admittedly, within grades, professional meatmen detect minor differences usually not discernible to the untrained eye, but by and large you will have excellent beef if you confine yourself to these two top echelons. Don't buy beef marked *good, commercial* or *utility*. Some of the big meat-packers use their own nomenclature for grading, and you can follow this if you're familiar with their meaning. The chances are, however, that the packer's self-imposed standards are hardly as objective as those of the government graders. In some parts of the country, beef that is slaughtered locally and delivered locally may not be graded at all. In such cases you must depend upon the good judgment of your butcher, and you should select him with the same care with which you choose a decorator, an architect or any of the other experts who advise you in the art of not just living, but living intelligently and pleasurably.

Finally, beyond the ranks of *prime* and *choice* there remains the very highest caste in the animal kingdom —*aged beef*. This is beef kept on the butcher's hook for several weeks, where it becomes more tender and more juicy through the friendly action of enzymes. During the aging process, the meat changes from a cherry-red color to a dull red. Veteran beefeaters want their meat aged not only to maximum tenderness, which takes about three weeks, but even beyond this stage until the meat acquires a sharp, almost gamy flavor. Don't try to age beef in your own refrigerator. It must be kept under controlled temperature and low humidity, which only the trained meatcutter can manage effectively. Now, if there's one kind of man the butcher hates more than the vegetarian, it's the man who demands aged beef. The reason for his hate is simple: Aging shrinks meat. The fresher it is, the more it weighs and the more the butcher collects. If it were possible, he'd love to sell his meat even before *rigor mortis* has set in. There are, however, in some cities, gourmet butchershops where aged beef is available at premium prices. Sometimes wholesale butchers who store aged beef for fine hotels and taverns will sell it at retail prices. Certainly for the best of all possible beef blowouts, you should make every attempt to buy well-ripened beef.

The best ribs for roasting are sometimes known as "the first three ribs." Anatomically, these are the ribs farthest from the neck and may also be called the 10th, 11th and 12th ribs. In order to avoid confusion, simply tell the butcher that you want three ribs cut from the small end right alongside the short loin. These ribs will contain the large, solid center piece known as the "eye" and will be relatively free from gristle, excess fat and the tough end known as the flank. The ribs should be no more than seven inches long. Tell the butcher to cut off any meat beyond the seven-inch goal line. Use these ends for boiling or braising. Have him also cut off the backbone for easy carving.

Undergraduate carvers are often partial to boned rib roasts. These are sometimes called Spencer or Newport roasts. Offhand, they would seem to be easier to handle, but actually they present some difficulties that should not be overlooked. Boned roasts take a longer cooking time per pound than roasts with the bone left in, because the meat is much more compact and chunky after it is tied. The butcher, in boning and tying the meat, will sometimes include the tough flank, which would otherwise be eliminated. Then, when you go to carve the boneless meat, the cord used to hold the meat together will sometimes drop off prematurely, and the wobbly, unsupported meat will actually be harder to slice than a roast in which the stalwart bone remains.

For handling a rib roast properly, there is certain basic equipment you should own. First of all, you want a shallow, uncovered roasting pan at least 10 by 14 inches. You'll want a carving board, and it should be a thick, hard maple board, not the thin, warped affair used for slicing bread or buns. The widely used spiked board is helpful to some carvers and a damned nuisance to others. The spiked board is particularly bothersome when you stand a rib roast on its end for carving, for the meat stubbornly bends like a leaning tower. To set the roast aright, it may be necessary to place a saucer or other supporting object beneath the meat. This is rather difficult on a spiked board.

The best knife for carving is known appropriately as the roast-beef slicer. This long, narrow weapon of uniform width is rounded at the blade's end, making it easy to swing the knife up to and around the bones. For steadying the meat and lifting the slices, you'll need a carving fork with genuinely sturdy prongs and handle.

Before any tenderfoot chef places his roast in the oven, he should take heart and understand that the interior of roast beef isn't a deep, dark continent full of mystery but something that can be easily gauged at every stage of the roasting procedure by the use of a meat thermometer. Insert this instrument and you'll be able to tell whether the meat is rare, medium or well done. A word of warning, however: For some years now, the manufacturers of meat thermometers have held a somewhat naïve idea of what constitutes "rare." Most meat thermometers indicate rare as 140 degrees (the internal temperature of the meat). In our opinion, beef is rare at 130 degrees. Let the temperature go to 140 degrees for medium and 160 degrees for well done. Usually there's someone at a roast-beef party who asks for the crisp, well-done endpieces, but most adult roast-beef lovers will not tolerate beef that isn't rare.

Never buy a roast containing less than two ribs. Small roasts are subject to excessive loss of flavor in the oven because the cut sides may be just as large in a one-rib roast as in a four-rib roast. A three-rib roast is a good average size.

Raw roasting beef that has been stashed away in the deepfreeze is never equal to unfrozen beef roasts because of the huge flood of juice which is unloosed when the large cuts are thawed prior to roasting. If you roast frozen beef without thawing it beforehand, you must allow from 15 to 20 minutes more cooking time per pound than for the unthawed roast. This additional cooking time varies with the shape and size of the roast. You should insert the meat thermometer as soon as the meat is soft. In either case there will be a pronounced loss of juice with a corresponding loss of flavor.

Butchershop browsers will discover a number of other cuts that are used for roasting. Plain sirloin of beef, called "boned shell" by the butcher, is luxurious eating and quite expensive. The real potentialities of this cut, however, are best realized when the meat is cut into steaks for broiling. Top-sirloin or sirloin-butt roasts are semitender and must always be roasted quite rare or they lose their savor. They are sold boneless, and although the meat can be quite succulent at times, they lack the robust flavor of the ribs. Top-round roasts are quite coarse in texture, semitender at best, and though containing very little waste, they are definitely of hash-house caliber. Lastly, roast filet, or tenderloin, of beef is the most expensive and kindest cut of all. In French restaurants, roast filet of beef is usually featured with a lush wine sauce. The sauce is added because, though the winsome meat melts in your mouth, the flavor is flat alongside the unmatched palatability of roast ribs.

The amount of beef to buy naturally depends upon the capacities of your guests. For instance, if you're entertaining the unabashed when-do-we-eat sort, you may want to provide oversize portions, and you should allow a pound of raw beef per person. Thus, a three-rib roast weighing nine pounds trimmed and ready for the oven would satisfy nine such hefty appetites. Naturally, after cooking the meat will weigh considerably less. If your guests, on the other hand, are noted for the slim waistlines they keep, you might allow from ½ to ¾ pound of raw beef per person.

No supporting dish has ever upstaged roast ribs of beef on the table. Before the roast is ushered in, you might serve some plump oysters on the half shell or offer a cup of clear green-turtle soup. Under no circumstances should you dull your palate with a heavy pureed soup. Along with the roast beef itself, there are some alluring time-tested consorts—fluffy baked and stuffed potatoes flavored with chives, the youngest of baby green string beans, the natural gravy known as *jus* and Yorkshire pudding—a thin, tender shell or crust baked with the drippings of the beef itself. Certainly, with roast beef it would be hard to imagine a more buoyant or amicable beverage than cold beer or ale freshly poured into oversize tankards.

## ON THE FIRE

Remove beef from refrigerator at least an hour before roasting in order to bring it as close as possible to room temperature. Preheat oven to 425°. Place ribs fat side up in an uncovered roasting pan. Insert meat thermometer through the fatty side of the roast. Don't salt or pepper the meat. Salt penetrates meat to only about ½ inch from the surface. Excess salt draws off beef juice. Roast-beef slices may be sprinkled with salt only after they're carved. Roast the meat at 425° for 20 to 25 minutes. Then lower temperature to 325°. Roasting at a constant high temperature causes excessive shrinkage. Keep the roast on the fire until it is done as indicated by the meat thermometer. From time to time you may have to pour off the light beef drippings for Yorkshire pudding. If you don't have a meat thermometer, allow about 18–20 minutes per pound for rare roast beef, 20–22 minutes per pound for medium and 25 minutes for well done.

## AU JUS

The thin roast-beef gravy, with no thickening whatever added, should look like a dark consommé. To give it an authentic roast-beef flavor, two steps are necessary: First, you must use the dark drippings on the pan bottom or sides (not the light melted fat of the beef). Then you must carefully capture the pink juices that flow out as the roast sets after it is removed from the oven. If possible, the beef juices that flow out as the meat is carved should be added to the gravy boat, too. First, pour off all fat from the pan. Add (for a three-rib roast) 1½ cups boiling water. Scrape the pan bottom and sides to loosen the drippings. Add 2 bouillon cubes and a dash of brown gravy color. Add 2 teaspoons sweet butter, ⅛ teaspoon Worcestershire sauce and salt and pepper to taste. Bring to a boil. Reduce flame and simmer 3 minutes. You may have to use two top burners to simmer the liquid in the large pan. Strain the *jus* if necessary.

## AT THE CARVING BOARD

Before taking your command post at the head of the table, be sure that the roast has been removed from the oven at least 20 minutes. A 25- to 30-minute interval is even better. During this time the beef sets— that is, the internal juices stop flowing, the cooking subsides and the meat is now amenable to easy, clean slices. Usually, a three-rib roast will remain hot during this time. If the roast should be cooled by a kitchen draft, you can reheat it by placing it in an extremely slow oven, 200°, for 5 to 8 minutes. Place the meat upright on the meat-carving board with the rib bones on your left. Support the meat, if necessary, so that it is on a level plane by placing a small plate or dish beneath it. Be sure your roast-beef slicer is razor-sharp. If necessary, sharpen it on a whetstone and pass it over a knife steel to temper the edge. Keep a large-size napkin or towel handy. Steady the meat by inserting the meat fork between the top rib bones. Be sure to use a long, steady motion with the knife blade, not a short, staccato movement. Starting at the right side and carving toward the bone, cut off the end slice, making it fairly thick—about ½ inch. Cut down to free the meat from the rib bones. Lift the meat, using both knife and fork or fork and serving spoon. Cut subsequent slices about ¼ inch thick, checking frequently to make sure the slices are parallel. Cut away the rib bones when necessary. Pour escaped beef juice into gravy boat.

## YORKSHIRE PUDDING

This light, airy pudding rises in the oven and falls when it is cut. It's really a hollow shell like a popover, since it's made from a popover batter. Since Yorkshire pudding is baked at 400° and beef is roasted at 325°, you'll have a minor problem in kitchen strategy here. It can be solved as follows: Prepare the pudding batter. Ten to 15 minutes before the roast is removed from the fire, turn up the heat to 400°. Put the pudding in the oven for about 15 minutes. Remove the roast to let it set. Continue baking the pudding until it is done, about 25 minutes longer. To make Yorkshire pudding batter, beat 2 eggs in a deep bowl. Add 1 cup milk. Beat well again. Gradually add 1 cup sifted all-purpose flour and ½ teaspoon salt. Beat with a rotary eggbeater until the batter is very smooth. Strain the batter. Pour ¼ cup light drippings into an 8-by-8-inch square baking pan. Add the batter. Bake at 400° for 35 to 40 minutes. Serve at once, cutting the pudding into squares. This formula will make about six portions. A martini or two before eating is, as always, a grand idea if you tend toward waggish ways.

* * *

However sumptuous a staple, even roast beef is oft enhanced by absence from the festal board. Your beef-smitten taste buds may grow fonder with an occasional switch of allegiance to such saporific *spécialités* as roast of lamb and pork, herewith proffered:

## ROAST LEG OF LAMB
### (Serves 8)

*1 leg of lamb, 6 to 7 lbs.*
*½ cup salad oil*
*3 large cloves garlic, smashed*
*1 teaspoon ground cumin*
*1 teaspoon rosemary*
*1 teaspoon dry mustard*
*1 teaspoon salt*
*¼ teaspoon freshly ground black pepper*
*½ cup dry white wine*
*2 cups chicken broth*
*2 tablespoons butter*
*Brown gravy coloring*

Have the butcher remove the fell (outer skin) from lamb, remove the hipbone and truss up the leg for proper roasting and carving. Combine oil, garlic, cumin, rosemary, mustard, salt and pepper. Place lamb in a shallow pan or casserole. Rub the oil mixture thoroughly into the meat and marinate at least 3 hours before roasting, overnight if possible. Rub the oil mixture in again just before roasting. Place the leg fat side up in an uncovered roasting pan. Insert meat thermometer into thickest part and roast in preheated 325° oven until thermometer registers about 160° for medium to well done (about 2½ hours). About ½ hour before cooking is completed, pour off all fat from pan, but let brown drippings remain. Then pour wine over meat and return to oven to finish roasting. Remove meat from pan and place pan over a top flame. Add chicken broth and bring to a boil. Reduce flame and simmer 5 minutes. Add butter, brown gravy coloring and salt and pepper to taste. Let the leg set at least 20 minutes before carving. Then pour hot gravy over meat and serve.

# SHORT RIBS OF BEEF BURGUNDY
### (Serves 4)

Short ribs have a magnificent beef flavor. They are somewhat fatty, but this is balanced by the very dry red-wine sauce in which they are potted. The gravy should be skimmed of every globule of fat before serving. Short ribs should be escorted to the table with fluffy egg noodles, French-cut green string beans and a bottle of fine Pommard.

> *3 lbs. short ribs of beef*
> *3 tablespoons butter*
> *1 large onion, sliced*
> *1 clove garlic, chopped fine*
> *4 sprigs parsley*
> *2 pieces celery, sliced*
> *1 carrot, sliced*
> *1 small bay leaf*
> *1 pinch thyme*
> *2 tablespoons flour*
> *1 cup dry red wine*
> *1 cup water*
> *1 bouillon cube*
> *¼ teaspoon Worcestershire sauce*
> *¼ teaspoon brown gravy color*
> *Salt and pepper*

Place the short ribs in a shallow roasting pan in an oven preheated to 450°. Keep the meat in the oven until brown, about 30 to 40 minutes, turning once during the browning. In a heavy Dutch oven or stewing pot fitted with a lid, melt but do not brown the butter. Add the onion, garlic, parsley, celery, carrot, bay leaf and thyme. Sauté slowly until the onion turns deep yellow. Stir in the flour, mixing well. Add the wine, water and bouillon cube, mixing well. Bring the liquid to a boil, stirring frequently. Reduce flame so that liquid merely simmers. Transfer the short ribs from the roasting pan to the stewing pot. Cover and simmer slowly until the meat is very tender, about 2 hours. Remove pieces of meat from pot. Skim all fat from the surface of the gravy and strain the gravy through a fine wire strainer. Add the Worcestershire sauce and gravy color, plus salt and pepper to taste.

## ROAST FRESH HAM, BURGUNDY CABBAGE
### (Serves 8)

*1 fresh ham, 8 to 10 lbs.*
*1 cup chicken broth*
*4 lbs. red cabbage*
*2 medium-size onions, minced*
*2 cloves garlic, minced*
*¼ teaspoon ground allspice*
*⅛ teaspoon nutmeg*
*½ cup dry red Burgundy*
*¼ cup red-wine vinegar*
*3 tablespoons granulated sugar*
*¼ cup brown sugar*
*½ teaspoon ground cloves*
*Salt and pepper*

Place ham fat side up on a wire rack in an uncovered roasting pan. Insert meat thermometer into thickest part and roast in preheated 350° oven, allowing 33 minutes' roasting time per pound or until thermometer registers 185°. After about an hour, pour the chicken broth into pan and baste ham with it from time to time. Trim cabbage, removing bruised or spotted leaves. Cut into wedges and cut out and discard core; then slice into ¼-inch strips. Put with onions, garlic, allspice, nutmeg, Burgundy, vinegar and granulated sugar into a deep, heavy saucepan or pot. Cover with a tight lid and simmer until cabbage is just becoming soft. When ham is done, slice off outer rind. Pour liquid from roasting pan over cabbage. If there are more than 3 tablespoons of fat in the liquid, pour off excess. Cook the cabbage slowly until almost all liquid has evaporated, stirring frequently to avoid scorching. Season with salt and pepper. Rub the brown sugar and ground cloves over the fat side of the ham. Sprinkle with salt and pepper and return to a 450° oven for 20 minutes or until fat begins to brown. Let set in a warm place at least 20 minutes before carving. Place ham slices over cabbage on serving plates or platter.

# ROAST VEAL LOIN,
## FRESH MUSHROOM SAUCE
### (Serves 4)

*1 boned loin of veal, about 4 lbs.*
*Salt and pepper*
*2 tablespoons Dijon mustard*
*2 tablespoons minced parsley*
*¼ teaspoon minced fresh thyme or ⅛ teaspoon*
  *dried thyme*
*1 tablespoon minced fresh dill*
*3 tablespoons butter at room temperature*
*1 onion, sliced*
*1 piece celery, sliced*
*1 small carrot, sliced*
*1 cup chicken broth*
*½ lb. fresh mushrooms*
*2 tablespoons butter*
*2 tablespoons flour*
*1 teaspoon onion juice*
*1 teaspoon Dijon mustard*
*Brown gravy color (optional)*

Sprinkle veal with salt and pepper. Make a paste of the 2 tablespoons mustard, parsley, thyme, dill and 3 tablespoons butter. Spread half the paste on the inside of the veal. Roll up and tie with heavy twine in four or five places. Spread balance of paste on outside and place veal in a baking pan with the onion, celery and carrot. Roast in a preheated 300° oven for 2½ hours or until tender, basting from time to time with meat juice in pan. Remove from pan. Pour in broth and place over a low flame, scraping bottom and sides to loosen drippings. Simmer 5 minutes. Separate mushroom caps from stems and cut both into slices about ⅛ inch thick. Sauté in 2 tablespoons butter in a heavy saucepan until tender. Stir in flour, mixing very well. Strain gravy from baking pan and pour into saucepan slowly, stirring constantly. Bring to a boil and simmer 5 minutes. Add onion juice, 1 teaspoon mustard and brown gravy color if desired. Cut veal into slices about ¼ inch thick and pour mushroom sauce over veal.

## ROAST LAMB SADDLE, BEARNAISE MINT SAUCE
### (Serves 4 to 5)

*1 saddle of lamb, about 5 lbs.*
*Olive oil*
*Salt, garlic salt and pepper*
*4 large or 5 medium-size egg yolks*
*1½ teaspoons tarragon vinegar*
*¾ cup melted sweet butter*
*1½ teaspoons meat extract*
*1½ tablespoons finely minced fresh mint*

Be sure the butcher understands that the saddle must be a double loin (no rack included) cut across the back. (Kidneys and flank should be removed; both can be cut up for a stew at another meal.) Brush saddle with olive oil. Sprinkle with salt, garlic salt and pepper. Place fat side up on a wire rack in an uncovered roasting pan. Roast in preheated 500° oven for 15 minutes. Reduce heat to 350° and continue roasting—allowing 25 minutes per pound for medium or 20 minutes per pound for rare. Lamb epicures, it should be noted, prefer the latter. Pour egg yolks and vinegar into the well of an electric blender and blend for a few seconds. Heat butter over a moderate flame and add very slowly, about a teaspoon at a time, to slow-blending egg yolks. Remove sauce from blender. Add meat extract, mint and dash of salt and pepper. Keep sauce in a warm (not hot) place until serving time. Excessive heat will curdle it. Let meat set in a warm place at least 20 minutes before carving. Turn on underside and cut the fillet into long, thin strips the entire length of the saddle. Turn on other side and cut long strips alongside backbone; slices will be somewhat wedge-shaped at first. Then cut along rib bones to loosen slices. Carve the other side of the backbone in the same manner. Slices may be replaced on bone as frame and served from it at table or may be placed on a large platter. Pass sauce in a sauceboat.

# Chop Talk

The word *chop,* if it doesn't suggest cherry trees or suey, usually brings to mind the ubiquitous broiled lamb chop—a morsel both quickly prepared (brown, turn, brown, serve) and quickly devoured. But *chop* in the generic sense is an immense continent of pleasure, comprising the entire succulent expanse of an animal's tender midsection—a region with which every self-respecting trencherman should become intimately acquainted. In deepening this rather one-sided but nevertheless gratifying friendship between man and beastie, one must first learn to distinguish between the two best-known areas of contact: steaks and chops. The phrase itself is a clarion call for the brandishing of cutlery, and yet it is actually double-talk of a sort, because steaks *are* chops, and chops *are* steaks, in the sense that both are thick slices taken from those tender and toothsome central regions that have mercifully been spared the rigors of physical exercise. The distinction in terms is really a distinction in animals: When this choice cut is taken from a steer, it is called a steak; from lamb, mutton, pork, veal or venison, it is properly called a chop. It should be pointed out, however, that there are at large in the chop kingdom certain illegitimate claimants to these venerated titles which the true *bon viveur* should learn to ignore scrupulously; among them are such feeble impostors as the shoulder lamb "chop" and the round beef "steak" —both refugees from the gristly forequarters. But long acquaintance with the genuine article will perfect your ability to judge character in meats.

Don't expect to further this acquaintance in the average chophouse, however. On the standard menu, "(1) or (2) lamb chops," clothed daintily in ruffled pink panties, is the classic choice, as though these two pathetic numerals and the benign lamb were the alpha and omega of the chop world. Back in the days of Addison and Steele, a hungry man had an easier time of it. A visit to *his* local chophouse—a dependable, oak-beamed lair with crackling fireplaces, sturdy serving wenches and foaming mugs—yielded not the isolated broiled lamb chop we often eat today, but a great, juicy, pink-centered slab from the succulent heart of mountainous roast ribs of beef or loin of mutton.

For modern men, the chop field is still wide open to those who can perceive its riches. But one significant fact must be kept in mind: Beef, either rib or loin, asks for little in the way of culinary alchemy, but chops must be braced with burly sauces and spices to elicit their full range of subtleties. If you're eating a beautifully broiled steak, you're not going to degrade it with bottled sauce. But if lamb chops are your delight, you'll want to bathe them in olive oil, lemon juice, crushed garlic and rosemary before they're committed to the flames; the result is triumphantly toothsome. Or try young spring lamb steeped in a marinade of soy sauce, chopped fresh ginger and garlic (the latter two being just about the most bombastic flavors on the spice shelf); it is irresistible.

But let us venture even further into chop country. Consider the mixed grill—a dish in which the chop, playing the lead role, is surrounded by a quartet or quintet of compatible tidbits, broiled and fried. Most frequently one finds a broiled lamb chop in the pivot spot, flanked by bacon, broiled tomato, sausage link and tender mushrooms. In a traditional version, the lamb chop is joined by a slice of shell beefsteak, a stuffed tomato, sausage and French-fried onions. But earthy companions such as broiled lamb kidneys, chicken livers, sweetbreads or even calf's brains often show up, too. As a switch from the thin-sausage gambit, you might add a new fillip with a fresh or smoked fat country sausage, a pungent bockwurst or bulging bratwurst. Or if you want to gallicize your chop, serve it with a redolent French garlic sausage, stuffed fresh mushrooms, artichoke bottoms and souffléed potatoes. There's no limit to the variations on this theme, for chops—unlike many other meats—have countless friends and almost no enemies.

One point worth remembering: Any chop less than an inch thick isn't worth bringing home. A thin chop, after cooking, turns into a tire patch. Even the delicate "French" lamb chop—a rib chop in which all the meat has been scraped from the bone end—must have a plump and juicy eye. So buy the best chops from the best meatman in your fief; ask him for thick chops cut to order and don't recoil from the price. When you get them, examine the color—prime-quality chops will have an adolescent pink cast and not the brick-red complexion of an elderly lush.

When you're broiling lamb, mutton or venison, you'll want a fierce fire for browning, then a gentler flame for finishing. To tell when a chop has achieved rareness—that most perfect edible state—press it gently with the back of a spoon; the more resilient the meat, the rarer it is. A well-done chop, if you insist on it, is quite firm to the touch, although the tender fillet from a loin chop is so pliable that it always yields unresistingly. For broiling a 1-inch chop, allow 6 to 8 minutes per side; for 2-inch or 2½-inch chops, 10 to 12 minutes each side. But be careful with veal and pork chops; they wince at a strong fire. Sautéing over a moderate or low flame is the treatment they demand. Another tip: Never stab a chop in the back. If you must pierce it for turning, sink the fork into the outside rim of fat where you won't tear the flesh and forfeit the juices. The respectful utensil for chop handling is a pair of long outdoor-type tongs—not those little toys designed for ice-cube manipulation.

If your chop is part of a mixed grill or if it's veal, pork or venison, one per person usually provides an adequate meat course. When lamb chops are served solo, two comprise a man-sized portion. There may be some fastidious gourmets, of course, who wish to emulate Louis XVIII, who insisted that his chops be prepared à la victime: Three chops were tied tightly side by side and carefully charred; the two outside chops were then deliberately discarded and the soft, pale center chop was served in quivering solitude. The recipes here, you may be relieved to learn, involve no such wasted riches.

## ALSATIAN PORK CHOPS
### (Serves 4)

1 lb. sauerkraut
2 tablespoons butter
2 tablespoons salad oil
4 center-cut loin pork chops
Salt and pepper
1 medium-size onion, minced
1 medium-size clove garlic, minced
⅛ teaspoon chervil
⅛ teaspoon rosemary
¼ teaspoon sage leaves
4 juniper berries, chopped fine
1 cup dry white wine
1 cup fresh or canned chicken broth

Drain and squeeze the sauerkraut to eliminate as much juice as possible. Melt the butter in a Dutch oven or heavy saucepan and add the oil. Sprinkle the chops with salt and pepper and sauté until light brown on both sides. Add onion, garlic, chervil, rosemary, sage and juniper berries. Continue to sauté about 5 minutes longer. Add sauerkraut, white wine and broth. Place lid on pan and simmer over a very low flame about 1 hour or until liquid has almost evaporated from kraut. Season to taste.

## PORK CHOPS WITH PEPPER STUFFING
### (Serves 4)

1 cup soft bread crumbs
2 tablespoons butter
2 tablespoons minced onion
3 tablespoons minced green pepper
3 tablespoons minced pimiento
¼ teaspoon creole seasoning
1 egg, well beaten
Salt and pepper

*4 center-cut loin pork chops*
*Salad oil*

To make bread crumbs, cut Italian or French bread, at least one day old, into ½-inch cubes. Blend electrically at high speed, ¼ cup at a time, until 1 cup of crumbs is formed. To melted butter in a small saucepan, add the onion and green pepper. Sauté slowly until onion is yellow. Remove from fire and add pimiento, creole seasoning, bread crumbs, beaten egg and salt and pepper to taste. With a sharp paring or boning knife, cut a deep pocket in the side of each pork chop and stuff with the sautéed mixture. Fasten the open side of each chop with toothpicks inserted diagonally, using about three or four for each. Preheat oven and electric skillet to 350°. In ¼ inch salad oil in skillet, brown chops on both sides. Then transfer to a shallow baking pan. Bake 30 to 40 minutes or until chops are well browned and very tender. Serve with ice-cold applesauce spiked with horseradish.

## LAMB CHOPS, FRITTO MISTO
### (Serves 4)

*2 green peppers*
*1 cup sifted flour*
*2 tablespoons dry vermouth*
*2 egg yolks*
*½ cup cold water*
*Salt and pepper*
*Salad oil*
*2 egg whites, beaten stiff*
*4 slices eggplant with skin, ¼ inch thick*
*8 medium-size fresh mushroom caps*
*2 tomatoes, halved crosswise*
*4 loin lamb chops*

(*Fritto misto* is a no-holds-barred Italian dish in which anything from shrimps to sheep's brains to hominy is fried in batter. This version is an assortment of vegetables served as in a mixed grill with lamb chops.) In preheated 450° oven, place the whole peppers for 18 to 20 minutes. Rub off as much of the transparent pepper skin as possible with a dry towel. Cut peppers lengthwise into ½-inch strips, discarding seeds and stems, and set aside. In a mixing bowl, put the flour, vermouth, egg yolks, cold water, ½ teaspoon salt and 1 tablespoon salad oil. Beat just until smooth. Fold in beaten egg whites. Dip peppers, eggplant, mushrooms and tomatoes into the batter. While chops are broiling until brown on each side, heat salad oil, poured to a depth of ½ inch in an electric skillet set at 370°. Fry batter-coated vegetables until brown on both sides. Sprinkle chops with salt and pepper, place on serving platter and surround with vegetables.

## BREADED LAMB CHOPS ITALIENNE
### (Serves 4)

4 loin lamb chops
Salt and pepper
Flour
1 egg beaten with 1 tablespoon cold water
⅓ cup bread crumbs
2 tablespoons grated Parmesan cheese
Salad oil
2 ozs. sliced boiled ham
1 8-oz. can tomato sauce
¼ cup water
½ teaspoon chervil
½ teaspoon chives
2 teaspoons butter

Preheat oven to 350°, electric skillet to 325°. Sprinkle chops with salt and pepper. Dip first into flour, then into beaten egg, finally into mixture of bread crumbs and Parmesan cheese, until well coated. In ¼ inch salad oil in skillet, sauté chops until light brown, using two spoons or a pair of tongs for turning—not a kitchen fork, which might break the bread-crumb coating. Remove and place in a shallow pan, propping them as nearly upright as possible. Bake 30 minutes or until very tender. Meanwhile, cut ham into small matchstick slices about 1 inch long and combine in saucepan with tomato sauce, water, chervil and chives. Simmer 15 to 20 minutes. Add butter and pour onto serving plates. Place chops on top.

# VEAL CHOPS WITH HAM AND TRUFFLES
(Serves 4)

*4 loin veal chops*
*4 tablespoons deviled ham*
*Flour*
*1 egg beaten with 1 tablespoon cold water*
*½ cup bread crumbs*
*2 tablespoons finely minced truffles*
*Salad oil*
*1 10½-oz. can cream of mushroom soup*
*¼ cup dry sherry*
*¼ cup light cream*

Spread the deviled ham on the chops. Dip into flour, into beaten egg, then into mixture of bread crumbs and truffles, until well coated. In ¼ inch salad oil in an electric skillet set at 300°, sauté chops until brown on both sides. Transfer to a shallow baking pan and bake in preheated 325° oven 40 to 50 minutes. Heat soup, sherry and cream to boiling point and serve with chops.

# VENISON CHOPS, CUMBERLAND SAUCE
(Serves 4)

*4 loin venison chops*
*½ cup French dressing*
*2 tablespoons minced shallots or onions*
*2 tablespoons butter*
*1 10¾-oz. can brown gravy*
*¼ cup currant jelly*
*¼ cup port*
*Grated rind of 1 orange*
*Juice of 1 orange*
*2 teaspoons Worcestershire sauce*
*Salt and freshly ground black pepper*

Marinate chops in the French dressing for about 1 hour before cooking. In a saucepan, sauté the shallots in butter until yellow. Add the brown gravy, jelly, port, orange rind, orange juice and Worcestershire sauce and bring to a boil. Simmer 5 minutes while broiling or panbroiling the chops over a high flame until brown on both sides and rare inside.

# The Stalwart Steak

"You are what you eat" has long been a contention among some students of gastronomy. Romans believed that one who favored rabbit stew would become timid. A man, on the other hand, who chewed tough lion meat bought from the butcher's stall outside the amphitheater would develop a stiff upper colon and be brave. In Sparta during the Fourth Century, if you were male and over 20 years of age, you were required by law to eat two pounds of meat a day. It was supposed to make you brave. Meat-eating Tartars were known for their warlike activities, whereas vegetable-eating Brahmans were peaceable. As late as the 19th Century, certain scientists were developing the hypothesis that if you ate fish, you'd be brainy. Reason: Fish contain phosphorus, which is present in the human brain.

The argument seesawed back and forth for years, with some sociologists arguing that food habits set our cultural pattern and shape our emotions, while nutritionists insisted that there was no laboratory basis for the claim. The sociologists present an intriguing theory which we hate to kill, but it can be demolished by one word: *steak*.

Everybody digs and devours this *pièce de résistance* from the thick side of a steer, this charcoal-burned-outside and blushing-red-inside masterpiece of American cookery. Even Charles Dickens, who doted on vilification of American manners and customs, couldn't help expressing his passionate enjoyment of American porterhouse steak. But a steak eater can usually find no actual words to describe his animal delight. When a man eats fried chicken, he can stop between the second joint and the thigh to exclaim, "Superb!" But a beefsteak eater is a silent man. He carves the oozing broiled club steak; with his fork he swashes it for a second in the drippings on the platter; he lifts the thick, crimson slice to his lips. He may be able to utter, "Mmmmm!" but he can't converse.

Though both sexes eat T-bone constantly, the cooking of steak has always been a male art. A woman may make the greatest chicken patty in the world, but it seems to take a man to place a thick shell steak over a bed of live ashen-white charcoal, season it, brush it with butter and finally carve it properly. For men who hanker to perfect this aggressive art, we are happy to offer a few instructive details.

The first thing to learn about steaks is that there's no such thing as a thin steak. The word steak *means* a thick cut of food, and it can include anything from an eggplant steak to a salmon steak. But beefsteak must be cut at least an inch thick if it's to be broiled over or under the flames. If it's thinner than this, the heat of the broiler penetrates the inside of the meat before the outside is browned. The inside then becomes well done, the rivulets of juice seep out and the flavor is flat and steamy. Even a first-rate minute steak that is quickly seared in a frying pan should be no less than a half inch thick or it will be overdone, gray inside and insipid in flavor. As a matter of fact, the best broiled beefsteaks range from two to six inches in thickness. Big steaks of the latter size, served at banquets or beefsteak parties, are quickly seared on the outside under a fierce broiler flame and then transferred to the oven for 20 or 30 minutes, where the heat completes the interior cooking. However hefty the steak, the genuine intrinsic flavor, the red rivulets of goodness, as well as the nutrients, will all flow out if it is cooked to the well-done stage. A beefsteak must be rare or medium rare; any other steak is a perversion. If you like your beef well done, you should order boiled beef with horseradish, sauerbraten or pot roast.

Many chefs and hotel butchers still use an extremely simple method of telling the tenderness of steak. They hold a piece with the thumb on one side and forefinger on the other; then they press the fingers together. If the fingertips meet easily, it will be just as amenable to the knife and fork after it is cooked. (You cannot test veal or lamb in the same manner.) Naturally, a retail butcher will not permit you to manhandle steak in his shop. But the test is still a valid one, and in the privacy of your own kitchen you may test beefsteak in this way.

The jargon of the meatshop is enough to stump any sane man when he hears butchers and chefs talking about their loins, short loins, top sirloins, short hips, ribs, shells, chucks, sides and hindquarters. One single kind of steak, for instance, is called filet mignon, tenderloin and chateaubriand; each is taken from the same cut of beef. We don't wish to add to the Choctaw; so we'll just give you a quick rundown of steak nomenclature commonly used in butchershops and restaurants throughout the United States.

First of all, there is the *porterhouse,* named after old American inns where porter rather than ale was the specialty of the house. At the top of the porterhouse steak, there is a small coarse-grained piece called the flank or tail. It should be ground for hamburger rather than used for broiling. The porterhouse is divided by a bone into two main sections, the smaller called the *tenderloin* or *filet mignon*—the tenderest cut of the entire beef carcass. More flavorful than the filet mignon and firmer in texture is the larger section of the porterhouse; when served without the filet, it is called a *boneless loin steak, shell steak* or *strip steak*. It is the specialty of most of the famous U.S. steakhouses. A small porterhouse steak is called a *T-bone*. As it becomes still smaller at the end of the loin, where there is practically no filet left, it is called a *club steak*. *Rib steak* is similar to club in appearance since it is cut from the rib section of beef right alongside the club steaks. Although flavorful, rib steak tends to be loose in texture. *Sirloin* is less tender than porterhouse but just as flavorful. From the smaller section of the sirloin comes the *pinbone sirloin*; a steak from the larger section is identified as *wedge-bone*.

When buying steaks, you should allow about eight ounces per person for a filet mignon. Any other steak should weigh from 12 ounces to a pound for a man-size portion. This weight allowance includes fat and bone.

The cooking time for steaks will vary, depending on the intensity of the flame, the distance the meat is placed from it and the thickness and quality of the meat. If the meat is extremely cold when placed on the broiler rack or over the charcoal, it will naturally take a longer time to cook than at room temperature. Steak veterans always use a strong flame or a high temperature rather than a moderate flame. The strong heat quickly sears the meat and gives it its magnificent crisp brown crust. Set the thermostat at 550 degrees, preheating at least ten minutes before putting the steaks under the fire. If you are cooking the steaks over an outdoor charcoal fire, there should be a uniform bed of live charcoals with white ash showing, and the steaks should be about five inches above the flame.

For broiling rare 1-inch steaks which are at room temperature—such as rib, club, sirloin, T-bone and porterhouse—allow about 4 to 5 minutes' cooking time for each side. For medium rare, allow about 1 minute more on each side. To broil 1½-inch steaks rare, allow 6 to 7 minutes for each side, and 7 to 8 minutes for medium rare. A 2-inch steak will take 8 to 9 minutes on each side for cooking rare and 10 to 11 minutes for medium rare. A rare 1-inch filet mignon will take 3 minutes on each side, a 1½-inch filet 4 to 5 minutes on each side, and a 2-incher will take 6 minutes.

There are two ways of telling whether a steak is cooked sufficiently. A rare steak, when pressed quickly with the fingers or the back of a spoon, will feel somewhat resilient. A medium-rare steak will have less resiliency, and a well-done steak will feel firm. Since this touch method requires considerable experience, amateur chefs slit the meat in the very center with a small, sharp knife. The place where the steak is slit will naturally produce a spurt of juice and lose some flavor. But if the cut is small, not too much goodness will be lost.

To keep the steak from curling as it broils, ask the butcher to slash the side of the meat in three or four places. To help sear the meat quickly, brush it with salad oil or melted butter just before broiling. Sprinkle it rather liberally with pepper just before broiling, and to give the crust a deep-brown color, sprinkle with paprika. Keep the broiler door open to check the browning of the steak. If one part turns brown faster than another, move the steak for uniform broiling. Use a pair of tongs rather than a meat fork for turning, and don't cut a steak the instant it is removed from the broiler. Let it stand for four or five minutes so that the flowing juices will be absorbed into the meat tissue; then salt to taste. And for cutting steak, use sharp steak knives, serrated or straight-edged, rather than ordinary table knives.

Most conservative beefeaters insist that beefsteak must be *au naturel* if its incredibly wonderful beef flavor is to be preserved. For the most part, this is true. Any man who splashes catsup or chili sauce or barbecue sauce over a fine broiled steak is dead to the finer things. But simple steak butters—largely derived from French culinary art—when combined with the juices of the meat on the platter, can make several heavenly varieties of natural gravy. Such butters are brushed or spread over the steaks after the cooking is completed. Some of them call for shallots—a small yellow-skinned bulb of the onion family, not to be confused with spring onions. Shallots are available in fancy-fruit-and-vegetable stores. Mild onion may be substituted for shallots if necessary.

## MAITRE D'HOTEL BUTTER

This is the best known of the steak butters. Let ½ cup sweet or slightly salted butter stand at room temperature until soft but not melting. Add the juice of ½ lemon and 1 tablespoon finely chopped parsley. Brush or spoon the butter over the steak on serving plates.

## RED-WINE STEAK BUTTER

On French menus this is listed as *marchand de vin*. Smack 3 medium-size shallots with the flat side of a

knife blade—to loosen the skin. Remove skin. Chop
shallots as fine as possible and place in a small saucepan with 2 tablespoons butter. Simmer until tender but
not brown. Add ½ cup dry red wine and continue
cooking until the wine is reduced to ¼ cup. Allow
shallots and wine to stand in the refrigerator until
cold. Then combine with ¼ cup softened butter. Mix
well and spoon or brush over steaks on serving plates.

## MARROW BUTTER

When you buy your steaks, ask the butcher to give
you a small piece of beef marrow removed from the
shinbone. Peel 6 shallots and chop very fine. Place
with 2 tablespoons butter in a small saucepan and
cook slowly until tender but not brown. Cut ¼ cup
of the marrow into small slices about ½ inch thick.
Add to saucepan and cook slowly until marrow melts.
Remove from the flame. Add 1 tablespoon very finely
chopped parsley, the juice of ¼ lemon and ½ teaspoon Worcestershire sauce. Spoon over steaks on serving plates.

## FRENCH-FRIED POTATOES
### (Serves 4)

Potatoes may be French-fried in one or two steps.
The two-step technique, which we favor, permits you
to get all the scullery work done hours before eating
time; the potatoes can then be browned at the last
minute while the thick steaks are being sliced or the
chops are being crowned with mushrooms. You'll need
2 lbs. potatoes for four—Idaho or California baking
potatoes, if you please. Peel them, cut with a French-
fry cutter and drop into cold water to prevent discol-
oration. Dry thoroughly with a clean cloth or paper
towel before cooking. Preheat fat (⅔ full) in an
electric fry kettle to 360°. Fill the fry basket ⅓ full
of potatoes and lower slowly into fat, being prepared
to withdraw the basket if fat rises too high. Cook
only until barely tender (they will not be deeply
browned). Remove from basket and spread in a
shallow pan lined with absorbent paper. Fry the rest

of the potatoes in this way and let cool until chowtime.
When ready to serve, preheat the fat to 390° and fry
until golden brown. Drain for a moment above fat
before turning them onto absorbent paper. Sprinkle
generously with salt and quickly surround the waiting
steak with a mountain of these crispy spud slivers.
Then surround the dinner table, choose your weapon
and attack at will.

## FILET MIGNON, MUSHROOM CANAPE
### (Serves 4)

> 1 4-oz. can sliced mushrooms
> 3 tablespoons liver pâté
> 1 tablespoon dry sherry
> 4 slices toast
> Grated Parmesan cheese
> Paprika
> 4 filets mignons, 6 to 8 ozs. each
> Salt and pepper
> ¼ cup dry red wine
> 1 cup water
> 1 packet instant beef broth
> ¼ cup butter
> 1 teaspoon meat extract
> ¼ teaspoon onion powder

Put the mushrooms with their juice, the liver pâté
and sherry into the well of an electric blender. Blend,
turning the motor on and off as necessary and forcing
the mixture into the center of the well, until mushrooms
are a smooth puree. Spread the toast with the puree
and sprinkle with grated cheese and paprika. Pan-broil
the filets in an electric skillet preheated to 400° until
medium brown on both sides. Sprinkle with salt and
pepper and place on a warm platter. Add the red wine,
water, instant beef broth, butter, meat extract and
onion powder to the skillet and mix well. Scrape pan
bottom to loosen drippings and boil until liquid is
reduced by half. Place mushroom canapés under a
preheated broiler and broil until cheese browns. Place
filet on each canapé and pour pan gravy on top.

A FEAST OF FOOD
IN PICTURES

roast beef

mixed vegetables

spices

veal

sauces

lobster

boiled whole salmon

cherries jubilee

crepes suzette

## MINUTE STEAK STANLEY
(Serves 4)

¾ cup light cream
⅓ cup bread crumbs
1 teaspoon grated onion
3 tablespoons horseradish
1 teaspoon Dijon mustard
4 medium-size bananas
2 tablespoons melted butter
Cinnamon and sugar
4 boneless shell steaks, 8 to 10 ozs. each
Salt and pepper

Put the cream, bread crumbs, onion, horseradish and mustard into the top part of a double boiler over simmering water. Stir well and heat 10 minutes, adding salt and pepper to taste. Peel bananas and cut in half crosswise. Brush with melted butter. Sprinkle with cinnamon and sugar. Place in a greased shallow pan and bake in a preheated oven at 475° until tender. Slash the fat edge of each steak in several places and pan-broil with no added fat, in electric skillet preheated to 400°, until medium brown on both sides. Sprinkle with salt and pepper. Place the steaks on warm serving plates. Alongside each steak, pour the horseradish sauce. Place the baked bananas on the sauce.

## MINUTE STEAK, CAPER BUTTER
(Serves 4)

4 boneless shell steaks, 8 to 10 ozs. each
Salt and pepper
2 tablespoons minced parsley
2 tablespoons minced chives
4 tablespoons drained capers
4 tablespoons butter
Juice of ½ lemon

Slash the fat edge of each steak in several places. Preheat an electric skillet to 400°. Pan-broil the steaks with no added fat until medium brown on both sides.

Place on a warm platter. Sprinkle with salt, pepper, parsley, chives and capers. Heat the butter in the skillet until nut-brown, then pour over the steaks. Sprinkle with lemon juice.

## ROUND STEAK, RUSTIC STYLE
### (Serves 4)

*4 pieces round steak, ½ inch thick, 6 to 8 ozs. each*
*Salt and pepper*
*2 cups water*
*1 envelope instant beef broth*
*1 8-oz. can tomatoes, coarsely chopped*
*¼ cup minced fresh parsley*
*4 anchovies, minced*
*¼ teaspoon oregano*
*¼ teaspoon Worcestershire sauce*

Heat a Dutch oven or heavy saucepan over a moderate flame with no fat added. Sprinkle bottom of utensil with salt. Brown steaks on both sides. Add remaining ingredients. Bring gravy to a boil; then reduce flame so liquid barely simmers. Cook, stirring occasionally, until meat is tender, about 2 to 2¼ hours. Season to taste. These steaks are excellent when cooked one day, kept in their gravy and then reheated for lunch or dinner the next day.

## PORTERHOUSE STEAK, STUFFED MUSHROOMS
### (Serves 4)

*2½ lbs. porterhouse steak*
*½ lb. large, fresh mushrooms*
*Butter*
*Salad oil*
*Salt and pepper*
*4 boiled white onions from can or jar*
*¼ cup bread crumbs*
*2 tablespoons tomato paste*
*Grated Parmesan cheese*
*Paprika*

Have butcher remove flank from steak and grind it.

Detach mushroom stems from caps by hand and wash mushrooms well. Heat 1 tablespoon butter and 1 tablespoon oil in a wide saucepan until butter melts. Add mushroom caps and stems. Sprinkle with salt and pepper and sauté until tender. Remove mushrooms from pan and sauté the ground meat in the fat remaining, breaking it up as much as possible with a fork. Remove pan from fire when meat is brown. Put the mushroom stems and onions into the well of an electric blender and blend until pureed. In a mixing bowl, combine sautéed beef, pureed vegetables, bread crumbs and tomato paste and salt and pepper to taste. Pile the filling into the mushroom caps, making even mounds with a table knife or spatula, and sprinkle stuffing with cheese, salad oil and paprika in that order. Bake in oven preheated to 370° for 20 minutes or until brown. Brush porterhouse steak with oil and broil over a charcoal fire or under a hot broiler flame until brown on both sides. Brush with butter and sprinkle with salt and pepper. Serve mushrooms alongside steak on serving platter or plates.

# Variations on Veal

Veal has been synonymous with sumptuous supping ever since the Prodigal Son sat down to that feast of fatted calf. For veal, of course, is meat from a calf, and a very young calf at that—usually no older than three months. In fact, for cooking purposes, *veal* and *calf* mean the same thing.

When a goodly number of French, German and Italian chefs migrated to our shores in the recent past, proudly carrying their choicest veal recipes with them, American enthusiasm for cooking calf began to look up. For it was thanks to these gastronomic missionaries that America made two great discoveries: (1) Veal is versatile; (2) veal tastes great. Veal *parmigiana* and Wiener schnitzel are only two examples of how good veal can taste, no matter how widely separated by homeland and method of preparation.

But veal has other remarkable attributes that recommend it to the do-it-himself gastronome: It can be prepared in the well-known jiffy, and it provides a perfect medium for the experimenter with seasoning. Should your eye skim down a Continental menu, you're likely to find versatile veal anywhere from the hors d'oeuvres to the desserts. It's served as cutlets, chops, roast and scallopini, in sautés, sauces, stews and ragouts. The *Larousse Gastronomique* alone has more than 145 listings for veal.

As hors d'oeuvres, try an unusual tidbit such as Italian tunnied veal. Here, a cut of the leg is simmered until tender, chilled and then marinated in a piquant sauce of tuna fish, anchovies, lemon juice and oil to form a combination that brings instant peace to the stomach while the first martini is going down.

Veal will beget the mellowest possible gravies and sauces. When the *saucier* in a fine restaurant starts to make demiglace or basic brown sauce—from which dozens of other sauces are derived—he'll use veal bones as the foundation. And the juices of a veal stew will merrily marry with cream, stock, brandy, sherry, red and white wines, vermouth, beer and almost any conceivable vegetable or spice.

Mock turtle soup is another surprising variation of veal—for that rich, brown brew sees not hide nor hair of the turtle but is made with veal stock and pieces of calf's head. Meat isn't often served as a dessert, but cold calf's-foot jelly, served with port or sherry and covered with sweet cream, is a grand old charmer.

Veal is an exception to the rule that good food takes time to prepare. Consider the speed with which veal scallopini or cutlets can be turned out. Grace Moore's renowned recipe for a chafing dish of veal sautéed with brandy and simmered with cream takes all of seven minutes. And Toscanini's scoring for veal Marsala requires no more time. But since veal does warm so readily to the occasion, don't overcook it.

Veal can be delicate and subtle, but it also derives encouragement from (instead of being clobbered by) spicing. It may be accompanied by vivid garnishes of tomatoes and peppers and onions, crunchy crumb coatings or hefty servings of pasta and cheese.

In selecting veal, look for the lightest possible pink, a sort of faint grayish pink which indicates that the meat is young. Since there are always a few butchers willing to ignore the three-month upper-age limit to gain a few extra pounds of flesh, avoid brick-red veal; this darker hue indicates that the veal has lost its youth. Such meat will lack both the sensitive flavor of young veal and the mature flavor of beef. After a few surveys of the display case, you'll be able to spot the ideal color at a glance.

Although veal is immature meat, it will still require tenderizing, because it contains many tough connective tissues. Butchers perform this task when they cut the so-called Italian-style veal cutlets, but further tenderizing usually helps. Slap the slices of meat with the side of a cleaver or use a meat mallet or meat tenderizer.

Now, with an anticipatory appetite as a passport, let's disregard national boundaries and examine a group of Continental veal recipes:

## VEAL SCALLOPINI WITH HAM
### (Serves 4)

> 1¼ lbs. Italian-style veal cutlets, sliced thin
> Salt, pepper and ground sage
> Flour
> ¼ cup salad oil
> 8 thin slices prosciutto ham
> ½ cup dry white wine
> ½ cup water
> 1 teaspoon meat extract
> ⅛ teaspoon onion salt
> 3 tablespoons butter
> 2 tablespoons minced parsley

Cut veal into eight pieces of equal size. Pound meat with a metal meat tenderizer; then sprinkle with salt, pepper and sage. Dip each piece into flour and pat off excess. Preheat an electric skillet to 300°; a heavy saucepan may be substituted, but keep the flame moderate. Add the oil and sauté the veal until it is brown on one side only. Remove meat from skillet. On the browned side of each piece, place a slice of ham and fasten with diagonally inserted toothpicks. Return veal to skillet and sauté the uncooked side until brown. Then turn veal on the ham side and let it sauté about 1 minute more. Remove meat from skillet. Place it on serving platter or plates and remove toothpicks. Meat should be ham side up. Drain fat from skillet, but let the brown drippings remain. Add the wine, water, meat extract, onion salt, butter and parsley. Let boil about 1 minute, then pour over the meat.

## VEAL SCALLOPINI MARSALA
### (Serves 4)

Omit ham in the first recipe. Substitute dry (not sweet) Marsala wine or dry sherry for white wine and complete cooking as directed.

# VEAL SCALLOPINI WITH MUSHROOMS
(Serves 4)

Omit ham in the first recipe. Sauté ½ lb. sliced fresh mushrooms in skillet. Spoon mushrooms over veal before covering with gravy.

# BAKED VEAL CHOPS
(Serves 4)

2  *large cloves garlic*
½  *cup French dressing*
1  *teaspoon imported Dijon mustard*
4  *veal chops, 4 ozs. each*
1  *small onion, minced*
3  *tablespoons butter*
1  *cup bread crumbs*
2  *tablespoons grated Parmesan cheese*
*Salt and pepper*

Smash the cloves of garlic and combine with French dressing and mustard, mixing well. Place the veal chops in this mixture and marinate for 1 hour. While the meat is marinating, sauté the minced onion in the butter until the onion turns light yellow. Add the bread crumbs and cheese to the onion, mixing well. Sauté for 1 or 2 minutes. Remove from fire and set aside. Preheat an electric skillet to 360° or use a heavy saucepan with a moderate flame. Remove chops from the marinade. The oil clinging to the chops will suffice, so add no fat to the skillet. Sauté the veal until brown on both sides. Sprinkle with salt and pepper and place in a shallow baking pan or casserole. Spread the bread-crumb mixture on top of each chop. Cover them with aluminum foil. Bake in a slow oven, 325°, for 1 hour or until very tender. Serve with a prepared sauce.

# WIENER SCHNITZEL A LA HOLSTEIN
(Serves 4)

4  *thin veal cutlets, 4 ozs. each*
*Salt and pepper*
*Flour*
2  *eggs beaten with 2 tablespoons cold water*

*Bread crumbs*
*Salad oil*
*1 lemon*
*1 hard-boiled egg, chopped fine*
*4 anchovies*
*Capers*
*4 eggs*
*1 8-oz. can tomato sauce*
*1 tablespoon butter*

Pound the cutlets with a meat tenderizer. Sprinkle with salt and pepper. Dip into flour and pat off excess. Dip first into beaten eggs, coating thoroughly, then into bread crumbs. Pat crumbs well into cutlets. Chill cutlets for an hour or so, which will help the crumb coating adhere to the meat. In an electric skillet heated to 300°, pour salad oil to a depth of ¼ inch. Sauté the cutlets until deep golden brown on both sides. Place on a serving platter or plate and keep warm. Cut four thin slices of lemon and place a slice at one end of each cutlet. Squeeze the balance of the lemon juice over the cutlets. Sprinkle the lemon with the chopped hard-boiled egg. On each lemon slice, curl an anchovy around several capers. Fry the eggs and place one on each cutlet opposite the lemon. Bring tomato sauce and butter to a boil and pour around the cutlets. Serve balance of sauce in a sauceboat. (Lemon wedges, instead of slices, are also popular.)

## VEAL CUTLETS PARMIGIANA
(Serves 4)

*4 thin veal cutlets, 4 ozs. each*
*Salt and pepper*
*Flour*
*2 eggs beaten with 2 tablespoons cold water*
*Bread crumbs*
*Salad oil*
*½ lb. mozzarella, Bel Paese or Port du Salut cheese*
*1 8-oz. can tomato sauce*
*¼ teaspoon oregano*
*Grated Parmesan cheese*
*Paprika*

Prepare the cutlets as in the recipe for *Wiener schnitzel,* sautéing them only until light brown on both sides. Then place in a greased shallow baking pan or ovenproof casserole. Slice the mozzarella or shred the Bel Paese or Port du Salut. (The mozzarella will be stringy after cooking; the Bel Paese or Port du Salut merely soft.) Place the cheese over the cutlets. In a small saucepan, combine the tomato sauce and oregano. Bring to a boil and pour over the cutlets. Sprinkle the cutlets heavily with grated Parmesan cheese, then with paprika and salad oil. Bake in a moderate oven, 350°, for 20 to 25 minutes or until Parmesan cheese turns brown.

## BLANQUETTE OF VEAL
### (Serves 4)

(*Blanquette* of veal is a classic French stew. In the traditional recipe the veal is merely boiled until tender. In other French kitchens, however, and in this recipe, the veal is sautéed before it's simmered. During the sautéing, the juices that collect in the pot give the *blanquette* its rich, silken flavor.)

2 tablespoons butter
2 lbs. boneless shoulder of veal, cut into 1-inch cubes
2 tablespoons flour
1 quart water
3 envelopes instant chicken bouillon
¼ teaspoon prepared chopped bouquet garni
Salt and white pepper
1 lb. fresh button mushrooms
3 medium-size carrots, cut diagonally into ½-inch slices
1 8-oz. can small boiled onions, drained
2 tablespoons minced parsley
2 egg yolks, beaten
1 cup light sweet cream

In a deep stew pot or Dutch oven, melt the butter over a slow flame. Add the meat and sauté slowly, stirring frequently, keeping the pot covered, until meat loses red color, but do not brown meat. Stir in the flour. Add water, chicken bouillon, bouquet garni, ¼ teaspoon salt and ⅛ teaspoon white pepper. Bring liquid to a boil, reduce flame and simmer until veal is almost tender, about 1 to 1¼ hours. Add the mushrooms and carrots and cook until carrots and meat are tender. Add the onions and parsley. In a small bowl, combine egg yolks and cream, beating well. Add slowly about ¼ cup hot gravy, stirring well. Slowly pour mixture into the pot, stirring constantly. Heat slowly, still stirring constantly, approximately 2 or 3 minutes longer. Do not permit the gravy to boil or it will curdle. Remove from flame and add salt and pepper to taste. If stew must be reheated, use a double boiler.

## BAKED VEAL CUTLETS WITH VERMOUTH
### (Serves 4)

½ lb. fresh mushrooms
1 Spanish onion
1 green pepper
2 tablespoons butter
1 clove garlic, minced very fine
Juice of ¼ lemon
Salt and pepper
3 tablespoons salad oil
1 lb. Italian-style veal cutlets (not pounded thin)
¼ cup dry vermouth
2 tablespoons tomato paste

Wash mushrooms, separate caps from stems and cut into slices about ⅛ inch thick. Cut onion in half through stem end, then crosswise into thinnest possible slices. Cut green pepper in half, discard stem and seeds and slice into thinnest possible slices. Melt butter in a large saucepan. Add mushrooms, onion, green pepper, garlic and lemon juice and sauté until vegetables are limp, not brown. Season with salt and pepper. Heat the salad oil in an electric skillet preheated to 350° and sauté the veal only until it loses its pink color. Sprinkle with salt and pepper. In a shallow casserole, place slices of veal and vegetables alternately until all are used; a layer of vegetables should be on top. Combine the vermouth and tomato paste. Pour over veal and bake uncovered in a 300° oven for

1½ to 2 hours or until veal is very tender. Tip casserole and baste with liquid occasionally during cooking. Serve in casserole with saffron rice on the side.

## VEAL CUTLETS, TUNA SAUCE
### (Serves 4)

*1 lb. Italian-style veal cutlets, pounded thin*
*Salt and pepper*
*Flour*
*1 egg beaten with 1 tablespoon water*
*Bread crumbs*
*Salad oil*
*1 3½-oz. can tuna fish*
*1 8-oz. can tomato sauce*
*1 tablespoon sweet butter*
*1 teaspoon minced chives*
*2 tablespoons heavy sweet cream*
*2 tablespoons dry white wine*

Season cutlets with salt and pepper. Dip into flour and shake off excess. Dip into beaten egg, then into bread crumbs, coating thoroughly. Pour salad oil to a depth of ¼ inch in an electric skillet preheated to 370° and sauté cutlets until light brown on both sides. Transfer to a shallow baking pan and bake in a preheated 350° oven for 20 minutes. Drain tuna fish well. Cut into small dice and combine in a saucepan with tomato sauce, butter and chives. Heat to the boiling point, remove from fire and slowly add cream and white wine. Pour sauce onto serving plates or platter and place cutlets atop sauce.

## VEAL CAKES WITH WHITE WINE
### (Serves 4)

*2 slices stale French bread, ½ inch thick*
*¼ cup dry white wine*
*1 lb. boneless shoulder of veal*
*1 small onion*
*¼ green pepper*
*1 teaspoon salt*
*⅛ teaspoon pepper*
*⅛ teaspoon ground sage*

1 egg, beaten
Flour
3 tablespoons salad oil
1 10¾-oz. can beef-flavored mushroom gravy
1 8-oz. can tomato sauce
¼ teaspoon Worcestershire sauce
1 cup water

Soak the bread in the wine until wine is absorbed. Put the veal, bread, onion and green pepper through a meat grinder twice, using the fine blade. Combine the ground meat with the salt, pepper, sage and egg and mix well. Shape into eight flat cakes and dip the cakes into flour. Pour the oil into an electric skillet heated to 360°. Brown the cakes well on both sides and remove from pan. Drain fat from skillet, but let drippings remain. Return cakes to pan. Add the mushroom gravy, tomato sauce, Worcestershire sauce and water. Bring to a boil, reduce heat to 280° and simmer 20 minutes. Be sure to make enough. These cakes taste so good you'll want to eat them and have them, too.

# The Hearty Ham

When Cicero said, "Things perfected by nature are better than those finished by art," he couldn't have been thinking of the smoked thigh of a pig. A fresh ham is the product of nature and has much to recommend it. But a smoked ham is a work of art. Certainly, if Cicero had lived long enough to taste a genuine Smithfield taken from a peanut-fed razorback hog, carefully buried in salt, rubbed with freshly ground pepper, smoked over slow-burning hickory wood and then aged for two or three years, Rome's honeymouthed orator might have thought twice before making that rash utterance.

Ham fanciers fall into three classes: First of all, there are the backwoods boys who, from the age of two, have been raised on hog-ham gravy and bearlard biscuits. At the opposite extreme are those fastidious gentry who will eat ham only if it's served with fresh calf's sweetbread and crepes sautéed in whitewine sauce *sous cloche*. The third and largest class is the great majority of ham lovers who enjoy anything from deviled ham on a cracker to oversize ham steaks from the cornfields of Iowa.

All of these types appreciate the one salient fact about ham—integrity. There is no such thing as a fake ham. It's one of the least disguised and least doubtful of meat flavors. Even in a croquette or soufflé, the matchless flavor comes through unaltered. When you leave roast beef in your refrigerator for four or five days, the juices evaporate and the flavor becomes stale and weary. But you can keep a ham in the icebox for four weeks and the tangy miracle of the smokehouse remains unchanged. When meats such as corned beef or smoked tongue are canned, their original flavor and texture become almost unrecognizable. But a canned ham never loses its rich natural savor.

For all young gastronomes who aren't equipped to struggle with sole in aspic, joints of mutton and pressed wild duck, the plump ham on the carving board is the easiest way to satisfy a ravenous appetite. A loaf of crisp sour rye bread, a jar of snappy mustard and some cold bottles of bubbling ale are all that are needed to start the revival meeting.

Until the late Twenties, any amateur chef who undertook to cook a whole ham in his bachelor apartment usually found out that a course in food engineering was necessary in order to do the job properly. Nowadays, the old process of soaking, scrubbing and simmering is for the most part unnecessary. In the early Thirties, tenderized or quick-cooking hams were introduced. These required no soaking or simmering and could be baked by merely placing them in the oven in the same manner as a turkey or a large rib roast. Later, completely cooked, ready-to-eat hams were introduced, and this type dominates the market today. In restaurants and hotels with proper cooking facilities, hams are still scrubbed, soaked, simmered, baked and glazed. The finished ham may be slightly more moist and more subtle in flavor than the cooked ham you buy in the butchershop, but the results are simply not worth the outlandish efforts required to bake a raw ham starting from scratch.

Over the United States you will find ham sold in an almost unlimited variety of forms and sizes. First of all, there are the aristocrats from the ham capital of the world, Smithfield, Virginia, population about 1000. Hams from this area are not to be confused with so-called Virginia-style hams which many restaurants and delicatessens offer and which are merely baked hams from any part of the country, stuck with a few cloves and browned in the oven. The real Smithfields are taken from a lean, aristocratic strain of porker turned loose in the woods in the spring and fattened on peanuts in the fall. Their shape is somewhat long and flat. The meat is deep brick red, the fat amber rather than white. The difference in flavor between a genuine Virginia ham and other hams is the difference between brandy and *vin ordinaire*. Native epicures in Virginia like their ham cut paper-thin, and for better carving they prefer cold ham over hot.

Throughout the South you'll find country hams many of which are prepared in the same manner as Smithfields. Some country hams are not smoked but merely cured in salt and then hung in a cold place for months to age. They are consumed locally for the most part. Smithfields, however, are available in fancy-food shops all over the United States. For apartment bachelors, a whole Smithfield is sometimes hard to handle; even half of a Virginia ham may be unwieldy. Those who want the real thing in small quantities can now buy sliced and cooked Smithfield in cans and jars. The price of a genuine Smithfield is about twice that of another ham, but for the special blowout, it's the ham what am. It is now offered cooked and glazed with brown sugar, ready for the carving knife.

Of course, the greatest number of hams sold in the United States are the moderately smoked hams typified by the brand names of nationally known meat-packers. They may be bought raw, partly cooked (tenderized) or completely cooked, ready to eat. Those who don't dig the intense flavor and saltiness of the Smithfield ham prefer this milder cure. For such respectable fare as ham with cabbage, beans or potato salad, or ham steaks, these hams are excellent.

The mildest of all hams are the canned Dutch, Danish and Irish specimens. Their bland flavor is just opposite that of their Virginia counterparts. They are sold in sizes ranging from 1 pound to 15 pounds. When buying the very small-size tins, you sometimes take the chance of getting excess fat and gristle, since the small cut may come from the extreme shank or butt end. Here again, the variety of brands you can buy is tremendous. If you're looking for a gastronomical novelty, you might try such sophisticated versions as ham in champagne sauce or Burgundy.

Finally, there are such hard hams as the Italian prosciutto or the imported Westphalian style. These hams are both slow-cured, with flavors that are pure enchantment. They must be cut like tissue paper. Both of them are served cold as appetizers. Prosciutto ham with ice-cold melon is now one of the best-known dinner preludes. Westphalian ham, cut into small, transparent slices, rolled up and eaten as is or filled with watercress salad, will stir the most slothful appetite into motion.

## BAKING A HAM

Buy a quick-cooking or tenderized ham. Place it fat side up on a wire rack in an uncovered roasting pan. Insert a meat thermometer in the thickest part of the meat. Bake in a slow oven and let it cool sufficiently so that it can be handled. Then cut away the skin from the fat side. If you do not like too much fat, cut away any fat in excess of ½ inch. The depth of the fat can be told easily by inserting the tip of a sharp knife in the ham. You can feel the firm meat when the tip of the knife reaches it. The distance the knife was inserted shows the depth of the fat. Score the ham (i.e., cut the fat to a depth of ⅛ inch in long diagonal lines about an inch apart). Cut again, in the opposite direction, to make diamond-shaped pieces. Make a paste of 1 cup brown sugar, 2 tablespoons flour, 2 tablespoons sherry and 1 teaspoon dry mustard. Spread the paste over the fat. Place the ham in a hot oven, 425°, for 15 to 20 minutes or until the top is golden brown.

We don't look kindly upon the old practice of jabbing cloves into every baked ham. In the first place, the flavor of the cloves doesn't spread beyond the small point where they're inserted. Besides, the flavor of whole cloves is extremely intense. If you happen to bite into one, it's as harsh as a toothache. If you like a clove flavor in ham fat, you can blend it more easily by mixing some powdered cloves with the sugar mixture before glazing the ham.

For kitchen hobbyists who like to ad-lib with easy ham dishes, we offer the following recipes:

# GLAZED HAM STEAK WITH BOURBON
(Serves 2)

¾ to 1 lb. ready-to-eat ham, center-cut slice, ½ inch
thick
2 tablespoons melted ham fat or shortening
¼ cup brown sugar
¼ cup bourbon whiskey
2 tablespoons bread crumbs
Paprika

Slash the edge of the ham steak in three or four places
to prevent curling during cooking. Preheat the broiler
to 400°. Heat the fat or shortening in a large frying
pan until it shows the first wisp of smoke. Lower the
ham slice carefully into the pan. Cook over a moderate
flame, turning once, until medium brown on both
sides. Transfer to a shallow baking pan or large metal
pie pan. Mix the sugar, whiskey and bread crumbs to a
smooth paste. Spread over the top of the ham and
sprinkle lightly with paprika. Place under the broiler
flame about 4 inches below source of heat—not too
close to the fire or the whiskey may flame. Broil only
until the glaze is medium brown. Serve at once.

# FRIED SMITHFIELD HAM, CREAM GRAVY
(Serves 2)

⅓ cup milk
⅔ cup cold water
1 5-oz. jar sliced, cooked Smithfield ham
2 tablespoons butter
2 tablespoons sherry
1 cup light cream
2 teaspoons cornstarch
2 tablespoons cold water

Combine the milk and the ⅔ cup cold water in a deep
dish. Place the ham in the milk mixture for 1 hour.
Then transfer *in toto* to a saucepan and slowly heat
until the liquid boils. Discard the liquid from the
ham and replace with butter. Let the ham sauté over
a slow flame for 3 minutes. Add the sherry wine and
light cream and cook over a slow flame until the liquid

just begins to bubble around the edge of the saucepan. Mix the cornstarch with the 2 tablespoons cold water to form a smooth paste. When the cream begins to boil, add the cornstarch mixture, stirring well, and cook until thick. Remove from the flame, season to taste and serve over hot, crisp toast.

## HAM CORNUCOPIAS
### (Serves 4)

*1 lb. fresh crab or 13-oz. can crab meat*
*¼ cup thinly sliced black olives*
*⅓ cup mayonnaise*
*2 tablespoons minced parsley*
*Juice of ½ lemon*
*1 teaspoon grated onion*
*½ teaspoon Worcestershire sauce*
*2 hard-boiled eggs, chopped fine*
*Salt and pepper*
*8 large, thin slices canned ham*

Remove carefully any pieces of shell or cartilage from the crab meat. In a mixing bowl, combine the crab meat, the olives, mayonnaise, parsley, lemon juice, onion, Worcestershire sauce and the eggs. Add salt and pepper to taste and more mayonnaise if a richer mixture is desired. Place the mixture on the ham slices and roll up in cornucopia fashion: with one end closed and the other showing the crab meat. Place the cornucopias on a deep bed of watercress and serve with French bread or Russian pumpernickel.

## BARBECUED HAM STEAK
### (Serves 2)

*1 8-oz. can tomato sauce*
*¼ teaspoon ground allspice*
*⅛ teaspoon cayenne pepper*
*Juice of 1 lemon*
*3 tablespoons salad oil*
*3 tablespoons brown sugar*
*1 lb. ready-to-eat ham steak*

Combine all ingredients except ham, mixing well. Pour

mixture over ham steak in a shallow pan or casserole. Let it stand for 1 hour at room temperature. Remove ham from sauce and place over a hot charcoal fire or under a preheated broiler, basting frequently with sauce. Broil 20 to 25 minutes or until brown on both sides. Heat remainder of sauce and serve in a sauce-boat.

## HAM SAUTE WITH GRAPES MADEIRA
### (Serves 4)

½ lb. seedless grapes
3 tablespoons salad oil
2 tablespoons butter
3 6-oz. pkgs. round ham slices, ⅛ inch thick
1 lb. button mushrooms
1½ cups light cream
¼ cup Madeira wine
1 dash freshly ground nutmeg
Salt and pepper
4 slices toast

Remove grapes from stem. Put into a saucepan with cold water. Bring to boil and simmer for 1 minute. Then pour off water and set grapes aside. Pour oil into an electric skillet heated to 350°. Add butter and ham slices and sauté only until ham begins to brown around edges. Remove from skillet and set aside. Add mushrooms and sauté, covered, until tender. Add cream and Madeira. Simmer 5 minutes. Return ham to skillet. Add grapes and simmer, uncovered, 3 to 4 minutes. Add nutmeg and salt and pepper to taste. Arrange toast on serving dishes or platter. Put ham on toast. Pile mushrooms on top and ladle gravy with grapes atop mushrooms.

## HAM STEAK WITH CRUSHED PEPPER
### (Serves 2)

1 large onion, sliced
2 cloves garlic, smashed
1 teaspoon leaf sage
¼ cup olive oil
2 tablespoons red-wine vinegar

    *1 lb. precooked ham steak*
    *2 teaspoons crushed whole pepper*
    *Butter*

In a shallow pan or casserole, combine well the onion, garlic, sage, olive oil and wine vinegar. Scatter half the pepper over one side of the ham steak and pound it into the meat with a meat mallet. Turn the ham and repeat the procedure with the balance of pepper. Place ham in the oil mixture and let it stand at room temperature for 1 hour, turning several times to marinate thoroughly. Remove from mixture and place over a hot charcoal fire or under a preheated broiler. Broil 20 to 25 minutes or until brown on both sides. Brush with butter just before serving.

## HAM AND LEEKS AU GRATIN
### (Serves 4)

    *8 large leeks*
    *3 tablespoons butter*
    *3 tablespoons flour*
    *1½ cups hot milk*
    *1 tablespoon prepared mustard*
    *6 tablespoons grated Parmesan cheese*
    *1 dash freshly ground nutmeg*
    *Salt and pepper*
    *2 egg yolks, beaten*
    *8 large slices canned ham*
    *Paprika*

Trim ends of leeks so that each piece is about 4 inches long. Cut off root ends and wash leeks well under cold running water, separating leaves as much as possible to remove any sand. Boil in salted water until tender, drain and set aside. Melt butter in a saucepan. Remove from flame and stir in flour. Slowly add hot milk, stirring constantly. Add mustard, 2 tablespoons grated cheese and nutmeg. Season with salt and pepper. Return to a low flame and simmer slowly 10 minutes, stirring frequently. Remove 2 or 3 tablespoons hot sauce and mix with the egg yolks. Slowly pour yolks into saucepan. Simmer 1 minute longer, stirring constantly. Remove from fire. Wrap a slice of ham around each leek. Place in a shallow casserole. Pour sauce on top. Sprinkle with balance of cheese and a dash of paprika. Bake in oven preheated to 375° for 20 minutes or until top of sauce is lightly browned.

## CROSTINI OF HAM
(Serves 4)

> 4 hero rolls
> ⅓ cup butter
> ⅔ cup finely diced celery
> ⅔ cup finely diced onion
> ½ cup finely diced green pepper
> 2 tablespoons minced parsley
> ⅛ teaspoon ground sage
> ⅛ teaspoon leaf thyme
> 2 tablespoons deviled Smithfield ham
> 2 eggs, beaten
> 6 ozs. sliced cooked ham, diced
> Salt, pepper and paprika
> 4 tablespoons melted butter

Cut rolls in half lengthwise; then cut top halves into ½-inch cubes and place in a shallow pan in preheated 375° oven for 20 to 30 minutes or until cubes are crisp and firm. Remove from oven. When cooled to room temperature, soak cubes in cold water for 5 minutes; then squeeze dry gently. Put the ⅓ cup butter, celery, onion, green pepper, parsley, sage and thyme into a saucepan. Cover with cold water. Bring to a boil, reduce flame and simmer until water is evaporated. Avoid scorching vegetables as water reduces. Add deviled ham, mixing well, and combine with bread cubes, eggs and diced ham. Add salt and pepper to taste. Pile the mixture on the bottom halves of the rolls. Sprinkle with paprika, then with the 4 tablespoons melted butter. Bake in 375° oven for 30 minutes and serve piping hot.

## HAM HASH, COUNTRY STYLE
(Serves 4)

Any leftover, canned or sliced boiled ham may be used. Be sure the ham and seasoning vegetables are minced or chopped fine. Mashed potatoes should be prepared without any milk or liquid.

> *Vegetable fat*
> *¼ cup minced onion*
> *¼ cup minced green pepper*
> *¼ cup minced celery*
> *2 cups minced cooked ham*
> *1 cup mashed potatoes*
> *1 teaspoon Worcestershire sauce*
> *Salt and pepper*

Melt 3 tablespoons fat in a saucepan. Add the onion, green pepper and celery—minced very fine—and sauté until tender but not brown. Mix with ham, potatoes and Worcestershire sauce. Add salt and pepper to taste and place in the refrigerator to chill thoroughly. Shape into eight round cakes about ½ inch thick. Brown on both sides on a lightly greased griddle or heavy frying pan. Serve with chili sauce or catsup. Then sit down at the table right away, before your guests demolish the whole batch.

# Burgermastery

Some people spend too much time worrying about aphrodisiacs. Everyone knows the type who won't take a girl to a restaurant unless he can engage a *chambre séparée,* fitted with midnight-blue drapes and scented with mists of Virile Night perfume. He is the type who worries about ordering oysters or crayfish. He asks the headwaiter to make him a salad of watercress and ginseng root, since both of these vegetables, he has heard, are supposed to be effective sources of sexual stimulation. The voluptuary who makes all of these elaborate preparations usually finds that the glorious moment in which he has imagined his girl would melt like drawn butter turns out to be a bad mistake. You can tempt a girl with the promise of oysters or fresh beluga caviar, lure her with sherried lobster or ravish her with filet mignon. But any sensible man knows when to stop.

When dalliance is done, there is only one manly thing to do—give her a hamburger. There's something so right-side-up about a grilled brown hamburger, something so keen about its honest beef juice oozing into a split feathery bun, something so unpretentious about eating it, that it just comes naturally as a wonderful postlude.

You can get a bad steak but seldom a really bad hamburger. You'd be committing a crime if you doused a club steak with catsup, and you'd be mad to put a slice of raw onion on a lamb chop. And yet a hamburger will take both the catsup and the onion and toss them down as charming bystanders.

159

It would be hard to find a food as easygoing as hamburger. Park Avenue tycoons who have given up struggling with their venison steaks find the chopped sirloin easy pickings. Truck drivers freewheeling on long hauls over the country swallow them by the bagful. For the man who prefers to look into his angel's eyes instead of the dinner plate, the hamburger is indispensable. For the girl who loves rare meat cooked over charcoal, ground beefsteak is a succulent staple. For some time now, surveys of public eating places have shown that more hamburger is eaten than any other meat dish, even edging out the frankfurter comfortably. Its nearest rival is ham and eggs.

Hamburger is named after the German port of Hamburg, where old sea dogs during the last century ate their scrambled T-bone raw, the dish now known in this country as cannibal or tartar steak. The whole history of chopped-meat patties is an account of how a simple dish—chopped meat—can be ruined by over-spicing, overgrinding, overcooking and overdressing. Hamburgers in ancient Rome, for instance (they called them Ostian meatballs), illustrate the point. The Latin writer Apicius tells how the Romans made them. "Clean, scrape and shape the meat. Crush pepper, lovage, cumin, caraway, silphium and one laurel berry moistened with broth. In a square dish, place the meat cakes and spices. Cover them crosswise with twigs. Pickle them for two or three days. Roast them. Mix the broth in the pan with crushed pepper, lovage and raisin wine. Thicken the broth with a mixture of fat and flour." With hamburger recipes like this, it's easy to understand why Rome declined and fell flat on its face. During the Middle Ages, hamburgers were made in a thousand varieties. Almost all beef as well as pork, mutton and chicken were chopped fine for the simple reason that forks were unknown and the knife was a kitchen utensil rather than a piece of tableware.

Undoubtedly, the modern hamburger owes a lot to Cornelius B. Paulding, who, in 1870, led a movement to eat without knives, forks or spoons. Paulding wanted to junk all tableware, claiming that if people ate with their fingers, the pioneer spirit that made

America great could be recaptured. Paulding's movement never gathered momentum, but the hamburger on the bun accomplished the same ends.

It took generations for cooks to discover that the more unadorned the meat, the more natural is its goodness. The smartest hamburger heavens these days advertise the fact that their meat consists of only chopped prime beef and a little salt. In some hotels a little grated onion and perhaps some milk or cream are added to the meat. But the seasonings are conservative and never overpowering. Strangely, in France, where simplicity and subtlety of flavors are almost worshiped, raw hamburger is so dressed up it seems like a hangover from Nero's days.

Hamburgers masquerade under a host of names. Tartar steaks are preferred by gents with balloon heads, who have had too much to drink the night before and who think that the best way to restore the digestive tract is to give it the shock treatment with raw meat and onions. In roadside stands and other honest eating places, however, a hamburger is called a hamburger. In hotels it will assume such noms de plume as bitock of beef, meat patties, Salisbury steak, chopped tenderloin steak or chopped sirloin steak. But in any instance it is chopped beef shaped into a cake ranging in thickness from an eighth of an inch to a full inch. It may weigh anywhere from an ounce to a full half pound before cooking.

You can buy two frankfurters that are alike, but seldom will two chefs turn out quite the same hamburgers. Chopped beef is a kind of magnifying mirror: Let the chef use chopped round instead of chuck, add a little more onion or salt, prowl around ever so carefully with a few grains of paprika or add an ounce or two more suet—and the hamburger will reflect the difference immediately. The net result, however, if the chef is a square shooter, must be succulent, unadulterated beef flavor. Anything else is a fraud.

Any educated bachelor who has cut his wisdom teeth should know something about meat when he sets about making a hamburger. Meat which has been preground and is resting in the display cases should be avoided. It usually includes a large proportion of fat—revealed by the large number of white specks. It frequently includes such unsalable odds and ends as beef hearts, scraps of veal and pork, stray kidneys, slightly mildewed flank steaks and other vagrants of the refrigerator.

The best rule is to buy your beef and have it ground to order or grind it yourself. Buy chuck of beef if you want it somewhat fatty, round of beef if you prefer it lean and top sirloin for the finest flavor. To all lean meat, an ounce or two of suet may be added per pound. Better still, ask the butcher to add an ounce or two of marrow taken from the shin of the beef.

Although hamburger is our great national specialty, our great national offense is grinding the meat so that it emerges with the consistency of mush. Tell the butcher to put the meat through a grinder with a medium blade only once; twice will often turn it into puree. In hotel kitchens years ago, when the butcher had sufficient time, the meat was actually chopped with two cleavers until it was ready to be shaped into a hamburger.

The bachelor who attempts to make a hamburger should have a thorough orientation in the art of petting. Before chopped beef is made into a hamburger, it is mixed with seasonings and sometimes milk or cream. You shouldn't overmix it or it will become tight and tough. When you put it into a mixing bowl, you are not going into a grudge battle with both mitts slugging in every direction. You are touching flesh that should be cajoled lightly and lovingly until it is in the shape you want it to be. If you own an ice-cream scoop, you should use it to divide the meat into equal portions. Other containers, such as glass sherbet dishes, may be used for dividing the meat into equal-size servings.

A hamburger should be brought to the fire with the respect of a votary. If the flame is too hot, the outside will be seared too quickly and the inside left raw. Too low a flame will cause the meat to steam and the outside of the burger will be a grayish brown instead of a deep, rich brown. Thin hamburgers from ¼ to ½ inch thick should be cooked on a griddle or in a frying pan. Thicker hamburgers from ½ inch to 1 inch in thickness, known as hamburger steaks, should be cooked under a broiler flame or in an infrared broiler. For playboys and playmates who dig this frisky, facile dish, the following formulas should be invaluable:

## HAMBURGER STEAK
### (Serves 4)

1½ lbs. chopped beef
1½ teaspoon salt
¼ teaspoon pepper
3 tablespoons light cream
1 teaspoon grated onion
4 teaspoons butter

Remove meat from refrigerator. Let it stand until it reaches room temperature. Put into a mixing bowl. Carefully break apart with the fingertips. Sprinkle with the salt and pepper. Add the cream and onion. Mix lightly until there is no pool of cream visible in the bowl, but don't overmix. Divide into four portions. Shape each into a ball between the palms. Press gently to flatten into cakes ½ inch thick. Place the patties in the refrigerator to chill at least 2 hours; cold burgers will be less inclined to break when they are put under the broiler flame. Preheat the broiler flame at least 10 minutes. Brown the burgers on both sides and dab a dollop of butter on each morsel just before serving. Note: Burgers are rare inside when they yield easily to the touch of a finger or the back of a spoon. When they are medium done, they feel less resilient. When they are well done, they feel firm.

Serve hamburger steaks on toast, piling the plates with French-fried potatoes or warm potato chips. Catsup and sliced sweet Bermuda onions are *de rigueur*. Foamy dry beer should be served in tall Pilsner glasses. For athletes, the pound of meat should be divided into two or three portions rather than four. For sandwiches, divide a pound of meat into about six portions and cook on a griddle very lightly greased or in a heavy cast-iron frying pan. Split the buns and toast them on the cut side only before serving.

## HAWAIIAN HAMBURGER STEAKS
(Serves 4)

*1½ lbs. chopped beef*
*¾ teaspoon monosodium glutamate*
*1½ tablespoons finely minced fresh ginger*
*¼ cup soy sauce*
*2 large cloves garlic, minced fine*
*1 tablespoon lime juice*
*1 tablespoon salad oil*

Remove meat from refrigerator and let stand until it reaches room temperature. Mix beef with monosodium glutamate and ginger. Shape into four flat cakes and chill in refrigerator. Mix soy sauce, garlic, lime juice and oil and brush generously on hamburgers. Charcoal-broil, basting frequently with soy sauce, until deep brown on both sides. Serve with grilled pineapple.

## HAMBURGER CLARET STEAKS
(Serves 4)

*1½ lbs. lean chopped beef (round)*
*¾ cup dry red wine*
*3 tablespoons finely minced shallots or onions*
*3 tablespoons butter at room temperature*
*1½ teaspoons salt*
*¼ teaspoon freshly ground pepper*
*½ teaspoon monosodium glutamate*

Remove meat from refrigerator and let stand until it reaches room temperature. In a small saucepan, simmer wine and shallots until wine is reduced to about ¼ cup; then chill. Combine wine, butter, salt, pepper and monosodium glutamate. Add beef and mix very gently until ingredients are blended. Shape into four flat cakes and chill in refrigerator. Broil over charcoal or cook on griddle until deep brown on both sides.

## HAMBURGER ORDINAIRE

For a straight beef flavor, omit the onion or the cream or both. Add 2 or 3 tablespoons ice water, however, to keep the meat juicy.

# DEVILED HAMBURGERS

Add 1 teaspoon prepared mustard and 1 teaspoon Worcestershire sauce to meat before shaping into cakes.

# HAMBURGER PIQUANTE

Add 1 tablespoon catsup, 1 teaspoon horseradish sauce and 2 tablespoons finely chopped parsley to meat before shaping into cakes.

# BARBECUED HAMBURGERS

Brush the meat generously with prepared barbecue sauce before and during broiling. Pass additional barbecue sauce at the table.

# CHEESEBURGERS

Place a slice of sharp process cheese on the browned side of the meat right after it has been turned. If burgers are being broiled, brown both sides and then place a slice of cheese on top. Broil about 2 minutes more or until cheese begins to soften; shortly after (if you've done everything by the book), so will she.

# HAMBURGERS TEMPURA
## (Serves 4)

*1 lb. chopped beef*
*1 teaspoon soy sauce*
*⅛ teaspoon pepper*
*¼ teaspoon powdered ginger*
*1 cup sifted all-purpose flour*
*1 egg yolk*
*1 cup cold water*
*1 teaspoon salt*
*1 large green pepper*
*Salad oil*
*4 slices tomato, ¼ inch thick*
*8 scallions, trimmed to 3-inch lengths*

Combine beef, soy sauce, pepper and ginger, mixing

gently. Shape into four round patties. Mix flour, egg yolk, water and salt in an electric blender for 30 seconds. Cut green pepper lengthwise into ½-inch strips, discarding seeds and stem. Pour salad oil to a depth of ¼ inch in an electric skillet preheated to 370°. Dip patties into batter and sauté until well browned on both sides. When patties are half-done, dip tomato slices, pepper strips and scallions into batter and sauté until tender. Serve with hot Chinese mustard and prepared duck sauce.

## SALISBURY STEAK
(Serves 4)

> 1¼ lbs. chopped top-sirloin steak
> ¼ cup light cream
> 1 teaspoon salt
> ¼ teaspoon pepper
> 2 tablespoons minced parsley
> ½ teaspoon onion powder
> Bread crumbs
> Paprika
> Salad oil
> 2 tablespoons butter

Let meat stand at room temperature 1 hour. Mix gently with light cream, salt, pepper, minced parsley and onion powder. Shape into four oval patties, ¾ inch thick. Sprinkle generously with bread crumbs, lightly with paprika and salad oil. Place on a greased rack under preheated broiler and broil until brown on both sides. Brush with butter just before serving.

## HAMBURGERS MADRID
(Serves 4)

> 1¼ lbs. chopped beef
> 1 teaspoon salt
> 2 tablespoons finely minced canned chili peppers
> ½ teaspoon monosodium glutamate
> 2 tablespoons ice water
> 4 bananas
> Brown sugar
> Cinnamon

2 tablespoons butter
1 10½-oz. can cream of mushroom soup
3 tablespoons dry sherry
3 tablespoons light cream

Let meat stand at room temperature 1 hour. Mix gently with salt, chili peppers, monosodium glutamate and ice water. Shape into four patties about ¾ inch thick. Cut bananas in half crosswise and place on a shallow, greased broiler pan. Sprinkle with brown sugar and cinnamon, dot with butter and bake in oven preheated to 400° until tender. Place hamburgers on a lightly greased, preheated electric skillet or griddle and cook until well browned on both sides. In a saucepan, combine cream of mushroom soup, sherry and cream. Bring to the boiling point; then pour onto serving plates. Place hamburgers on sauce and flank with baked banana halves.

## ROQUEFORT HAMBURGERS
### (Serves 4)

1¼ lbs. chopped beef
½ teaspoon salt
⅛ teaspoon pepper
¼ cup finely crumbled Roquefort cheese
Bread crumbs
Paprika
Salad oil
2 tablespoons butter at room temperature
½ teaspoon lemon juice
1 tablespoon minced parsley
4 slices French bread, about 3-inch diameter

Combine meat with salt, pepper and Roquefort cheese, mixing gently. Shape into four round patties about ¾ inch thick. Dip these into bread crumbs. Sprinkle lightly with paprika and salad oil and place on a well-greased wire broiler rack. Broil under a preheated broiler flame until brown on both sides. Combine butter, lemon juice and parsley. While hamburgers are cooking, toast French bread. Spread with butter mixture and place hamburgers atop.

# Let's Stew It

*God maye sende a man good meate, but the Deuyll maye sende an euyll coke to dystrue it.* So ran a medieval adage that must surely have been written by a sage with a stomachful of bad stew. For stew—known variously as slumgullion, dumb funk, Black Mike and sometimes slop—too often is *Deuyllish* indeed: a turgid, mongrel mixture covering a multitude of culinary sins. Certainly the heavy bowl of mediocre mutton that masquerades as lamb stew in many a roadside restaurant is an excellent example of *dystrued meate,* and army men of every nation can recall a variety of horrors called stew ladled into their mess kits by *euyll cokes* called mess sergeants.

Never mind—one taste of real stew will dispel the nightmarish memories of a hundred vile ones. From the French *navarin de mouton* to the Hungarian *gulyás,* from the Irish *scouse* to the South American *puchero,* the fragrance of a fine stew slowly simmering on the kitchen range will set aquiver the nostrils of the most rabid antistew man. When professional chefs take the day off and retire to the quiet precincts of their own kitchens at home, they eat stew. It may be a delicate veal stew with mushrooms or a heady venison in red wine, but it's the kind of homey dish that satisfies the chef's peasant heart as well as his aristocratic head.

One of the criticisms that foreign chefs often level at American cooking is the dryness of so many of the American specialties. American fried chicken, ham, breaded pork chops and even hamburgers are wrong—

in the eyes of foreigners—because these foods are relatively dry even when they're good. A stew, on the other hand, with its rivulets of glossy gravy, its bright scattering of vegetables and tender chunks of moist meat, is a deep mealtime oasis, the kind of liquid joy to sink your teeth into.

Culinarians have always suspected that the chief trouble with stews is the fact that they're so easy. The big, wide pot known as the Dutch oven is an open invitation to laziness. You can mix pork with veal, forget the herbs, add too much fat, throw in old turnips, leave the gravy unskimmed and still come up with a distant relative of a stew. You can't do that— and get away with it—when you prepare a fine roast, a pie or a lobster. This doesn't mean that you should never change stew recipes or invent your own recipe for stew. However, you shouldn't diddle-daddle around, throwing in anything from allspice to zucchini, unless you know what you're doing.

A stew is one of those creations in which the gravy is fully as important as the meat itself. As a matter of fact, you can test a good stew by merely sipping the gravy alone. If it's a beef stroganoff, for instance, a few drops of gravy on the tip of your tongue should convey a luscious blend of beef, onions, mushrooms and caraway seed. If any of these flavors singly hits you in the eye, the stew is wrong. It's still virginal and must stay on the slow fire until all the flavors are welded into a subtle composite blend. This leads to the heart of the stew man's skill. He must have a kind of Joblike patience. Only the languorous, barely visible lapping of the gravy around the meat must be allowed. Electronic cooking methods, pressure cookers and all other hurry-up gadgets or schemes will fail to produce a masterly stew. To any man who aspires to be a power behind the stewpot, we're happy to proffer the following eight-part advice direct from our test kitchen:

1. When you go to the butchershop, never lay your money on so-called stewing meat assembled in the display case. This is normally a conglomeration of meat from every portion of the carcass, cut into cubes and marked at a very low price. Instead, order meat from a particular cut specified in the recipe. Tell the

butcher, for instance, that you want chuck of lamb or rump of veal or top round of beef or whatever specific cut is indicated as best for the stew you're making.

2. Don't buy meat that's excessively fatty. A moderate amount of fat, such as one finds in some parts of beef chuck, helps to make a superb stew. If there's too much fat, however, it will merely melt as the stew cooks and rise to the top of the gravy, from which it must be skimmed. Every last particle of fat should be removed from the top of the stew before the stew is served. If the stew is kept in the refrigerator overnight, removal of the fat is very easy. As the fat becomes cold, it solidifies and can be easily lifted or scraped from the top of the stew. While the stew is still warm, remove the fat by tipping the pot slightly and skimming the fat from one end, using a gravy baster, a ladle or a large kitchen spoon.

3. For uniform cooking, stewing meat should be cut into uniform pieces about 1 inch or 1½ inches square. Don't let the butcher deal out an assortment of huge and teensy chunks.

4. Meat with bones, such as chuck of lamb, should be examined carefully before cooking to remove any small bone splinters.

5. Remember that the sheer weight of the meat, like a gridiron juggernaut, may cause the stew to stick to the bottom of the pot. To avoid scorching, stir the stew frequently but not constantly, scraping the bottom and corners of the pot. Use a heavy metal pot of the Dutch-oven type with a tight-fitting lid. Use a low, easygoing flame.

6. When piercing the meat to see if the stew is done, try three or four pieces of meat. One piece may require longer cooking than another even though both are from the same cut of meat.

7. The idea that a stew tastes better the second day than the first is often substantially true. The long standing of the stew's ingredients, like the "ripening" of a punch, makes for a mellower marrying of flavors. Of course, if the stew contains potatoes, the potatoes will lose their freshness the second day even though the meat and gravy flavors have perked up.

8. Finally, if the meat is quite tough (all stewing

meat, for reasons of flavor, is not very tender), the pot, in rare instances, may have to remain on the fire so long that the gravy becomes too intense or concentrated in flavor. In this case, the gravy should be diluted with stock or water.

So much for pointers. Here, now, are the pleasures:

## BEEF STEW WITH VEGETABLES
### (Serves 4)

This is the great all-American favorite. Buy the meat cut into 1-inch cubes. For color, sprinkle freshly cooked green peas over the stew on the serving plates. Bring on the main course with a giant tossed green salad. And for the epilogue, serve ripe Camembert cheese and coffee.

> 2 lbs. chuck of beef, cut for stewing
> 3 tablespoons vegetable fat
> 1 medium-size onion, minced
> 1 leek, white part only, minced
> ¼ cup flour
> 1 bay leaf
> ¼ teaspoon thyme
> 3 cups boiling water
> 3 bouillon cubes
> 1 10-oz. can tomatoes, minced
> 12 small silver onions, peeled
> 4 carrots, ½-inch slices
> 4 medium-size potatoes, quartered
> Brown gravy color (optional)
> 2 dashes Tabasco sauce
> Salt and pepper

Sauté the meat in the fat until light brown. Sprinkle the onion and leek over the meat and mix well. Sauté 5 minutes more. Sprinkle in flour, mix well and add bay leaf, thyme, boiling water, bouillon cubes and tomatoes, 1 teaspoon salt and ⅛ teaspoon pepper, stirring well. Bring to a boil. Skim. Reduce flame and simmer slowly for 2 hours. Add the whole silver onions, carrots and potatoes and simmer until meat and vegetables are tender. Skim fat and add brown gravy color, Tabasco, salt and pepper to taste.

# BEEF GOULASH
(Serves 4)

There are hundreds of goulash variations containing anything from sauerkraut to sour cream. Even in its country of origin, Hungarian goulash is served in countless forms. In all the versions, however, you'll find a pronounced flavor of paprika and a thick gravy crowded with more vegetables than stock. Bring on the goulash with boiled parsley potatoes, snappy crisp coleslaw and big steins of beer.

> ¼ cup vegetable fat
> 3 medium-size onions, sliced thin
> 1 green pepper, sliced thin
> 2 lbs. chuck of beef, cut for stew
> 2 tablespoons paprika
> 2 tablespoons flour
> 1 10-oz. can tomatoes, minced
> 3 tablespoons tomato paste
> 1 10-oz. can consommé (undiluted)
> 1 cup boiling water
> Salt and pepper

Sauté the onions and green pepper in the fat until the onions turn deep yellow; then remove from pot and set aside. Put meat into pot and sauté until brown, adding more fat if necessary to keep it from sticking. Return the onions and green pepper to the pot. Stir in paprika and flour, mixing well, then the tomatoes, tomato paste, consommé and boiling water. Mix well and simmer slowly until meat is tender, about 2½ hours. Finally, season to taste with salt and pepper. Pitch in with gusto and let the *Deuyll* take the hindmost.

# BEEF STROGANOFF
(Serves 4)

The beef for this elegant stew should be cut into 1-inch squares, ¼ inch thick. It should be lean beef from the top sirloin or top round. Along with it, you'll want buttered egg noodles and glazed young carrots, and for dessert, a piece of apple strudel and coffee.

¼  cup vegetable fat
2  lbs. lean stewing beef
½  lb. fresh mushrooms
¼  cup minced onion
1  clove garlic, minced
½  teaspoon dried chervil
3  tablespoons flour
4  cups boiling water
3  bouillon cubes
2  tablespoons caraway seeds
2  tablespoons minced parsley
2  tablespoons tomato paste
1  cup sour cream
Salt and pepper

Melt the fat. Add the beef and sauté slowly, stirring frequently, until brown. Detach the mushroom caps from the stems. Wash well. Cut the caps and stems into slices ¼ inch thick and add with onion, garlic and chervil to the pot. Sauté 5 minutes more. Stir in the flour, mixing well. Add 3 cups boiling water and the bouillon cubes, stirring well. In a *separate* small saucepan, combine 1 cup boiling water and the caraway seeds. Simmer 15 minutes. Strain the caraway broth and add it to the stew pot, discarding the seeds. Add the parsley and simmer slowly until the meat is very tender, about 2 to 2½ hours. Skim fat from surface. Stir in tomato paste. Turn off flame just short of boiling and slowly stir in sour cream. When ready to serve, reheat, bringing gravy up to boiling point, and add salt and pepper to taste.

## LAMB STEW WITH BEANS
### (Serves 4)

The extremely luscious combination of lamb and white pea beans is one which French chefs have had fun with for years. It is one of those savory salmagundes which definitely improve on the second or third day. With it, you'll do the right thing by offering buttered fresh broccoli, a bottle of fine rosé wine and, for the conclusion, a *baba au rhum.*

1  cup dried white pea beans
2  cups cold water

    3 tablespoons fat
    2 lbs. chuck of lamb, cut for stewing
    ¼ cup minced onion
    ¼ cup minced green pepper
    1 clove garlic, minced
    1 bay leaf
    1 10-oz. can tomatoes, minced
    2 cups boiling water
    2 bouillon cubes
    Salt and pepper

Soak beans overnight in the cold water. Then remove half the beans to a small saucepan. Cover with fresh water, add ¼ teaspoon salt and simmer until tender, adding water if necessary during cooking to keep from scorching. Set pan aside until stew is done.

Melt the fat in a stewpot. Add the lamb and sauté until brown. Add the onion, green pepper, garlic and bay leaf and sauté 5 minutes more. Add the tomatoes, the *uncooked* beans together with the water in which they were soaked, the 2 cups boiling water, bouillon cubes, 1 teaspoon salt and ⅛ teaspoon pepper. Simmer until lamb and beans are tender, about 1½ hours. Mash the cooked beans separately by forcing them through a food mill; then add to the pot and salt and pepper to taste.

## IRISH LAMB STEW
### (Serves 4)

The stew which in Ireland is known as *scouse* has never caught the fancy of American stew men. *Scouse* is merely layers of large lamb chunks, potatoes and onions, covered with water and simmered until tender. More to our liking is the following lamb stew with light gravy thickened with potatoes instead of flour. Dignify the proceedings with fresh green string beans, a crisp watercress salad and a tall pistachio parfait.

    3 tablespoons vegetable fat
    2 lbs. chuck of lamb, cut for stewing
    ¼ cup minced onions
    2 tablespoons minced green pepper
    2 cloves garlic, minced

3 tablespoons minced parsley
⅛ teaspoon leaf sage
4 cups boiling water
3 bouillon cubes
4 medium-size potatoes, pared
¼ teaspoon Worcestershire sauce
Salt and pepper
1 8-oz. can ready-to-bake biscuits

Melt the fat. Add the lamb, cover and sauté slowly only until meat loses red color—*do not brown*. Add the onions, green pepper, garlic, parsley and sage and sauté 3 minutes longer. Add the boiling water and bouillon cubes and simmer 1 hour. Cut 2 of the potatoes into slices about ½ inch thick and add with the remaining 2 whole potatoes to the pot. Continue simmering, keeping the pot covered, until the whole potatoes are tender, about ½ hour more. Remove the whole potatoes from the pot and mash them. Add them to the stew, mixing well. If the gravy is too thick, thin with stock or water. Add Worcestershire sauce and salt and pepper to taste. Add the biscuits to the pot and simmer slowly, covered, 12 to 15 minutes.

# The Gourmet Gobbler

The turkey is a full-blooded American. Before the New World was discovered, the fowl was unknown in Europe. The first explorers brought wild turkeys back with them, and Europeans soon domesticated the bird. As early as 1570, Charles IX of France celebrated a feast with a huge turkey dinner. Englishmen also started to breed and raise turkeys on farms. In fact, the first domestic turkeys in America were brought from the Old World to the New, where the original settlers were still munching on tough wild turkey taken from the woods.

Ben Franklin suggested the turkey should be our national bird instead of the eagle. Even a man with Ben's imagination might have had difficulty picturing the modern turkey, taken from the grass range to be raised in confinement, treated with ultraviolet rays and fed penicillin to stimulate growth. In Ben's time, a full-grown turkey weighed approximately 18 pounds. Today, you can buy a bronze giant that weighs 40.

The difference between a chicken and a turkey is, after all, immeasurable. The chicken is nice and inoffensive; the turkey is rich with breathtaking curves. If you are served a small portion of chicken, you excuse it, understanding that the chicken is a naturally limited bird. But when the roast turkey is brought on, with its herb stuffing and brown giblet gravy, it is a great mound of joy. A chicken leg is disposed of quickly; the leg of a turkey, however, is a real event.

Turkey tacklers who set out to carve the bird would be wise to take a tip or two from the professional cook, who never approaches a turkey unless it is resting on a wooden carving board. The board should be dry and free from grease. Carving boards suitable for home use are available at household stores. One type of board is equipped with chromium spikes to keep the bird from leaving the roost.

Secondly, the professional cook is equipped with a knife that is always razor-sharp. He uses the knife steel frequently during carving operations. Thirdly, he keeps a clean kitchen towel within reach to wipe the hands or the knife handle when either becomes slippery. Fourthly, a turkey, he knows, should never be carved until it has been out of the oven at least 30 minutes. This permits the inner cooking to subside; the meat sets, making for easier carving into clean, neat slices.

Here are the principal steps in carving a turkey:

1. Holding the drumstick in one hand and the carving knife in the other, cut down to separate the drumstick and thigh from the body of the turkey. Let the knife hug the side of the body as it moves downward. It may be necessary to twist the drumstick and thigh slightly to sever them from the body.

2. Cut between the drumstick and thigh. Use the knife tip to probe between the leg and thigh joint. Again, if necessary, twist the two parts to separate them.

3. Cut the drumstick into relatively thick slices, about ¼ to ½ inch thick. Turn the drumstick around as it is being sliced. Or pass the drumstick whole if someone clamors sufficiently for it. Cut the thigh into slices of the same thickness, cutting around the thighbone when you come to it.

4. Cut off the wing at the joint that connects it to the body.

5. Holding the bird with the fork inserted in breastbone or keel bone (the very top of the breast), start cutting the breast meat downward into slices about ⅛ inch thick or less. Cut parallel slices, using a long sawing motion with the knife. Avoid cutting slices that are too large in diameter or too thick. Four thin slices taste better than two thick slices. Be sure serving plates or platter are nearby so that the meat can be transferred easily from the carving board.

While the turkey is setting and the carving is being

done, the meat naturally cools. Be sure that the serving plates are warm, that the dressing is steaming and that the gravy poured over the turkey is bubbling hot.

For turkey parties, it is now possible to buy the bird roasted and ready for carving at a slight additional cost. Some dealers, in fact, will provide you with a turkey already carved or the turkey carved and the meat put back on the frame, looking just as it did when taken from the oven. For those who'll have no truck with breakaway birds, here's how it's done.

## ROAST TURKEY
### (Serves 8)

(If you want to stuff the bird, buy one of the prepared packaged stuffings and moisten it with cold chicken broth instead of water. After stuffing turkey, fasten the front and rear cavities with poultry pins. The drumsticks should be fastened under the skin flap, tied together or skewered close to the body to make the bird as compact as possible for uniform roasting.)

> 1 turkey, 8 to 10 lbs.
> ¼ lb. butter at room temperature
> Salt and white pepper
> 1 10½-oz. can chicken gravy
> ½ cup chicken broth
> ¼ cup dry white wine
> ¼ cup tomato juice
> Brown gravy color

Preheat oven to 425°. Brush turkey generously with soft butter. Sprinkle with salt and pepper. Cover with aluminum foil and place breast side up on a V rack in an uncovered roasting pan. After 1½ hours, turn heat down to 350°, remove all the aluminum foil and continue roasting until skin is light brown, 1 hour or so longer. Turkey is done when thickest part of drumstick is soft and shows no pink juices when pierced. Let the turkey set in a warm place about 30 minutes before carving. Remove all fat from pan, leaving drippings. Add gravy, broth, wine and tomato juice. Stir well. Place pan over top flame and simmer 5 minutes. Add brown gravy color, correct seasoning and serve.

## GIBLET GRAVY

Sauté liver until tender; boil turkey neck and gizzard until tender. Use ½ cup of this stock in place of chicken broth in the preceding recipe. Put gizzard and liver through meat grinder. Add to gravy and simmer 5 minutes.

## OYSTER AND CHESTNUT STUFFING

24 medium-size oysters, shucked
3 quarts old French bread cut into 1-inch cubes
1 23-oz. can chestnuts in water
1 cup diced onions
2 cups diced celery
½ lb. butter
1 tablespoon poultry seasoning
1 tablespoon salt
½ teaspoon freshly ground pepper
½ cup minced fresh parsley
6 eggs, beaten
½ cup cognac

Soak bread in cold water ½ hour. Drain, pressing lightly to remove excess liquid, but do not squeeze dry. Drain chestnuts and break into small pieces. Drain oysters and cut each into eighths. Put onions, celery and butter into a saucepan and sauté very slowly until vegetables are tender but not brown. In a large mixing bowl, combine bread, sautéed vegetables and all other ingredients and mix well. Put into cavity of turkey before roasting.

## TURKEY CUTLETS, CRANBERRIES AND COINTREAU
(Serves 4)

16 slices breast of roast turkey, ⅛ to ¼ inch thick
1 4-oz. pkg. cream cheese with chives
Salt and pepper
Flour
2 eggs beaten with 2 tablespoons cold water
Bread crumbs
Salad oil

*1 8-oz. can cranberry sauce, well chilled*
*Grated rind of 1 medium-size orange*
*2 tablespoons Cointreau*

Turkey slices must be chosen so that eight slices can be matched to eight other slices of approximately the same size. Work the cream cheese with a spatula or knife until it is soft enough to spread easily. Spread on eight turkey slices and fit the remaining slices on top, sandwich style. If there are any loose ends, they should be trimmed off to make the tops and bottoms of cutlets symmetrical. Sprinkle with salt and pepper. Dip into flour, then into beaten egg and finally into bread crumbs. Heat salad oil to a depth of ¼ inch in an electric skillet preheated to 370° and sauté the cutlets until brown on both sides. Drain on absorbent paper and sprinkle with salt. Combine cranberry sauce, Cointreau and orange rind, mixing well with a fork, and serve in a sauceboat at the table.

## BARBECUED BABY TURKEY
### (Serves 6)

*1 young turkey, about 6 lbs.*
*Salt and pepper*
*½ cup chili sauce*
*¼ cup cider vinegar*
*¼ teaspoon Tabasco sauce*
*2 teaspoons soy sauce*
*1 teaspoon Worcestershire sauce*
*¼ teaspoon ground coriander*
*2 tablespoons salad oil*

Have the butcher split the turkey for broiling. If the turkey is frozen, it must be thawed first, in which case you must order the bird at least a day before it is needed. Have the butcher remove the inside breastbone and crack the thighbones. Skewer the legs close to the body and bend the wing tips so that they fit under the back.

Wash the turkey well, dry with paper toweling and sprinkle with salt and pepper. Combine all other ingredients into a basting sauce, mixing very well. Preheat broiler. Place the turkey skin side down in a

shallow pan and brush with basting sauce. Be sure
turkey is not in contact with flame or so close that
parts of it burn while other parts remain undone.
Broil until light brown. Turn skin side up, brush with
basting sauce and broil again until light brown. Reduce heat to 300°. Transfer turkey to oven section of
range and bake 1 hour or until tender, brushing
frequently with basting sauce. Turkey may be served
hot or cold. Remove skewers and cut into chunks with
poultry shears.

## TURKEY AND CORNMEAL CAKES
## WITH SAUSAGE
### (Serves 4)

*1 teaspoon salt*
*3 cups boiling water*
*1 cup yellow cornmeal*
*1 cup cold water*
*1 small onion, grated*
*¼ cup minced green pepper*
*1 tablespoon butter*
*1½ cups cooked turkey cut into ⅛-inch dice*
*Salad oil*
*1 lb. small link sausages*

Add salt to boiling water. Combine cornmeal and cold
water, mixing well, and add gradually to boiling water.
Reduce flame and simmer very slowly, stirring frequently, 12 to 15 minutes, keeping pot covered. Remove from flame and add onion, green pepper, butter
and turkey, mixing well. Put cornmeal mixture into
greased loaf pan and chill in refrigerator until firm
enough to slice. Cook sausages, following directions
on package. Grease a griddle or electric skillet preheated to 370°. Unmold the cornmeal mixture. Cut
into ½-inch slices and fry until brown on both sides.
Serve sausages alongside fried cornmeal with chilled
whole-cranberry sauce.

# Fair Game

Once a year, men in practically every state of the union tromp out of the woods with dogs and guns, their game bags filled to the legal limit with things furred and feathered. That they enjoy the hunt there is no doubt—but whether their fallen quarry will put them in ecstasy as tasty table fare is something else again. Too often does the ring-necked pheasant turn out tough as timber, the mud hen muddy, the wild duck dry as Ibsen's play of the same name.

This culinary anticlimax, which occurs year in, year out, is completely unnecessary, since just a little care and savory savvy are all that is required to do justice to the fine flesh found in fields and forests. By drawing and skinning your game carefully, by ripening for the proper amount of time before cooking and by styling your cookery to the game's age, you can be sure of avoiding most of the pitfalls that may make your victory Pyrrhic as all get-out.

Let's face it, much of the game consumed nowadays is bought in gourmet butchershops or ordered from mail-order game farms. The quality and tenderness of such game is uniformly excellent because it's raised under controlled conditions. Everything from wild boar to pheasant is now sold in cans or jars. For men who love their hasenpfeffer, for example, frozen rabbit all ready for the stewing pan is now widely sold at frozen-food counters. The fact that game connoisseurs are quite willing to pay $16 for a brace of pheasant from a game preserve shows something of the value they put on the uniquely luscious taste of game. But there are those purists—and some buckoes—who get an added clout from bagging their own dinners, many of them guys who, except during hunting season, are unbloodthirsty, indoor types. For these, the following facts of wildlife are noted:

First of all, the knowing nimrod must never forget the simple fact that his game is shot. When lead pierces the innards of beast or bird, it can cause undigested food to spoil the adjacent flesh. Food left in the crop alongside the neck may taint the wild meat. It's important, then, for the gunner-gourmet to draw his quarry as soon as possible. To draw game merely means to remove the innards. If you can't do it yourself, you'll often find butchers, suppliers, *Hausfraus* or guides in well-known game areas who will perform this scullery work for you.

If you decide to draw the birds right in the field, it isn't necessary to pluck them immediately. Merely remove enough feathers from the neck and tail end to allow a reasonable working area. With your hunting knife, make a slit alongside the neck and remove the crop and windpipe. Cut another slit from the end of the breastbone to the tail and remove the internal organs. Don't wash the bird, merely wipe it dry.

If it's a hefty buck you've knocked down, the easiest solution, of course, is to take your kill to the butcher nearest your camp and ask him to skin, gut and cut the venison into pieces that will fit into your range or food freezer. However, if you are bound and determined to do it yourself, here's how: Make your incision at the top of the chest and draw it down vertically to and around the tail. Pull the flesh to the side and remove the lungs, heart, stomach and intestines. Wipe the adjacent flesh clean with a slightly moistened rag, and with small branches keep the torso spread open for airing until the body heat has dissipated. It is best not to skin the animal at once, but to leave it in the hide until it is aged and ready for butchering or at least until it can be aged under semirefrigeration. If this is the case and you do postpone skinning, you must remove the musk glands behind the leg and upper thigh of the animal or they will spoil the meat along the entire shank. This is easily accomplished, as they are located between the skin and flesh on the hind legs of the animal and can be pulled out with little difficulty from a vertical incision. Once the animal is ready for skinning—which certainly shouldn't be until you've returned from your trip—complete the cut you've made to remove the innards, extending it to the bottom of the chin, and remove the hide by pulling up and out. To remove the hide from the legs, cut along the inside of them, starting from just above the hoof and running to the center cut you have made in the torso. The head and hooves, of course, should be severed.

If your hunting trail isn't too far from your home, you can defer the job of drawing the game until you've returned. Often the butcher or chef in your own club kitchen, or any competent restaurant chef, will be able to take care of all cleaning operations. But in any event, as soon as the game is brought down, it should be kept as cool and well ventilated as possible. Don't throw the birds or small animals in an airless heap inside your game bag while they're still warm. Keep the birds hanging separately as long as possible. Don't toss your deer over the front fender right alongside the engine heat, particularly on a warm day, and then begin driving several hundred miles to your destination. If you do, you may find that you've crossed the line between ripe and rotten when you sit down to your roast saddle of venison.

Unlike fish, which should be transferred right from the hook to the frying pan, game must be aged before it's eaten. If it isn't hung, it will be flat-tasting, coarse and tough. In Scotland, pheasant are hung until they almost drop from the hook. In America, our tolerance for the mature fragrance of aged game is more limited. Sportsmen in years gone by were in the habit of aging their game outdoors, hanging it for days from the branch of a tree, a tent pole, a cornice or any other presumably cool place where its individual flavor could develop. The hazards of this old practice, still followed in some sections of the country, are countless. An occasional spell of hot weather can quickly ruin a man's entire bag. Varmints and insects can attack the hanging meat. Against their depredations hunters still douse birds with ground pepper, tie mosquito netting around small game animals or hang them from extra-tall trees. Game boxes, small contraptions with screens of fine-mesh wire, are helpful if you're too many miles from civilization. The best practice, however, is to age your game in the refrigerator. It takes a little longer than outdoor aging, but it's infinitely safer. If the refrigerator temperature is set between 38 and 42 degrees, the game will mature more satisfactorily than at 32 to 36 degrees. And, naturally, a butcher's walk-in refrigerator, where the game can hang in cool air circulated by a blower, does a better job than a bachelor's small, crowded refrigerator. Usually upland game birds such as pheasant, quail or grouse should be aged from three to six days, depending on individual taste. Wild duck should be aged two to three days. Venison, on the other hand, should be aged from one to two weeks.

In choosing a particular recipe, it's extremely important to know the age of the game you're about to prepare. Unless you can recognize the signs of maturity, you'll be in the position of the man who invites his chums to a dinner of broiled squabs and then discovers that what he's serving tastes like old soup fowl. One of the distinctive signs of age in a bird is the end of the breastbone. In a young bird, it's soft and may be twisted easily. In older birds the tip of the breastbone is quite rigid. The feet and shanks are another sign. They're pliable and smooth in a young bird but coarse and rough in older fowl. The claws of a young bird are quite sharp; as the bird grows old, the claws become blunted. The end wing feathers are pointed in a young specimen and somewhat rounded in an older bird. When judging waterfowl, note that the windpipe of the young is soft; as they mature, it becomes less pliable. In estimating the age of a rabbit, the ears and lips are your clues: The ears of the young are very soft, and the cleft in the upper lip is more definitely outlined than in an older hare. The age of deer, of course, is indicated by the antlers: The greater the growth, the older the animal, usually.

Once you've determined that your game is young, you can choose the dry forms of cookery, which are normally used in preparing tender meat, such as broiling or roasting. If game is old, it must always be cooked by moist heat as in braising, stewing or boiling (although the latter is rarely used in game cookery). Certain young game animals such as rabbit or woodchuck may be cooked by either method. The tender cuts of venison such as the rack or loin may be broiled or roasted, whereas the tough cuts such as the chuck should be stewed.

Game birds tend to be dry and lean in their natural state. To compensate for this dryness, most birds that are roasted are usually covered with a thin layer of salt pork, larding pork or bacon. Aluminum foil or a double thickness of cheesecloth dipped into salad oil may be used to prevent excessive drying when a fierce oven heat is used. During cooking, the birds may be brushed with butter or oil. Basting with stock or chicken broth is an aid in retaining natural juices. The electric rotisserie in which the bird is self-basted as it revolves before the heat is an excellent piece of equipment for the modern game cook.

Your first taste of game may be quite startling. The texture is unique, for one thing. Most game doesn't break under a fork unless it's cooked to death. And the flavor of game is pungent and racy rather than mild. It nips the taste buds and is generally more tart than mellow. That's what is meant by "gamy," and once you've grown accustomed to its special blandishments, you may very well join the ranks of those who declare game the most exciting fare there is. Here, now, from our own plush-lined pup tent are easy directions for the open season:

## ROAST PHEASANT WITH BREAD SAUCE
### (Serves 6)

> 2 pheasant, 2½ to 3 lbs. each
> Salt and pepper
> 4 thin slices salt pork
> ½ cup chicken broth
> 1 cup milk
> 1 medium-size onion
> 2 whole cloves
> 1½ cups bread crumbs
> 2 tablespoons dry sherry
> ¼ cup butter
> 2 tablespoons minced parsley

*2 tablespoons minced chives*
*¼ lemon*

Preheat oven to 450°. Wipe pheasant with damp cloth and sprinkle lightly with salt and pepper. Tie slices of salt pork over breasts and place pheasant breast side up in a shallow roasting pan. Roast 10 minutes and reduce heat to 350°. Add chicken broth to pan and continue roasting, basting about every 10 minutes with chicken broth. Roast until pheasant are tender—about 1 to 1¼ hours' total cooking time. Meanwhile, pour milk into a thick saucepan. Stick the cloves into the onion and add to the saucepan. Bring slowly up to the boiling point, but do not boil. Add ½ cup bread crumbs to milk. Stir well and simmer about 10 minutes longer, stirring frequently to prevent burning. Remove onion and cloves from saucepan. Add sherry to sauce. When pheasant are done, pour off fat from the roasting pan, or remove with a basting syringe, but save drippings. Add drippings to bread sauce. Add salt and pepper to taste. In another saucepan, melt the butter. Add the remaining 1 cup bread crumbs and sauté slowly, stirring constantly, until bread crumbs are light brown. Add parsley and chives to pan. Squeeze the juice of ¼ lemon into the bread crumbs and mix well. Serve the bread crumbs and the bread sauce in separate sauceboats at the table. Cut pheasant into portions with poultry shears. Serve with any tart jelly, such as red or black currant, cranberry or crab apple.

## ROAST DRESSED PHEASANT
### (Serves 6)

This way of presenting pheasant on the platter is strictly for display purposes, but if you have the time and the patience, it's a lot of fun for a buffet or holiday table. Before the pheasant is plucked, cut off in whole sections the plumage of the wings and tail. Cut the wings close to the body. Cut off the tail with enough of the appendage to keep the feathers intact. Also cut off the head and neck in one piece. For each section, take a length of rather stiff wire and force it through the solid part of each appendage to which the feathers are attached. Allow about two inches of wire to extend from the end for fastening each section later on. Roast the pheasant as described in the preceding recipe. For dressing 2 pheasant, take 2 small loaves of unsliced white bread or 1 large loaf cut in half crosswise. Hollow out the center of each loaf so that it resembles a trough, into which the cooked pheasant may be placed. Fry the bread in a large pan with deep fat heated to 370° or in a shallow pan containing 1 inch of hot fat, turning the bread as needed to brown evenly. Place the roasted pheasant on the bread on a large silver platter. Arrange the head, wings and tailpiece of each pheasant, fastening each section into the bread, so that the birds look as though they were reconstituted to their natural state. If you buy pheasant for this purpose, be sure to ask for male pheasant in the plume, since the male wears the more colorful feathers.

## ROAST QUAIL WITH GRAPES
### (Serves 4)

> 4 quail
> Salt and pepper
> 2 thin slices salt pork
> 1 onion, sliced
> 1 piece celery, sliced
> 2 sprigs parsley
> 1 cup chicken broth
> ¼ cup tomato juice
> 2 juniper berries, crushed
> Brown gravy coloring
> 1 tablespoon arrowroot or 2 tablespoons flour
> 1 8-oz. can seedless grapes
> 1 oz. cognac

Preheat oven to 500°. Sprinkle quail lightly with salt and pepper. Cut slices of salt pork in half crosswise. Tie a piece of salt pork over the breast of each quail. Place the quail breast side up in a shallow roasting pan. Add the onion, celery and parsley to the pan. Roast 10 minutes and reduce heat to 350°. Add ½ cup chicken broth to the pan and roast about 15 to 20 minutes longer or until quail are tender, basting about every 5 minutes. Remove quail from pan. Remove salt

pork from breasts. Skim fat from drippings and place
the roasting pan over a top flame. Add balance of
chicken broth, tomato juice, juniper berries and enough
gravy coloring to make liquid a rich brown. Bring to a
boil. Dissolve arrowroot or flour in ¼ cup cold
water, mixing until no lumps remain, and slowly add
to the gravy while stirring constantly. Simmer 10 minutes over a low flame and strain into a saucepan. Drain
grapes and add to gravy. Bring to a boil. Add cognac
and salt and pepper to taste. Place each quail on a
piece of toast. Pour sauce with grapes over quail on
serving plates or platter.

## BREAST OF MALLARD DUCK
### (Serves 4)

Many ducks on the eastern flyway live on a diet of
seafood, which creates a particularly strong fishy
smell when the ducks are roasted or broiled. The odor
that comes from the carcass isn't much of a problem
in this recipe because the breast meat is cut off the
carcass. The remainder of the duck, consisting of the
leg and second joint, is seldom eaten, since it is generally quite tough. Sometimes the discarded meat is
put into a duck press, where the juices are extracted
for the gravy. In roasting or broiling wild duck, the
meat should always be cooked rare for best flavor
and tenderness.

> 2 mallard ducks
> ¼ cup olive oil
> 2 tablespoons red-wine vinegar
> ¼ teaspoon rosemary
> 4 sprigs parsley
> 1 onion, sliced
> 2 pieces celery, sliced
> 1 clove garlic, crushed
> Salt, pepper and paprika

Pluck only the breast feathers from the ducks. With
a very sharp knife, cut into the skin—not the flesh—
starting at the neck and slicing straight back along
the top of the breastbone to the tail. Remove the skin
from the breast. To remove the meat, cut along

each side of the breastbone. Run the knife under the flesh and as close as possible to the carcass. Remove each side of the breast in one piece. Place the breasts in a bowl with all other ingredients except salt, pepper and paprika and marinate overnight. Preheat the broiler to 550°. Remove the breasts from the marinade. Sprinkle each lightly with salt, pepper and paprika and broil about 5 minutes on each side. Serve with wild rice, creamed silver onions, fresh green peas and guava jelly.

## ROAST PRESSED DUCK
### (Serves 4)

> 2 wild ducks, cleaned, drawn and singed
> Salad oil
> Salt and pepper
> 2 tablespoons sweet butter
> 1 teaspoon minced shallot or onion
> ⅔ cup red Burgundy
> 2 tablespoons currant jelly
> ½ teaspoon beef extract
> Juice of ½ lemon
> 1 oz. cognac
> 1 dash cayenne pepper

Be sure oil sac is removed from each duck near the tail end. Preheat oven to 550°. Place the ducks in a shallow roasting pan. Brush generously with salad oil. Sprinkle with salt and pepper and roast 15 to 20 minutes, no longer. Slice breast meat from ducks and keep in a deep, warmed platter. Save all juices when carving. In a chafing dish over a direct flame, melt the butter. Add the shallot and sauté about 1 minute. Add the Burgundy, currant jelly, beef extract and lemon juice and simmer 3 to 5 minutes. Place the carcasses of the ducks in the well of the duck press. Squeeze the juice several times and pour into the chafing dish. Add juice from platter, cognac and dash of cayenne pepper. Season to taste. Pour hot sauce over sliced breast of duck and serve with fried hominy, grilled tomatoes and a tossed garlic-flavored green salad.

## ROAST VENISON
### (Serves 4 to 6)

1 leg or saddle of venison
1 carrot, sliced
1 onion, sliced
1 large clove garlic, smashed
4 sprigs parsley
1 teaspoon crushed whole pepper
1 small bay leaf
1 pint dry white wine
½ cup vinegar
1 quart water
3 thin slices salt pork
1 10½-oz. can chicken gravy
1 tablespoon currant jelly
1 jigger cognac or bourbon

Steep venison in a marinade of carrot, onion, garlic, parsley, crushed pepper, bay leaf, wine, vinegar and water in the refrigerator for 2 days, turning it several times. Then remove vegetables from marinade and place in an uncovered roasting pan. Save 1 cup of the marinade. Drain venison well. Rest it on bed of vegetables in pan. Cover with pork slices and roast in 425° oven, allowing about 10 to 12 minutes per pound. When done, remove venison from pan. Add the cup of marinating liquid, chicken gravy, currant jelly and cognac. Mix well. Bring to a boil over top flame and simmer 5 minutes. Skim fat from gravy. Correct seasoning, strain gravy and serve.

## VENISON CHOPS, CHESTNUTS ESPAGNOLE
### (Serves 4)

4 venison chops, ¾ inch thick
½ cup French dressing
2 tablespoons butter
½ cup celery, small dice
¼ cup onion, small dice
¼ cup green pepper, small dice
1 8-oz. can tomatoes

*1 12-oz. can imported whole chestnuts*
*½ teaspoon sugar*
*⅛ teaspoon garlic powder*
*Salt and pepper*
*Prepared mustard*

Marinate the venison chops in the French dressing for 2 hours. In good-sized saucepan, melt the butter. Add the celery, onion and green pepper. Sauté only until onion turns yellow. The celery and green pepper may be crisp. Chop the tomatoes coarsely, saving the juice. Add tomatoes and their juice to the saucepan. Simmer slowly 5 minutes. Drain the chestnuts and add to the pan with the sugar and garlic powder. Season generously with salt and pepper and simmer 10 minutes. Remove venison chops from French dressing. Brush each chop lightly with mustard. Sprinkle with salt and pepper and broil under a preheated broiler flame about 5 to 6 minutes on each side. Serve chestnuts alongside chops on serving plates. Garnish each plate with a large sprig of watercress and prepare for an evening of fun and game.

# The Secrets of Saucery

"Cooking and roasting are things to teach," said Brillat-Savarin. "It needs a genius to make a sauce." Possibly. But a genius without a recipe might find himself outclassed by a lesser talent equipped with a really sound set of instructions. Such a fellow, if he keeps his wits about him, can turn out a fine sauce that will do much more than merely flatter food—it will also stand in its own right as an exciting experience in eating, for few snacks are more savory than a saucy sauce and a small heel of French bread.

What the novice American *saucier* does lack, and what his French brother has in abundance, is tradition. Ever since the Middle Ages, when hawkers drove their carts through the streets of Paris shouting their latest sauce creations and professional *sauciers* had already set up their own independent guild, a great culinary tradition has been nurtured. Sauces like the *mère*, or "mother," sauces—the basic brown and white sauces from which other sauces are derived—were developed literally over hundreds of years of labor, experimentation and criticism. Fortunately, Americans can dip into this tradition and select for their own repertoire innumerable sauces that no longer require 14 hours of stirring, reduction and despumation. Luscious, velvety sauces can now be prepared in a matter of minutes.

It's important to understand the two main ways in which sauces are concocted: First of all, there are the sauces that are made apart from the food with which they are served. The tomato sauce under a breaded veal cutlet or the egg sauce poured over boiled fresh salmon are examples of this type. Then there is the second category—sauces created as part of the preparation of other foods. For instance, if you sautéed breast of chicken, then added sherry and light cream and simmered the liquid slowly until it reached the consistency of heavy cream, you'd have this second type of sauce. In America we often call this type of sauce a gravy, such as the gravy of a lamb stew.

The quantity of sauce accompanying a particular dish may vary greatly. It may completely cloak the food as does the robe of golden hollandaise poured over fresh asparagus. At other times it may be merely a small liquid ribbon like the dark devil sauce poured around a grilled pork chop. But, in either case, it must be so luscious that it transmutes the food it punctuates. Naturally, there are some foods that require no sauce at all. A broiled thick spring lamb chop, for instance, should be adorned with nothing more than a light brushing of butter and perhaps a drop of lemon juice. But other dishes—such as calf's liver, smoked ham, veal chops, duckling and fillet of sole, to mention only a few—fairly cry for a fine, piquant sauce.

A sauce cook's worst potential enemy is flour. Now, in most sauces, flour is indispensable as the thickening agent. But if the flour remains raw or semicooked, as it does too often, you don't have a sauce but a thick mucilaginous mess that suffocates any food with which it is served. The graduate sauce cook simmers his sauce not merely until it is thick but until it is glossy, the signal that every bit of raw floury taste has disappeared. The most nearly perfect thickening agent (that is, the one which conveys practically no flavor of its own to a sauce) is arrowroot, a powder made from the root of a West Indian plant. It takes only one-third as much arrowroot as flour to thicken an equal quantity of sauce, but arrowroot leaves the sauce transparent rather than opaque and is therefore not widely used. Other sauces in which rich flavors must be maintained intact, such as hollandaise, are thickened with egg yolks. Finally, there are sauces that are self-thickening—such as the tomato sauces served with spaghetti, which become thick as their own ingredients are gradually reduced in the saucepan. Just remember, the best sauce betrays as little floury taste as possible.

The sauce cook and the soupçon are inseparable. In no other branch of cookery does the shred of herbs, the scintilla of spice, the gleam of sherry or the hint of garlic count for so much. When completing sauces, immediately before they go to the table, you may wish to avail yourself of such finishers as monosodium glutamate, Worcestershire sauce, cayenne pepper, garlic powder and others, never forgetting to use them in grains or droplets, not shovelfuls.

The soul of a fine sauce is its liquid or stock. Some liquids, such as milk, cream, tomato juice or melted butter, are all ready for the saucepan and require no previous preparation. Others, such as the stock for brown sauces, once took hours, even in some cases days, to make. During the dark ages of American cookery, ordinary tap water was used. In France the *fonds* or foundation stocks were always the long-cooking variety. Here is where the old-line sauce cook and today's bachelor chef part company. The modern kitchen benedict uses the bouillons now available in a bewildering variety of concentrated powders, cubes, granules, pastes and soups. Even in hotels noted for their *haute cuisine,* you will now find such concentrated stocks in common use. Many of them are actually superior to the ordinary run of stocks found in the average restaurant.

Men who are absolute neophytes in cookery can now buy prepared sauces that require no toil whatever. First of all, there are the frozen sauces. These frozen gourmet sauces merely need thawing and heating. For some time, fresh hollandaise sauce put up in jars and kept under refrigeration has been available in specialty food stores. It may not be as superb as the best fresh hollandaise sauce, but it excels the average hollandaise you'll find in public eating places. There are now instant hollandaise and instant béarnaise sauces put up in powdered form. They are reconstituted with butter and water. Gourmet items include imported sauces from France. There is also an eight-ounce can of basic white sauce that can easily be converted to such varieties as curry sauce, paprika sauce and others.

Many of the thick concentrated soups are quickly adaptable as sauces. Thus frozen shrimp soup may be thawed, laced with sherry or brandy and cream and poured over fish, seafood and egg dishes.

Of course, all these sure-fire ready sauces include a certain cost in addition to the money you pay. That cost is simply that you give up some of your own creative fun for a certain standardization. Some fellows don't mind if their palates react in exactly the same way as everybody else's. Others prefer the unique experience that comes from coaxing their own individual miracles out of a saucepan.

The following oddments of culinary advice will be helpful for all disciples of the sauce maker's art. Whenever possible, use shallots, those small, yellow bulbs that look like miniature onions, instead of onions. Shallots give a lush, mellow flavor to any sauce, but unhappily are seldom available at ordinary fruit-and-vegetable stands. When melted fat and flour are combined to make a sauce, use a fine wire whip to prevent lump formation. If lumps do form in spite of every care, force the sauce through a fine wire strainer or simply spin in a blender. While sauce is simmering, stir it with a wooden or stainless-steel spoon to prevent a thick layer from forming around the bottom rim of the saucepan. Continued beating with a wire whip in a soft aluminum pan may discolor a white sauce. For eye appeal, brown gravy color may be added to any brown sauce and a drop or two of yellow color to any white sauce. When wine is added at the end of the cooking period rather than at the beginning, use a fine table wine rather than ordinary cooking wine if possible, since the wine flavor will emerge rather distinctly.

In the following recipes for basic sauces and their variations, no portions are indicated, since there is actually no such thing as a portion of sauce. Most of the recipes will yield approximately one measuring cup of sauce, which usually serves four.

## ESPAGNOLE SAUCE

This is the basic French brown sauce called espagnole, or Spanish, because it's dark, or brunette. It should not be confused with the thick Spanish sauce made largely of unstrained tomatoes, frequently served with omelets. Be sure the consommé used for the stock is the condensed type that normally requires an equal quantity of water for serving as soup. In the recipe below, however, it should *not* be diluted with water. The dried onion flakes, parsley flakes, chervil and dried mushrooms in this recipe are all excellent labor-savers that perform just about as nicely as the fresh vegetables for this particular job. Fresh vegetables, of course, can be used, if such is your fancy. Use espagnole sauce on smoked beef tongue, baked ham, veal steaks or chops, calf's liver, broiled veal kidneys or lamb kidneys, Salisbury steak or hot meat sandwiches.

>   *1 10½-oz. can condensed consommé or bouillon*
>   *¼ cup tomato juice*
>   *¼ cup water*
>   *2 tablespoons butter*
>   *2 tablespoons flour*
>   *1 tablespoon onion flakes*
>   *½ teaspoon parsley flakes*
>   *⅛ teaspoon dried chervil*
>   *3 medium-size pieces dried mushroom*
>   *⅛ teaspoon Worcestershire sauce*

Into a small saucepan, pour the consommé, tomato juice and water. Slowly bring to a boil. In another saucepan, melt the butter slowly, without browning it. Stir in the flour. Mix with a wire whip until well blended. Let the mixture, called a *roux,* remain over a very low flame and stir it constantly until it turns a deep golden color similar to coffee ice cream. Slowly stir in the hot liquids from the first saucepan. Add the onion and parsley flakes, chervil and mushrooms. Simmer over the lowest possible flame 25 to 30 minutes. Skim when necessary. Strain the sauce and add Worcestershire sauce and seasoning to taste.

## SAUCE CHASSEUR

Omit dried mushrooms and onion flakes from espagnole recipe. Slice thin 3 medium-size fresh mushrooms. Mince fine 1 small onion. Sauté mushrooms and onion in butter before adding flour. Add 3 tablespoons sherry to sauce when finished cooking. Use the sauce, unstrained, for glorifying braised beef, roast chicken or guinea hen, veal cutlets or venison steak.

## DEVIL SAUCE

Follow recipe for espagnole sauce, adding 12 crushed peppercorns to consommé mixture, and cook as directed. Make a paste of 1 teaspoon dried mustard, 1 teaspoon prepared mustard and 1 tablespoon cold water. Add mustard mixture and ¼ cup finely chopped sour pickle to strained brown sauce. Ladle it around roast fresh ham, roast loin of pork, grilled pork chops, smoked tongue or broiled fresh mackerel.

## RED-WINE MARROW SAUCE

Prepare espagnole sauce. In a separate pan combine ½ cup dry red wine and 1 tablespoon minced shallots, or spring onions if shallots are not available. Cook wine and shallots until wine is reduced to ¼ cup. Strain wine into brown sauce. With a paring knife, gouge out enough marrow from raw beef marrow-bones to fill ¼ cup. Cut marrow into small dice, wash and add to the strained brown sauce. Heat for ½ minute and spoon over minute steaks, London broil or broiled lamb kidneys.

## SAUCE BIGARADE

Remove the peel, in large pieces, from 1 medium-size California orange. With a very sharp knife, cut away the inner white membrane from the outer peel. Cut the peel into very thin slivers about 1 inch long. Cover with water, boil for 1 minute and drain. To strained brown sauce, add orange slivers, 2 tablespoons orange juice, 2 tablespoons dry white wine, 2 tablespoons curaçao and ⅛ teaspoon lemon juice. Simmer 1 minute. This is the classic sauce used with roast duckling or broiled baby duckling.

## BECHAMEL SAUCE

This sauce named after Louis de Béchamel, an officer in the court of Louis XIV, may seem similar to the usual white sauce untutored brides learn before they know how to boil an egg, but a few small additions transform it into an epicurean elixir.

>1 cup hot milk
>¼ cup light cream
>2 tablespoons butter
>2 tablespoons flour
>1 small onion, sliced
>½ small bay leaf
>2 tablespoons dry sherry
>½ teaspoon salt
>1 dash white pepper

Heat the milk and cream in a small saucepan, but do not boil. In another saucepan, melt the butter and remove the pan from the fire to keep from browning. Stir in the flour and blend well. Slowly add hot milk and cream and stir. Add onion and bay leaf. Return to a slow flame and simmer; don't boil or sauce may burn. Cook for 20 minutes, stirring frequently. Add sherry, salt and pepper. Strain and combine with cooked fresh mushrooms, crab meat or shrimps. Use as an escort for croquettes or cutlets or as a base for cream soups.

## VELOUTE SAUCE

In place of milk in preceding recipe, use a strong chicken broth. Add a chicken-bouillon cube if sauce seems weak in flavor. Pour over fricassee of chicken, grilled sweetbreads, hot chicken or hot turkey sandwiches. Combine with chicken cut into hash-size pieces for creamed chicken hash.

## MORNAY SAUCE

First prepare a béchamel sauce. Add ¼ cup of strained béchamel sauce to 2 well-beaten egg yolks and mix well. Pour this mixture slowly into the balance of the béchamel, stirring well. Add 2 tablespoons grated Parmesan cheese and a dash of cayenne pepper and pour over boiled or baked fish. Sprinkle with additional Parmesan cheese and paprika and place under broiler until cheese melts.

## HORSERADISH SAUCE

Add 3 tablespoons prepared horseradish to velouté sauce. Dissolve 1 teaspoon dry English mustard in 1 tablespoon cold water. Add to sauce. Indispensable with boiled beef, it may also be used for boiled corned beef, tongue or chicken.

## RUM SAUCE

2 tablespoons confectioners' sugar
3 tablespoons brown sugar
¼ cup light rum
2 tablespoons dark Jamaican rum
2 tablespoons Falernum
1 tablespoon butter
Juice of ¼ lemon

Put all ingredients into a heavy saucepan. Heat only until butter melts, no longer or the alcohol will evaporate. Pour warm over plum, fig or date pudding or ice cream.

## VODKA FRUIT SAUCES

Brandied fruits and fruits in rum have long been luscious accompaniments for ice-cream desserts. We've found that the liquor harmonizes beautifully with black cherries and frozen strawberries.

To make the strawberry mixture, thaw one 10-oz. can or package of sliced, sweetened strawberries. Add 1½ ozs. vodka. Let the mixture stand 1 hour to ripen before serving. Spoon over vanilla or strawberry ice cream.

Vodka and black cherries are combined as follows: Drain a No. 2 can of pitted black cherries (not the sour red pie cherries). Drain well to remove as much cherry juice as possible. Combine the cherries with 3 ozs. vodka. Let the mixture stand at least 5 or 6 hours in the refrigerator. Place the cherries and vodka in a saucepan and heat until the liquor bubbles. Remove from the fire. Add another jigger of vodka. Light the liquid with a match. Let the blue flames play around the fruit for a few seconds, and then spoon the hot cherries over vanilla ice cream.

## HOLLANDAISE SAUCE

The richest and most delicate of all French sauces (named after Holland because that land was once the source of the best butter in Europe) is largely a combination of egg yolks and butter. For best results, use sweet rather than salted butter. Hollandaise sauce is used in generous portions with fresh asparagus, broccoli or cauliflower and, of course, for eggs Benedict. Since it curdles easily when hot, always serve just lukewarm.

> 4 large egg yolks
> ½ lb. sweet butter
> 1 tablespoon cold water
> 1 teaspoon lemon juice
> ¼ teaspoon salt
> 1 dash cayenne pepper

Beat the egg yolks in an electric mixing machine until deep lemon-colored and thick. While the egg yolks are being beaten, melt the butter over a moderate flame. Remove the butter from the fire as soon as it is all melted. While continuing to beat the egg yolks, begin adding the melted butter in the smallest possible stream, almost drop by drop at first. The butter will be emulsified by the egg yolks into a sauce somewhat resembling mayonnaise in appearance. Gradually add the balance of the butter in small driblets. When all the butter has been added, stir in the water, lemon juice, salt and cayenne pepper. Remove sauce from mixing bowl. It may be cold. To reheat, place over warm, not hot, water, stirring occasionally.

## BLENDER HOLLANDAISE SAUCE

> 3 egg yolks
> Juice of ½ lemon
> ½ cup hot melted sweet butter
> Salt and pepper

Into the well of an electric blender, pour the egg yolks and lemon juice and mix well for a few seconds. Then, with the blender at high speed, add the hot melted butter a teaspoonful at a time until it is completely absorbed. Remove from blender and season with salt and pepper to taste. Serve lukewarm.

## SWEET-AND-SOUR SAUCE

*½ medium-size green pepper, diced*
*½ medium-size sweet red pepper, diced*
*1 cup water*
*1 chicken-bouillon cube*
*3 tablespoons brown sugar*
*1 teaspoon soy sauce*
*¼ teaspoon brown gravy color*
*3 tablespoons cider vinegar*
*4 teaspoons cornstarch*

Place green and red pepper and water in a saucepan.
Bring to a boil and simmer 1 minute, no longer. Add
the chicken-bouillon cube, brown sugar, soy sauce
and the gravy color. Make a smooth paste of the
vinegar and cornstarch and slowly add it to the simmering liquid. Cook a minute or two until sauce is
thick and clear.

## REMOULADE SAUCE

*1 cup mayonnaise*
*¼ cup sour cream*
*2 tablespoons finely minced sour pickle*
*1 tablespoon finely minced parsley*
*2 teaspoons finely chopped capers*
*1 teaspoon finely chopped fresh or*
*½ teaspoon dried chervil*
*2 teaspoons anchovy paste*
*1 teaspoon Dijon mustard*

Combine all ingredients in a mixing bowl. Stir well
and chill until serving time.

## BEARNAISE SAUCE

Omit water and lemon juice from hollandaise sauce.
Add 2 teaspoons tarragon vinegar, 1 teaspoon finely
chopped tarragon, 1 tablespoon finely chopped parsley
and 1 teaspoon melted beef extract. Pass béarnaise with
filet mignon, broiled chicken, broiled scallops or
brochette of sweetbread. Remove beret before eating.

# The Life of Spice

"Variety's the very spice of life," wrote William Cowper, and spices can be the very life of cooking in the infinite variety they provide. This fact, while mouthwatering, is hardly news, since men have been setting sail since Columbus's time, and before, in hopes of returning laden with precious condiments. What *is* new is that more spices, and more different spices, are being used now than ever before.

To set things straight at the outset, by *spices* we mean all the culinary catalysts the French call *aromatiques,* including the familiar dried seeds, roots and buds (celery seed, ginger, cloves), the leaves of plants we commonly call herbs (basil, bay leaf) and many concentrated products such as onion juice and powdered garlic. The owners of spice emporiums can vouch for the fact that men are the chief purchasers in the present-day spice rush. Male traffic at their counters has sent sales of parsley flakes, dried chili, red pepper and garlic powder zooming 500 percent since the war, and pizza partisans have boosted oregano consumption 5000 percent in the same decade. There's also been a corresponding boom in the sale of comparatively exotic items such as coriander, fennel seed, cumin, lovage and tarragon. This masculine interest is understandable, since it's always been the male chef who's had the daring and imagination needed to experiment with spices.

A few assorted tips for the would-be connoisseur on selection, storage and preparation: Whenever possible, spices should be freshly chopped or ground. The obvious superiority in taste of pepper milled at the table, whole nutmeg grated into terrapin stew or mint leaves bruised in the julep glass testifies to the importance of this dictum. Then there's the trick of warming spices before they're used. To literally curry favor with your guests, warm the curry powder for a few minutes in an oven or double boiler before you add it to a sauce. And when you add sage to a stew, don't drop it in cold—simmer it in a little water for a minute or two before it goes into the pot.

Many spices surrender their full flavor only after long, slow simmering. The bouquet garni, for instance, a trio or quartet of spices tied in cheesecloth and used in soups and stews, will be effective only after about an hour's cooking. Very long cooking, on the other hand, can dissipate a spice's benefits. If you're simmering a whole corned beef for four and a half hours, you'd do best to add your spices about an hour before you take the beef off the fire.

If using herbs is new to you, you should know that the dried varieties are three to four times stronger than the fresh. Sometimes the flavors and fragrances of fresh and dried herbs are poles apart. Fresh chives and dried chives, for instance, hardly seem like the same botanical specimens. In cream cheese, fresh chives are best. In a clam chowder, fresh thyme would seem like a weak sister alongside the traditional dried thyme. For the average cuisinier's cupboard, many fresh herbs just can't be obtained, but fresh chives, chervil and tarragon are usually available throughout the year from wholesale vegetable dealers catering to the better bistros. For best results, buy spices in tightly closed glass containers, in the smallest possible quantities at a time, and store them in dry, cool places.

Here, in convenient alphabetical order, are some of the spices you'll most often use and when and how to use them:

ALLSPICE: Not, as it would seem to be, a combination of spices, but a dried aromatic berry. Adds a mild spicy-sweet zip to stews or meat pies. Add it to the water in which fresh salmon is boiled. Use ground in Swedish meatballs.

ANISEED: A licoricelike spice which blends well in fruit compotes, especially apple compote. May be used with certain vegetables such as glazed carrots or mashed sweet potatoes, but don't overwork it.

BASIL: One of the mainstays of Italian *cucina,* basil is indispensable for all tomato soups or even stews containing tomatoes, and a bit of it does wonders for French green beans. It enhances minestrone soup. Sprinkle fresh basil over mackerel or eel before cooking.

BAY LEAF: Necessary for almost all marinades, sauerbraten, venison stew and for the water in which tongue or corned beef are cooked. Fasten a leaf here and there on the skewer the next time you make shish kabob.

CARAWAY SEEDS: If you have an addiction to sour rye bread, you'll enjoy caraway seeds in beef stroganoff, in sauerkraut, especially when cooked with pork, and in noodles. Very congenial with cream-cheese or cottage-cheese spreads.

CARDAMOM SEEDS: Enclosed in a paper-thin pod which breaks easily with finger pressure, the little dark seeds are often served in cocktail lounges to be chewed as an antidote to liquor breath. Delightful in demitasse or hot coffee drinks.

CAYENNE PEPPER: Unlike black or white pepper, which are dried berries, cayenne pepper is derived from the *Capsicum* pod and is also known as chili pepper. In its ground form, it's very hot and should be used sparingly. Add it to mayonnaise, mild sauces and gravies, lobster Newburg, patty of chicken, cream of mushroom soup or any dish that may need spark.

CHERVIL: Cousin to parsley in flavor, chervil serves well in thick puree soups such as split pea or black bean, in butter sauces brushed over steaks or broiled fish and in seafood spreads. Fresh chervil enlivens spring salads marvelously. Together with fresh chives and tarragon, it forms the trio of chopped herbs known as *fines herbes* used in omelets.

CHILI POWDER: Besides its obvious use in chili con carne and tamales, chili powder adds a fine earthy touch to avocado spreads, corn chowder, shrimp creole and other dishes of the bayou country.

CORIANDER: Goes well with such bourgeois fare as stuffed cabbage or with the most elegant lobster Newburg or lobster *américaine.* Canned rice pudding is improved with a sprinkling of ground coriander.

CUMIN: Essential for traditional Middle East dishes, including lamb stews, stuffed grape leaves and eggplant in thousands of forms. Especially welcome with lentils or dried beans. It makes curry currier.

DILLSEED: Use ground dillseeds for grooming cabbage, coleslaw, potato salad, beet salad and for the mayonnaise dressing in seafood salads, especially of Scandinavian or German origin.

FENNEL SEED: Similar to anise in its aromatic flavor, fennel finds its way into such meats as spareribs or roast pork, into vegetables such as zucchini and other squashes and into apple pie or apple compote.

GARLIC: On the spice shelf, this bulb of the lily family now appears as liquid garlic, garlic powder or garlic salt. All three forms eliminate the fussy job of peeling and mincing fresh garlic. Garlic powder is the easiest to manage. Though more vigorous than onion in flavor, garlic may be used in almost all recipes calling for onion. French and Italian chefs, who couldn't cook without garlic, add it only from the tip of a spoon or the fingertips. Keep it far away from bland chicken dishes and delicate seafood such as crab meat.

GINGER: Although dried ginger hardly needs any introduction to a man who's eaten pumpkin pie or plum pudding, the fresh ginger root is a delightful adjunct to countless Chinese and Polynesian dishes. It's normally available in shops catering to the Oriental or Caribbean population.

MACE: This outer husk of the nutmeg can be used like nutmeg as a sprinkling for eggnogs or sherry flips. Spray it lightly into oyster stew or Welsh rabbit.

MARJORAM: Tame oregano, appropriately called sweet marjoram because of its delicate aroma. In poultry stuffings or fish stuffings, it plays a minor but very essential role.

OREGANO: Distinctive in all pizzas and pasta sauces, oregano is almost brash in flavor. It is used effectively in braised dishes such as Swiss or potted steak. Sprinkle it lightly into prepared canned tomato sauce. In a green salad, used warily, it adds a rustic Sicilian accent to the olive-oil dressing.

PAPRIKA: Like cayenne, paprika is processed from a species of *Capsicum*. Unlike cayenne, it's quite mild.

Used by many cooks for its color—sprinkled over chops, steaks or fish before broiling to give added brownness—it's an innocuous pigment. The best Hungarian or Spanish paprikas, however, possess their own individual flavors. Indispensable in goulash, chicken *paprikash,* oyster or clam stew.

ROSEMARY: This thin, spiky herb possesses an all-out "herby" flavor. It has an especial affinity for lamb, but shouldn't be used with beef because of its bold pungency.

SAFFRON: The most expensive of all spices, saffron contains a deep-yellow pigment that colors all food it touches. Add saffron to rice dishes such as *arroz con pollo* or *risotto,* remembering that a little pinch will flavor a cup of liquid. Its concentrated though mild flavor is essential in bouillabaisse.

SAGE: Available in whole leaves or in the powder known as rubbed sage, its faintly bitter taste is especially good in the stuffing for goose or duck. If you can get it fresh, sprinkle it into a veal stew or over veal scallopini.

TARRAGON: One of the most aromatic of all herbs, tarragon enjoys its widest use, perhaps, in tarragon vinegar. Use it sparingly in marinades, ragouts and pot roasts. Add it to dressings for seafood salads and to tartar sauce.

THYME: Could almost be called the Friday herb because of its widespread use in clam chowder. It goes equally well in finnan-haddie chowder, pasta sauces and tomato aspics.

TURMERIC: A member of the ginger family, ground turmeric is effective in chowchow, pickle relishes and curries. Add a dash of it to the hot English mustard.

\* \* \*

*Ingenuity* is a key word in the proper use of spices. You want a bay leaf, for instance, to add to your lasagna sauce. You go to the spice shelf and you find bay leaves ranging in size from a half inch to two inches in length. You must decide whether you want the bay to rise like a crown of laurel (bay leaves *are* laurel leaves) or whether you want the bouquet to be barely perceptible. One clove is larger than another,

one brand of rosemary more pungent than another
one. Such differences, happily, force the casual cook
to be creative in spite of himself.

To use spices subtly doesn't mean that one must
always use them in little wisps and snatches. Consider
the French steak *poivrade,* in which freshly cracked
whole pepper is liberally sprinkled over thick beefsteaks, then pounded in with a mallet before the steaks
are broiled—a perfect example of spices used boldly
but not frivolously. Along the same lines, a genuine
beef goulash is doused with the best Hungarian paprika
so generously that it sinks into every atom of meat
in the pot.

On the other hand, the classical bread sauce for
pheasant and other game is a delicate compound of
fresh white-bread crumbs and milk or cream. And
when an experienced game chef makes this bread
sauce, he lowers a small onion into the milk just before
it's scalded. Before the onion goes into the saucepan,
however, he sneaks two whole cloves into the onion.
In this case, his *aromatique* is as modest as it can be.
Then, when the sauce is finished, the onion with its
cloves is removed. The end product is a richly com-
forting taste with the unobtrusive flavors merged in
the most pleasant manner.

The more common a spice is, the more imagination
is called for in its use. Good mustard, for instance,
when used to spike a French dressing, horseradish
sauce or salad, will add a tang that seems perfect
to the palate. Neophytes should know that there are
black and white peppers and that white pepper is used
in mashed potatoes, white sauces and other dishes
where black pepper's color might be objectionable.
But there's more than a color difference in the two
peppers. Ordinary black pepper is the whole dried
bud of the pepper bush with an all-out pungency.
White pepper is the same berry with the dark outer
husk removed, leaving only the light center, and it
has a gentler flavor, particularly compatible with
scrambled eggs, a bisque of clams, crab-meat Newburg
and other bland dishes.

A common confusion among those to whom herbs
and spices are a new and exciting territory is the
difference between *flavoring* and *seasoning.* Once this

is understood—and it's a simple matter—the determination of correct amounts of condiments is more easily arrived at. When you season a dish, then, you are using condiments to enhance and bring out its natural taste and aroma. When you flavor a dish, you are imposing the taste of the flavoring agent on the taste buds, combining the basic taste of the foodstuff itself with the taste of the spice. Examples of flavored dishes are the curries and chili con carne. Every dish you eat is seasoned in some way, if only with salt and pepper.

When all is said and done, the art of knowing how much of a particular spice or blend of spices goes into any dish must be more or less self-taught. Once these lessons are learned by taste and error, you may proceed without trepidation. From canapés to demitasse, your guests will agree that a good thyme was had by all.

# The Vegetable Kingdom

To most males, the subject of vegetables is strictly off
limits. Dissertations on roast pig, benisons to venison
and panegyrics to prime ribs are bandied about in a
spirit of hearty camaraderie, but let a man confide a
craving for brussels sprouts with chestnuts or young
artichoke hearts in olive oil and his name will be
summarily dispatched to the nearest grievance com-
mittee. Yet these selfsame meatniks will be the first
to wolf down baked stuffed potatoes with their roast
beef, sautéed onions with their calf's liver, corn on the
cob with their chicken terrapin, buttered mushroom
caps with their mutton chops, green cabbage with
their corned beef. Unabashedly, too, they will admit to
a fondness for Chinese food, though the emperor's
share of that infinitely varied cuisine consists of nothing
more than monumental vegetable stews, subtly half
cooked with a soupçon of seafood, chicken, pork or
beef. Antivegetarians unequivocally proclaim themselves among the votaries of Continental tablefare, but
even there meat pays deep obeisance to the vegetable
kingdom in such *spécialités* as broccoli or asparagus
Mornay with grilled ham. And in an audacious Italian
dish such as eggplant *parmigiana*, meat bows out entirely in the face of overpoweringly succulent odds.

Withal, meat-eating trenchermen can hardly be
blamed for recoiling from the tasteless wet shrubbery
that all too often appears on American dinner plates
under such misnomers as "peas," "limas," "string
beans" and "cauliflower." The sad truth is that vegetables are seldom cooked at all in this country—

they're sent to an agonizingly slow death on that immemorial instrument of vegetarian mayhem—the steam table. One has but to recall his last experience with boiled vegetables to appreciate anew the truth of the immortal Carl Rose line, "I say it's spinach and I say the hell with it." Before you curse it once again and turn back for succor to your double chateaubriand, let us suggest that you first forage about in the nearest Latin quarter for one of those intimate Italian cafés where nearly everything on the bill of fare is made to order. Walk in, sit down and order *spinace* (not under any circumstances to be confused with the swampy foliage ladled out in most American restaurants as spinach). After testing Popeye's provender conjured up in the grand Latin manner, the most single-minded meat man invariably vows that it's epicurean but that it can't be spinach.

Italian or American style; leaf, chopped or creamed; served with boiled egg slices or cooked with sautéed almond slivers—spinach is still a rather limited legume beside the ubiquitous onion whose company it so enjoys. Indeed, this eminently edible bulb—a rowdy member of the lily family—ranks second only to salt as the most garrulous and compatible seasoning agent in the world of gourmandise. Soups, sauces, salads, stews and stuffings would fall flat without it. To a delicate mousse, it can supply the subtlest of accents; yet it can hold uncontested sway over a mammoth casserole of Belgian onion pie. It can be eaten cooked, uncooked or half-cooked; steamed, boiled or broiled; grilled, sautéed, deep-fried or baked. Minced, it can stand with pride beside a $60 jar of beluga caviar; raw, it can perch saucily atop a two-bit hamburger. For those who really want to know their onions, it can appear as a marble-size white pickler in the bottom of a gibson glass or as an enormous Spanish specimen as big as a baseball. It can show up as a redskin or even purple—perfect for gumbos and Italian dishes— as a golf-ball-sized "silver" (white) onion, creamed whole as a toothsome side dish, or as a standard yellow onion, an all-purpose variety bound for French onion soup, potato pancakes and all intermediate points. A few drops of its potent juice will invigorate anything from lobster curry to cream-cheese spread.

Its volatile oil, which attacks the tear ducts when you slice into the bulb, is the very essence that gives it its lively tang. Rejoice, therefore, as ye weep—keeping in mind that the medium-size yellow onions grown in northern soil possess the sharpest flavor and consequently yield the most lachrymose fragrance; the large Bermuda types will be sweeter, milder, juicier.

Though less extravagant in versatility as well as in odor and flavor, corn is no less robustly enjoyable: on or off the cob, either as side dish or main event. Whatever its guise—as fritters with Canadian bacon at a penthouse brunch, as a casserole with crab meat at a midnight dinner or simply as roasting ears with heaps of butter at a midsummer barbecue—corn demands absolute freshness if its evanescent elixir of sweetness is to be saved and savored. The moment an ear is shucked, the sugar content begins turning into starch. If the ears are kept chilled from stalk to stove, the taste-thieving sugar-to-starch race is greatly decelerated. Fortunately, there are many vegetables whose edible lives don't run out within a few hours; even after several days in the cooler, such hardy garden bounty as eggplant, tomatoes and broccoli will please the discriminating palate in Gotham or L.A. no less than in them thar hills.

With the senses of sight, touch and smell also in play, the following short-order course in shopping should prove a snap. Among the edible plants, bleached blondes and doubtful redheads always betray themselves. All greengroceries must be richly verdant, without pallid or mottled stretches; broccoli must be bright green and bushy-headed, devoid of droop; mushrooms white, not freckly yellow; tomatoes a burnished cherry red; eggplant a deep, velvety purple. Artichokes should look like snugly fitted, silken green pinecones. Onions should have a dry, crackly skin without tendrils; wet necks mean senility. Brussels sprouts must be crisp, unblemished and tightly furled; cauliflower ivory white, not yellowing with age. Corn ears must reveal snugly spaced rows of plump, golden-yellow kernels; a few smaller grains at the narrow end of the cob are permissible, but more than this indicates bland, textureless immaturity. The husk should have a fresh, grassy smell.

If all this sniffing and squeezing simply isn't your forte, you can, of course, always take sanctuary in the deepfreeze department of the corner caterer. The proliferating new line of frigid prefab "gourmet" vegetable dishes leaves us particularly cold. Yet there are a few straightforward frozen legumes—innocent of mass-production saucery—for which no apology need be made. The best of these is asparagus; though certainly not comparable in subtlety or delectability to its fresh-picked counterpart, when properly prepared it can understudy quite competently during the off-season. Artichoke hearts, too, find a more than reasonable facsimile in a California-grown frozen version now widely available all year round.

To our palate, rural French restaurants have the right idea about vegetables. Regarding as an unthinkable culinary sacrilege the mere thought of gracing their pans with anything but the freshest of fresh legumes, these wayside inns lovingly practice the time-honored ritual of preparing legumes *en saison*—perhaps a redolent platter of zucchini au gratin or a fragrant dish of young cauliflower rolled in buttered bread crumbs—to be served as a magnificent separate course following, and often upstaging, the meat. Embodying this charming philosophy, the following *pièces de choix* have been designed as full-fledged entrees.

## EGGPLANT PARMIGIANA
(Serves 4)

2 eggs
Salad oil
2 tablespoons cold water
12 slices peeled eggplant, ½ inch thick, about 3 inches in diameter
Flour
Bread crumbs
2 medium-size tomatoes, sliced thin
2 8-oz. cans tomato sauce
⅛ teaspoon garlic powder
½ teaspoon oregano
½ lb. mozzarella cheese, sliced thin
Grated Parmesan cheese
Paprika

Beat eggs well. Add 2 tablespoons salad oil and the water and beat again. Dip eggplant into flour, then into beaten-egg mixture and finally into bread crumbs. In a wide saucepan, heat salad oil to a depth of ¼ inch until it shows the first wisp of smoke. Sauté eggplant slices until brown on both sides. Arrange them, slightly overlapping, in a single large casserole or four individual ones, putting tomato slices atop. In a small saucepan, heat the tomato sauce, garlic powder and oregano to the boiling point and pour over eggplant. Top with mozzarella. Sprinkle generously with Parmesan, lightly with paprika and oil. Bake in preheated 375° oven for 20 minutes or until topping is brown.

## ASPARAGUS POLONAISE, FRIED EGG
### (Serves 4)

> 4 10-oz. pkgs. frozen large asparagus spears
> ½ cup sweet butter
> 1½ cups light bread crumbs
> 2 hard-boiled eggs, chopped fine
> 4 teaspoons chopped fresh chives
> 4 eggs

While asparagus is still frozen, peel the bottom of each spear with a vegetable peeler to remove stringy outer fiber. Cook, following directions on package, and keep in a warm place. Melt butter in a saucepan. Add bread crumbs and heat until light brown. Add chopped eggs and chives. Fry the other eggs one at a time. Drain asparagus and place on serving plates or platter. Spoon bread-crumb mixture atop and crown with eggs.

## STUFFED MUSHROOMS ROCKEFELLER
### (Serves 4)

> 1½ lbs. large white mushrooms
> 3 tablespoons butter
> Salt and pepper
> Juice of ¼ lemon
> ¼ cup butter
> 4 scallions, white and green parts, minced
> Bread crumbs
> 1 tablespoon Pernod

*¼ teaspoon tarragon*
*¼ teaspoon chervil*
*6 slices bacon*

Wash mushrooms well. Detach stems and sauté caps in 3 tablespoons butter until just tender. While sautéing, sprinkle with salt and pepper and lemon juice. In another saucepan, melt the ¼ cup butter. Add finely chopped mushroom stems and the scallions and sauté until tender. Remove pan from flame. Stir in ½ cup bread crumbs, Pernod, tarragon, chervil and salt and pepper to taste. Fill each mushroom cap with chopped-mushroom mixture. Then dip filled end of each into bread crumbs and place filled side up in a greased shallow pan or casserole. Top each mushroom with a piece of bacon and bake in preheated 475° oven for about 10 minutes or until bacon is crisp.

## BROCCOLI MORNAY WITH HAM
### (Serves 4)

*1 medium-size bunch broccoli*
*¼ cup butter*
*¼ cup flour*
*1 cup hot milk*
*¼ teaspoon onion powder*
*Salt and pepper*
*1 6-oz. jar hollandaise sauce*
*½ cup heavy cream*
*½ lb. sliced boiled ham*

Remove all outer leaves from broccoli. Separate into stalks. Cut off and discard from ½ to ¾ inch from the bottom of each stalk and wash broccoli well. Cook in 1 inch of salted water in a covered pot until barely tender; then drain. Melt butter in a saucepan. Remove from flame. Stir in flour with a wire whip until mixture is very smooth. Gradually add hot milk, stirring constantly. Return pan to a low flame and cook slowly, stirring frequently, until all floury taste has disappeared. Again remove from flame. Add onion powder and salt and pepper to taste. Fold hollandaise sauce into white sauce. In a deep, cold bowl, beat cream until whipped. Fold into sauce. Broil ham slices in preheated broiler until edges curl. Transfer to four individual shallow casseroles. Place broccoli atop ham and spoon sauce atop broccoli. Place casseroles under broiler flame until sauce turns brown, taking special care to turn when necessary to avoid burning.

## ONION PIE
### (Serves 4)

*1 8-inch pie shell, unbaked*
*2 lbs. large Spanish onions*
*¼ cup butter*
*3 eggs, well beaten*
*1 cup sour cream*
*¼ teaspoon salt*
*⅛ teaspoon white pepper*
*1 dash cayenne pepper*
*Parmesan cheese*
*Paprika*

Unbaked pie shells ready for the oven are available in the baked-goods departments of many food marts. Peel onions. Cut each in half through the stem end, then crosswise into thinnest possible slices. Melt butter in a wide saucepan and sauté onions until limp but not brown. Meanwhile, combine eggs and sour cream in a bowl, mixing well. Add onions, salt, pepper and cayenne pepper. Turn onion mixture into pie shell. Sprinkle generously with Parmesan, lightly with paprika. Bake for 20 minutes in preheated 450° oven. Reduce heat to 325° and bake 20 minutes longer or until bottom of crust is medium brown.

## CORN BEIGNETS
### (Serves 4)

*Beignets* are a French form of fritter made from a cooked batter. Their lightness is due to the large number of eggs rather than the usual baking powder. You'll want to savor them with maple syrup or honey.

*1 cup water*
*2 tablespoons butter*
*½ teaspoon salt*

¼ teaspoon nutmeg
½ cup cornmeal
½ cup all-purpose flour
4 eggs
1 cup off-the-cob cooked or canned corn
Deep fat

In a heavy saucepan, bring the water to a boil. Add the butter, salt and nutmeg and stir until butter dissolves. Add the cornmeal and flour all at once. Remove from the flame and do not return to the fire. Stir well until all ingredients are well blended; the mixture will be very thick. Gradually add the unbeaten eggs one at a time, stirring well after each addition until the batter is very smooth. Add the corn and place the mixture in the refrigerator until cold. Heat a kettle of deep fat to 370°. (If deep fat isn't practical, heat shortening or salad oil to a depth of ½ inch in a shallow pan.) Drop the batter by heaping tablespoonfuls into the hot fat. Fry, turning once, until brown on both sides. Drain on absorbent paper. Serve while very hot. Fold back your cuffs and get with it.

# Salad Days

Never ask a woman to come up and see your salad bowl. If you do, don't let her go near it. A girl who may be an otherwise skillful cook and an unaffected creature often becomes coquettish when she makes a salad. When your back is turned, she'll come up with prunes and cottage cheese or pea and walnut salad or an elaborate bowl of mixed greens tasting exactly like a bale of wet hay. Even professional cooks are sometimes guilty of the same offense in their elaborate chaudfroid dishes and aspic salads, made solely for show-off purposes on buffet tables. But in the privacy of their own homes, they wouldn't think of eating such silly flimflam.

When a man's tired and hungry at the end of a broiling summer day, he yearns for a cold lobster salad as fresh and keen as the cold Maine water itself. He wants the very first taste of tangy mayonnaise to impart its lascivious delight. When a bowl of romaine is brought to his table, he wants the dark leaves to glisten with real olive oil and wine vinegar. He wants the beefsteak tomatoes to be so sweet that they taste as though someone had sprinkled them with sugar. He wants the French dressing to bite and yield at the same time.

A good salad maker must have meticulousness, patience, cleanliness and a very alert sense of touch and taste. For some reason, it takes a man to master this really fine art. One of the most noted salad makers of all time was Henri d'Albignac, a French nobleman who fled the revolution and went to live in London.

Unlike modern *émigrés*, who become doormen and dishwashers, the Frenchman took up the art of salad making. He became known as the salad king, and fabulous sums were paid to him to prepare the "sallets" for prominent dinners held in Grosvenor Square. In America at about the same time—when salads were relatively unknown—two famous Frenchmen, Brillat-Savarin, the noted food philosopher, and Collete, a Parisian chef, were teaching New Yorkers the subtleties of French dressing and vinaigrette sauce.

The kind of bowl you use will affect the salad that finally comes forth. Several decades ago, there was a rage for wooden salad bowls that's only now subsiding. The wooden bowls were peasantish, informal and bohemian. You were told that if you used the bowl often enough, the garlic, pepper and other seasonings would become impregnated into the wood. In time these flavors would be transferred to any salad mixed in the bowl. You were told not to wash the bowl— merely to wipe it clean each time. But wood is porous and therefore absorbent. When you rub it with garlic often enough, it may eventually acquire a built-up garlic odor. But it also absorbs the oil of the salad dressing. Oil in time turns rancid. No legerdemain will remove the unclean off-flavor of many of these wooden bowls. At the present time you can buy a number of wooden salad bowls made of extremely handsome hardwood, less absorbent than the old-fashioned wooden chopping bowl.

The part the bowl plays, however, is negative. It should give *no* flavor whatever to the salad. If you want to give a garlic scent to your salad, it's very easily done by merely rubbing the bowl with a cut clove of garlic or using a garlic press or placing in the salad a piece of French bread previously rubbed with garlic. Then there are a number of salads in which you don't want a garlic flavor to predominate. For instance, if you're making a crab-meat salad, garlic has no place whatever in the scheme of things. Finally, the bacteria that collect in the unwashed wooden bowl make for unsanitary food handling. Obviously, the best type of salad bowl is one made of glass, china or pottery. Bright crystal glass is especially nice for showing the sorcery of the salad man.

The old Spanish saying that to be a good salad maker you must be a miser with vinegar, a spendthrift with oil and a madman in mixing is not entirely true. The advice about oil and vinegar is sound as far as it goes. You should use four parts of oil to each part of vinegar in making a salad. But you should take special care that the total amount of dressing is only enough to coat all the greens with a thin film of dressing. You must not be such a spendthrift that the salad is drowned in dressing, leaving a lazy pool of liquid on the bottom of the salad bowl. When you mix the salad, you should do it thoroughly but with a light hand all the time. A madman will beat the tender leaves until they droop with despair. It takes a sage—not a madman—to mix a salad.

Much of the skill in conjuring up a slick salad is merely choosing the right raw material. If you buy the plump beefsteak tomatoes adorning the summer vegetable stalls, your salad will automatically be better than one made with dull winter hothouse tomatoes. If the avocado is soft, ripe and oily, it will seem almost a different fruit from an avocado that is hard, astringent and tasteless. When you make French dressing with the imported (genuine) olive oil, it will have a richness, body and superb olive flavor that you can't possibly create with domestic cottonseed oil or corn oil.

Every interested disciple of the salad bowl should keep in mind the fact that a salad isn't really a salad until it's marinated. This doesn't mean you must marinate it for hours. For some salads the mixing time itself, or 10 to 20 minutes' standing time, is sufficient for a proper blending of flavors. Others, like the French white-bean salad, require at least overnight marinating. In any case, you must allow sufficient time for the wine vinegar, chives, Dijon mustard and the other various ingredients in the bowl to blend, to cook without fire in a sense, until a liaison of flavors has occurred. When you bite into a cold shrimp, you should instantly taste the sweet pepper, the lemon juice, the pungent celery salt and any other condiment that went into the bowl before the salad was mixed.

In leafy green salads, this liaison is encouraged by olive oil and vinegar; for many of the more substantial salads, it's often formed with mayonnaise. A good rule of thumb for the salad beginner is seldom to use mayonnaise as it comes from the jar. Spreading un-mixed mayonnaise on toast is just right for a club sandwich. But for salads the mayonnaise should be softened so it clings to the ingredients and flows among them. Dilute it with milk, cream or lemon juice, or any combination of these. Use from one to four table-spoons of diluent per cup of mayonnaise. Now and then you will mix mayonnaise with a watery food, such as the mandarin-orange slices in the shrimp-salad recipe that will follow. In such instances, the food itself will provide its own *diluendo* and no other thin-ning will be necessary. Freshly boiled potatoes in a salad, on the other hand, will not only blot up the mayonnaise but will actually make it thicker than it was when taken from the jar. Around the Rouen area in France, chefs make a potato salad by adding only sweet cream and vinegar to the hot, sliced boiled potatoes. As the salad stands, the cream turns into a gentle, enticing cold sauce.

The kinds of individual dressings that you can make from a jar of prepared mayonnaise are practically unlimited. Such additions as capers, chopped tarragon, chopped hard-boiled egg, curry powder, sherry, sour cream, unsweetened whipped cream, chili sauce or chili powder, or even fruit juices or fruits, are only a few of the numberless variations.

Not many amateur chefs make their own mayonnaise these days. If, however, you are enamored of olive-oil flavor, you may want to make your own, since the prepared product is processed from comparatively tasteless vegetable oils. Whipping up your own may-onnaise is really a snap if you own an electric blender. You merely drop into the well of the blending machine 1 egg, 1 teaspoon prepared mustard, ½ teaspoon salt and a dash of cayenne pepper. Mix at low speed for about 5 seconds. Then, at low speed again, slowly add 1 cup olive oil or other salad oil if you prefer. If you own the type of blender that's fitted with a filler cap, merely remove it and pour the oil through the opening. After the oil has been added, stir in 1 tablespoon lemon juice and 1 tablespoon wine vinegar, and the mayonnaise is ready. Again you can reach for your apothecary jars and add turmeric, dillweed or any spiking ingredient that pleases your fancy, remembering to add a little at a time to taste.

When you make a salad, be conscious not only of flavors, but of textures as well. It's no accident that in one salad recipe after another you'll find diced celery listed as one of the ingredients because of its crispness. Crinkly lettuce, hard water chestnuts teamed with tender shrimp, soft pimientos paired with lobster chunks—all these are prime examples of delightful textural juxtaposition.

No man who ever had the right to hold a salad spoon has said anything more important than Sydney Smith in his famous recipe in rhyme for a salad dressing: "Let onion atoms lurk within the bowl / And, half-suspected, animate the whole." To keep raw onion half-suspected, however, isn't as easy as it sounds. Some fresh onions are much more volatile than others, and when the tear glands begin to flow too energetically, that's an indication to go easy. An onion that's grated will reach other foods in the bowl much more quickly than an onion that's diced or chopped. The most delicate member of the onion family is that thin, green herb, the chive. Shallots, the small, yellow bulbs that come in quart measures, have a lively yet delicate onion flavor, but must be chopped extremely fine before they can be used in salads; they're usually too small to grate. Scallions should be handled the same way. For those who can't tolerate onions in raw form, onion powder or onion salt may be substituted.

The proficient salad maker knows how to turn emergencies into assets. When a recipe calls for two cups diced boiled chicken and you have only one cup on hand, you won't be fainthearted about substituting cooked ham or tongue or sweetbread or chicken liver or even crab meat. And if you happen to have only a cup and a half of chicken when a recipe calls for two, and you decide to add a half cup of walnuts or chestnuts or frozen pineapple chunks, you'll learn that additions of this type, properly prepared, will invariably be credited to your creative ingenuity rather than to a shortage in your icebox.

A good salad maker must be a tyrant in insisting that fresh things be really fresh. He refuses to go to work if lettuce leaves are tired, tomatoes are wrinkled with age and cucumbers are shriveled. Perhaps the most fanatical people in this respect are the Danes. In Danish restaurants, when a customer orders salad, the waitress brings a tray of watercress still growing in the soil. The customer watches as the waitress carefully cuts off the small leaves for the salad bowl.

People eat salad with their eyes. The mere sight of white cabbage and shredded green peppers dropped into a big bowl for coleslaw will set the taste currents buzzing. This doesn't mean you must have screaming reds contrasting with loud greens just to create eye appeal. Even a salad of all greens—provided the greens are fresh and crisp—will set up a whole range of subtle but distinct notes on the green theme: the deep-sea green of the watercress, the pale green of the lettuce, the sturdy burgher's green of the romaine and the fresh green of the parsley. Let these delightful hues remain in the bowl *au naturel*. Don't pretty them up with carrot curlicues, celery canes or spiraled beets.

Salads, like other cold dishes, must be ice-cold and not served at tepid room temperature. Even the bowl, the mixing spoon and fork and the salad plates should be cold. Similarly, everything in a salad must, of course, be as clean as a new spoon. A tiny grain of sand will spoil an otherwise delightful salad. Some greens that are grown in sandy soil—such as spinach and certain kinds of lettuce—may have to be washed in six clear, cold waters before all sand is removed. All salad greens must be thoroughly drained and dried before going into the bowl. After washing the greens, place them between clean cloth towels or paper towels and press gently to blot out all trace of water. Excess water will not only dilute the dressing but will keep it from clinging to the greens.

Since most salads include lettuce, savants of the salad bowl know that there are two principal kinds of lettuce—iceberg and Boston. Iceberg is crisp, solid and heavy for its size. Boston lettuce is light, soft and tender. Of the two types, Boston has the more delicate flavor. French dressing will cling more readily to the Boston than to the iceberg. Iceberg lettuce is the more plentiful of the two, and in the wintertime Boston lettuce is obtainable only in fancy-fruit stores. Iceberg lettuce has always appealed to gourmets who eat with their jaws rather than with their taste buds. No matter which lettuce you use, be sure to remove any impurities or discolored pieces. To separate lettuce leaves from the head, cut a cone-shaped piece about one inch deep out of the core. Hold the lettuce under cold running water to wash. Press the head of lettuce and it will separate easily into leaves.

We would like to puncture one more old wives' tale before presenting our repertory of salads. This is the theory that salad greens should never be cut with a knife but should only be torn with the fingers. According to old cookbooks, the rusty color of the knife will stain the tender greens and spoil their natural appearance. The answer to this dictum is not to use a rusty knife. Whether you cut or tear such greens as chicory, escarole or romaine won't make much difference. Some salad materials such as chives, parsley and green peppers must be cut with good, sharp steel.

## FRENCH DRESSING

This dressing, after it has been stored in the refrigerator a day or two, will look something like mayonnaise. Many French dressings made with olive oil are not stored in the refrigerator, but since egg is included in this recipe, the dressing should be refrigerated. When this dressing is mixed with a tossed salad, it will melt and yet cling to the leaves. Use imported French or Italian olive oil. If a garlic flavor is desired, smash 2 or 3 large cloves of garlic and add to vinegar. Let the garlic remain in the vinegar overnight. Strain the vinegar before adding it to the other ingredients.

> 1 teaspoon powdered mustard
> 1 teaspoon prepared French Dijon mustard
> 1 teaspoon salt
> ½ teaspoon sugar
> ¼ teaspoon white pepper
> 1 egg, slightly beaten
> 1 pint olive oil
> ½ cup red- or white-wine vinegar

In a deep mixing bowl, combine the powdered mustard, French mustard, salt, sugar, pepper and beaten egg.

Mix well. Very slowly add the oil, pouring by half teaspoonfuls at first, beating with a wire whip or electric mixer so that all ingredients cohere. Continue to add oil in a very slow stream, then the vinegar. Store in a covered wide-mouthed jar in the refrigerator.

## ROQUEFORT DRESSING

Add ½ cup crumbled Roquefort cheese to the basic recipe for French dressing.

## ANCHOVY DRESSING

Add 3 tablespoons anchovy paste to the basic recipe for French dressing.

## SOUR-CREAM DRESSING

> *1 cup sour cream*
> *2 tablespoons wine vinegar*
> *½ teaspoon onion salt*
> *2 tablespoons sugar*
> *2 dashes Tabasco sauce*

Simply combine all ingredients, stir, then toss down.

## PLAYBOY'S GARLIC FRENCH DRESSING

> *1 egg*
> *2 teaspoons imported Dijon mustard*
> *⅓ cup wine vinegar*
> *1 tablespoon salad oil*
> *⅓ cup water*
> *⅓ cup bread crumbs*
> *¼ teaspoon chopped fresh garlic*
> *½ teaspoon salt*
> *1½ teaspoons sugar*
> *⅛ teaspoon monosodium glutamate*
> *⅛ teaspoon white pepper*

Put all ingredients into an electric blender. Blend at high speed for about 30 seconds. Chill thoroughly before serving. Serve with any type of tossed salad. Store in the refrigerator.

## TOSSED GREEN SALAD
(Serves 4)

This is the great all-purpose salad which may be used as the prologue or epilogue to the dinner. We list only one combination of greens, but obviously you can make hundreds of variations to suit your own taste. Remember to cut or tear the salad greens into small uniform pieces.

> *2  cups Boston lettuce*
> *1  cup chicory*
> *½  cup watercress*
> *¼  cup sliced scallions*
> *1  cup sliced cucumber*
> *1  cup romaine*
> *6 to 8  tablespoons French  dressing*

Combine all ingredients, adding dressing to taste. Toss lightly but thoroughly. Season with salt and pepper to taste.

## HAM SALAD A LA PLAYBOY
(Serves 4)

The partnership of ham and salad greens is a light but satisfying main course. Deliver a big basket of French or Italian bread to the table with this salad. A generous wedge of fresh blueberry pie topped with vanilla ice cream and a tall glass of iced coffee should satisfy the hungriest noonday warrior. Be sure the spinach is free of all root ends and sand. Use only the smallest spinach leaves.

> *¾  lb. sliced boiled ham*
> *4  hard-boiled eggs*
> *2  cups Boston lettuce*
> *2  teaspoons French Dijon mustard*
> *4  tablespoons salad oil*
> *1  tablespoon white-wine vinegar*
> *2  teaspoons chopped chives or scallions*
> *2  tablespoons grated Parmesan cheese*
> *2  cups spinach leaves*
> *Salt and pepper*

Cut the ham into small pieces about ½ inch wide and 1 inch long. Cut the eggs lengthwise into quarters. Cut or tear the lettuce into small pieces. Into the salad bowl, put the mustard, oil, vinegar, chives and Parmesan cheese. Stir well until blended. Add the spinach, lettuce and ham and toss thoroughly. Add salt and pepper to taste, plus more vinegar or oil if desired. Turn salad onto chilled dinner plates. Place egg wedges around perimeter.

## BEEF AND TOMATO SALAD
### (Serves 4)

This classic Parisian salad must be prepared the day before it is eaten so that all ingredients can marinate thoroughly. The beef must be cold boiled beef or potted beef—roast beef is not suitable.

> 2 cups boiled beef cut into ¼-inch cubes
> 2 medium-size boiled potatoes
> 2 medium-size tomatoes
> 2 tablespoons minced parsley
> ½ cup thinly sliced dill pickle
> ⅓ cup French dressing
> 1 teaspoon Worcestershire sauce
> 2 teaspoons grated onion
> Salt and pepper
> Lettuce leaves

Peel the potatoes. Cut the potatoes and tomatoes into the same size as the beef cubes. Mix all ingredients except the lettuce leaves. Season to taste with salt and pepper. Let the salad remain in the refrigerator 1 day. Serve on cold dinner plates lined with lettuce leaves.

## CAESAR SALAD
### (Serves 4)

Caesar salad from California has become a national institution. The original version included coddled egg, a tasteless affectation, which we omit.

> 2 tablespoons lemon juice
> 1 tablespoon tarragon vinegar

>    2 *cloves garlic*
>    2 *small- to medium-size heads of romaine*
>    3 *slices white bread, toasted*
>    ⅓ *cup olive oil*
>    ¼ *cup crumbled blue cheese*
>    2 *tablespoons grated Parmesan cheese*
>    *Salt and pepper*

Combine the lemon juice and vinegar in a small glass. Smash the garlic and add to the lemon-juice mixture. Let remain in the liquid at least 2 hours; then remove. Rub the salad bowl with the garlic. Cut or tear the romaine into 1-inch pieces. Cut toast into ½-inch squares. Put all ingredients into a large bowl, toss thoroughly and season with salt and pepper.

## SEASHORE SALAD A LA PLAYBOY
### (Serves 4)

>    2 *1-lb. lobsters, boiled*
>    ½ *lb. freshly cooked crab lump*
>    1 *lb. medium-size shrimps, boiled*
>    ¼ *cup French dressing*
>    1½ *cups diced celery*
>    *Salt, pepper and celery salt*
>    ¼ *teaspoon paprika*
>    1 *teaspoon horseradish*
>    *Juice of 1 lemon*
>    2 *tablespoons oyster-cocktail sauce*
>    2 *scallions, white part, finely chopped*
>    ½ *teaspoon Worcestershire sauce*
>    ½ *head lettuce*
>    2 *tablespoons capers in vinegar*
>    1 *cup mayonnaise*
>    *Lettuce leaves*

Cut the lobster meat into ½-inch cubes. Examine crab lump and carefully remove any shell or cartilage. Peel shrimps and remove veins. In a salad bowl, combine the lobster meat, crab lump, shrimps, French dressing, celery, 2 or 3 generous dashes each of salt, pepper and celery salt, the paprika, horseradish, lemon juice, cock-tail sauce, scallions and Worcestershire sauce. Mix thoroughly and chill in the refrigerator at least an hour. Cut ½ head of lettuce into fine shreds and combine with salad, capers and mayonnaise, mixing thoroughly. Line four dinner plates with lettuce leaves. Spoon salad on lettuce and garnish, if desired, with wedges of hard-boiled egg or wedges of tomato or both.

## CORNED BEEF SALAD
### (Serves 4)

*¾ lb. thinly sliced cooked corned beef*
*4 medium-size boiled potatoes, peeled*
*4 medium-size cooked or canned red beets*
*1 medium-size dill pickle*
*4 tablespoons salad oil*
*2 tablespoons garlic-flavored wine vinegar*
*2 teaspoons prepared mustard*
*1 tablespoon finely chopped chives*
*Salt and freshly ground black pepper*
*Lettuce leaves*
*2 hard-boiled eggs*

Cut the corned beef into ½-inch squares. Cut the potatoes, red beets and dill pickle the same size. In a salad bowl, combine the corned beef, potatoes, beets, dill pickle, salad oil, wine vinegar, mustard and chives. Add salt very sparingly, since the corned beef is salty. Hold the pepper mill over the bowl and give the handle a half-dozen turns. Toss all ingredients thoroughly. Let the salad marinate in the refrigerator at least 4 to 5 hours. Line cold dinner plates with lettuce leaves. Spoon the salad onto the lettuce leaves. Garnish with wedges of hard-boiled egg.

## ITALIAN MIXED SALAD
### (Serves 4)

*2 quarts salad greens*
*1 sweet green pepper, sliced thin*
*4 whole roasted sweet red peppers from jar, sliced thin*
*2 small hot green peppers, sliced thin*
*2 2-oz. jars artichoke hearts in oil, drained*
*2 3¼-oz. jars cocktail mushrooms, drained*
*12 large stuffed green olives*
*6 large black olives*

2 large tomatoes, cut into wedges
¼ cup capers in salt
1 cup diced celery
¼ cup olive oil
2 tablespoons red-wine vinegar
2 2-oz. cans boneless and skinless sardines

The salad greens may consist of any available assortment such as lettuce, romaine, chicory, endive and watercress, cut or torn into medium-size pieces, washed and dried until not a droplet of water shows. Use one of those special wire salad baskets, paper towels or clean cloth towels for drying the greens. In a large salad bowl combine all the ingredients (ice-cold) except the sardines. Toss slowly but thoroughly until well blended. The capers in salt will usually obviate the necessity for additional salt. Since the artichoke hearts, roasted peppers and mushrooms are marinated as they come from the jar, no further marinating is required for this salad. Spoon the salad onto the serving plates. Place the sardines on top of each portion.

## MANDARIN SHRIMP SALAD
### (Serves 4)

2 lbs. shrimps, boiled
1 5¼-oz. can water chestnuts, drained
⅓ cup heavy cream, whipped
½ cup mayonnaise
1 11-oz. can mandarin-orange segments, drained
2 dashes Tabasco sauce
Salt and white pepper
Lettuce leaves
1 bunch watercress
1 2-oz. jar pimiento strips, drained

Remove shells and veins from shrimps. Slice the water chestnuts as thin as possible. Fold the whipped cream into the mayonnaise. In a salad bowl, combine the shrimps, mayonnaise mixture, water chestnuts, orange segments and Tabasco sauce. Add salt and white pepper to taste. Let the salad marinate 30 minutes in the refrigerator before serving. Line cold dinner plates

with lettuce leaves. Spoon the salad onto the lettuce.
Place 2 large sprigs of watercress on each portion of
salad at opposite sides of serving plates. Place the
pimiento strips on top of salad just before serving.

### SCALLOP SALAD
(Serves 4)

1½ lbs. sea scallops
1 tablespoon dillweed
1 teaspoon grated onion
2 tablespoons salad oil
2 tablespoons lemon juice
Salt, pepper and celery salt
1 cup diced celery, including leaves
½ cup sour cream
½ cup mayonnaise
Lettuce leaves
8 large stuffed olives

Wash scallops well. Drop into boiling salted water
and simmer for 4 minutes. Drain and cut into slices
about ½ inch thick. (Bay scallops may be substituted
for sea scallops, when in season. They should be
boiled 2 minutes and left whole.) Put the sliced scallops into a salad bowl. Add dillweed, grated onion,
salad oil, lemon juice and 2 or 3 generous dashes
each of salt, pepper and celery salt. Let chill in the
refrigerator 1 hour. Add the celery, sour cream and
mayonnaise, mixing well and correcting seasoning as
needed. Spoon the salad onto lettuce leaves. Cut
stuffed olives in half crosswise and arrange, cut side
up, on top of each portion of salad.

# Saturnalian Sweets

Until recent years, the man-of-the-world paid scant attention to desserts. He was content to round off his meal with a wedge of ripe Camembert cheese while his gentle companion munched her *meringue glacée* with marrons. Naturally, there were exceptions now and then when a man might have been temporarily overcome by the aroma of a deep-dish apple pie or a warm brandied mince pie. But as a rule, the male of the species was quite willing to grant that sweets were designed for the sweet. This is true no longer, as can be seen during the holidays when the land is lit with flaming plum puddings, cherries jubilee and *crème Cognac*. To see how widely these food-and-drink desserts are now accepted by both sexes, we need only step into a gourmet store and observe guys as well as dolls loading their arms with sweet provender from the tiers of brandied fruitcake, *baba au rhum*, prepared crepes suzette, pears in crème de menthe, brandied apricots, peaches and dates and dozens of other easy and exquisite holiday morsels.

When serving such festive dishes, it's important to be aware of the bounds of good taste. There are still too many chefs who insist on serving gondolas of spun sugar, goddesses carved out of raspberry ice and layer cakes bedizened with fireworks showing Mt. Vesuvius in eruption. The lengths to which this old-fashioned kind of dessert can go were once vividly described by Horace Walpole, recalling a function celebrating the birth of the Duke of Burgundy. Walpole told how the intendant of Gascony "treated the noblesse of the province with a dinner and a dessert, the latter of which concluded with a representation by wax figures moved by clockwork of the whole labor of the dauphine and the happy birth of an heir."

The simpler a dessert's appearance, the greater the skill and savvy which should be accorded its concoction. A man may have a passion for peaches. He may idolize brandy. But when he merely drops a few peaches into a bowl and then sloshes some brandy over them, he discovers that he doesn't have brandied peaches at all. He may have chosen the wrong kind of peaches or the wrong brandy or both. The liquor may have been so potent that it killed the peach flavor. The fruit may have been too ripe or too firm, too flavorless or too sweet. Today's holiday host buys his own choice of brandied peaches in a jar, slices them, heats them in a chafing dish, adds a little more brandy for gentle flaming, spoons the warm peaches over smooth vanilla ice cream and—*voilà!*

In buying liqueurs for regal desserts, one can select any good domestic brand when straight fruit flavors such as cherry, apricot or blackberry are required. Naturally, elegant elixirs such as Benedictine or Chartreuse are available only in their original imported form. For such desserts as mince pie or fruitcake, it isn't necessary to buy imported brandy. If, on the other hand, you're serving a flaming fruit dessert to a connoisseur of cognac, it would be better to use the imported product. For some reason, American whiskeys have been unaccountably neglected for warming up desserts. Both bourbon and rye are actually delightful for flaming warm confections such as plum, date and fig pudding.

The whole subject of preparing liquored desserts, especially if you're making your own modifications of a recipe, should be approached with a certain caution. One should be aware of the fact that the mere presence of liquor doesn't automatically create an exemplary dish. Peaches in port wine may sound fascinating, but the chances are that if you've never tasted this dessert before, you won't be transported with ecstasy at the first bite. Maybe on the second or third trial, your taste buds will begin to feel a mellow afterglow—maybe not. Then there are desserts that may look very good but can be misleading. For example, if you should pour crème de violette liqueur over canned Bartlett pears, you'd have a luscious contrast of deep purple and creamy white colors. But the resultant mixture of flavors would hardly be happy. On the other hand, some desserts that have little eye appeal in themselves, such as the classic plum pudding, can be extremely delicious.

Flaming desserts will automatically be more pleasurable if served from fine buffetware. You can flame desserts in an old frying pan if you wish, of course, but the applause meter will register much higher if you perform the same fire ritual in a gleaming chafing dish or a properly proportioned pan of copper.

One of the perplexing problems for the apprentice at the buffet table is the flaming dessert that refuses to ignite. To avoid this minor disaster, observe the following rules: Be sure that the food that is to be flamed is heated and kept hot *before* the liquor is added. The liquor itself should be hot, too, if possible. If you pour cold liquor into a hot chafing dish or hot saucepan, you should wait at least a minute before applying the flame. After the inside of the pan is aflame, keep it directly over the heat. If the food contains a considerable quantity of its own liquid, like canned fruits in syrup, this liquid should be largely drained off before the alcohol is added. The alcoholic strength of the liquor that's used is a factor in building your crater of fire. Anisette, for instance, a liqueur sometimes bottled at 54 proof, will hardly contain the fire power that you'll find in kirsch or mirabelle (both 100-proof brandies) or in green Chartreuse (110 proof).

Normally, in homes, a lighted match is used to set the pan ablaze. Professionals at buffet tables, heating food over an open flame, will quickly move the pan back and forth in a rocking motion, and the small spray of alcohol vapors will set the inside of the pan afire. With a little practice you can learn to perform this bit of culinary showmanship. If you've never served distilled desserts before, it's a good idea to rehearse them privately before performing them publicly. Some flaming desserts will require considerable advance preparation.

Without further prologue, however, let us proceed to savor a sampling of these spiritous meal caps, both hot and cold.

# PINEAPPLE FLAMBE, COCONUT CREAM
(Serves 4)

> ⅓ cup milk
> ½ cup amber rum
> 4 egg yolks
> ¼ cup granulated sugar
> 1 dash nutmeg
> 1 dash salt
> ½ 4-oz. can shredded coconut
> ½ cup heavy whipping cream
> 1 No. 2 can pineapple spears, drained
> 3 tablespoons brown sugar
> 2 tablespoons butter
> 1 dash cinnamon

In the top part of a double boiler, combine the milk, ¼ cup rum, egg yolks, granulated sugar, nutmeg and salt, mixing very well. Cook over water simmering in bottom part of double boiler, stirring constantly with a wire whisk, until a thick sauce is formed. Remove from the fire at once. Add coconut and chill in the refrigerator until serving time. Just before serving, beat the heavy cream until thick and fold into the coconut mixture. In a chafing dish or saucepan, heat the drained pineapple spears, brown sugar, butter and cinnamon. When pineapple is hot, add the remaining ¼ cup rum. When the rum is hot, ignite it. When flames subside, spoon the pineapple spears onto serving dishes. Spoon hot sauce from pan over pineapple and top with coconut mixture.

## ZABAGLIONE
(Serves 4)

You will often see this dish spelled on menus as *zabaione*. Imported Marsala is authentic for the dessert, but this sweet wine is not available at all liquor stores. A dark, sweet sherry or Madeira may be substituted if necessary.

> 6 egg yolks
> 6 tablespoons granulated sugar
> ¾ cup Marsala wine
> ⅛ teaspoon salt
> ⅛ teaspoon ground mace or nutmeg

Arrange a double boiler so the water in the bottom part does not touch the top section. Combine all of the ingredients in the top section. Cook over simmering water, beating constantly with eggbeater, until mixture is thick and light. It will swell to about three or four times its original volume. Avoid overcooking or the mixture may curdle. From time to time, while beating, it may be necessary to scrape the corners of the pan with a spoon to prevent a thick layer from forming. While warm, serve in parfait glasses, glass punch cups or any glass dessert dish. May also be served over cooked or canned fruit such as pears or peaches or over light, plain sponge cake or ladyfingers.

## STRAWBERRIES SMETANA
### (Serves 4)

> 1 quart fresh strawberries
> 2 jiggers maraschino liqueur
> 1 jigger Grand Marnier liqueur
> Granulated sugar
> 1 cup sour cream
> Light-brown sugar

(If fresh strawberries are unavailable, frozen whole strawberries may be substituted.) Remove stems from strawberries. Wash, drain well and combine with both liqueurs. Add 2 tablespoons granulated sugar or more to taste and let marinate for 3 or 4 hours in the refrigerator. Spoon strawberries into serving dishes. Top with sour cream and sprinkle heavily with brown sugar.

## COUPE WITH BANANAS FLAMBE
### (Serves 4)

> 2 medium-size bananas, firm and ripe
> 2 tablespoons honey
> ¼ cup pineapple juice

1 tablespoon butter
1½ ozs. amber rum
½ oz. crème de cacao
1 pint coffee ice cream

Peel bananas. Cut in half lengthwise, then crosswise into 1-inch pieces. Place with honey, pineapple juice and butter in a saucepan or chafing dish. Heat over a low flame, turning frequently, until bananas are soft but not mushy and liquid in pan has been reduced to a thick syrup. Add the rum and crème de cacao. Ignite the liquors. When flames subside, spoon bananas and sauce over the ice cream in serving dishes.

## BLACK-CHERRY RUM FRITTERS
(Serves 4)

Most Americans now know that the story of Washington and the cherry tree was a whopping fable invented by Parson Weems. Although Washington didn't chop down a cherry tree, he did plant and graft hundreds of cherry trees on his estate and, of course, loved the fruit in all forms. Black-cherry fritters, dusted with confectioners' sugar, should be served at a late hour on a frosty night. Or serve them for luncheon as a main course with grilled bacon and hot maple syrup. In preparing this recipe, don't use sour cherries, but only dark, sweet cherries in heavy syrup. If there are pits, remove them.

1½ cups all-purpose flour
1½ teaspoons baking powder
½ teaspoon salt
2 eggs
½ cup cold water
3 tablespoons dark Jamaican rum
2 tablespoons salad oil
1 teaspoon grated lemon rind
1 cup drained, canned pitted black cherries
Deep fat
Confectioners' sugar

Sift together the flour, baking powder and salt. Separate the whites and yolks of the eggs. Beat yolks well and combine with the cold water, rum, salad oil and lemon rind. Add the liquid egg mixture and cherries to the dry ingredients. Stir only until the ingredients are blended, that is, until there is no pool of liquid in the mixing bowl and no dry flour is visible. Don't stir like a dervish or the fritters will be tough. In a separate bowl, beat the egg whites until stiff. Fold the egg whites into the batter; that is, add the whites using a down-over-up stroke with the mixing spoon.

Heat a kettle of deep fat no more than half-full to 380°—that is, until the first wisp of smoke appears. For best results, use a thermostatically controlled deep fryer. Drop the batter by tablespoonfuls into the hot fat. Don't make the fritters too big or they will be underdone in the center. (The fritters may also be fried in a shallow pan in ¼ inch of hot vegetable fat.) Remove from the frying kettle and drain on absorbent paper. Sprinkle generously with confectioners' sugar just before serving.

## CREPES SUZETTE WITH BRANDY-BENEDICTINE LIQUEUR
### (Serves 2)

Although the conventional crepes suzette are heated in a rather elaborate orange sauce, the recipe below is a simpler variation of the great French dessert. The procedure is threefold: The crepes are made in advance, spread with jam and rolled and, just before serving, flamed with brandy-Benedictine liqueur.

> ¾ cup all-purpose flour
> ¼ cup confectioners' sugar
> ⅛ teaspoon salt
> 2 whole eggs
> 2 egg yolks
> 1 tablespoon brandy
> 1¼ cups milk
> Salad oil
> Strawberry or raspberry jam for filling
> 2 tablespoons butter
> 2 tablespoons granulated sugar
> ½ cup brandy-Benedictine liqueur

Sift flour, confectioners' sugar and salt. In a separate bowl, combine the whole eggs, egg yolks, brandy, milk and 2 tablespoons salad oil. Beat well with a rotary eggbeater or wire whisk. Combine liquid and dry ingredients and beat well. Strain the batter through a wire strainer. Let the batter rest for 1 hour before making the crepes. Lightly grease a 7-inch frying pan with salad oil, using a pastry brush or crumpled paper towel for greasing. Heat pan over a medium flame. Pour just enough batter (about 3 tablespoons) to cover pan bottom, tilting the pan so that the batter reaches the edge. When bottom is brown, turn crepe over with a spatula. Cook other side only until it is not moist-looking. It needn't be browned. Cook crepes quickly, since long cooking toughens them. Continue until the batter is used up. On the lighter side of each crepe, spread 1 to 2 tablespoons jam. Roll up and place in chafing dish or crepe-suzette pan. When ready to serve, add butter and granulated sugar to chafing dish or pan. Sauté slowly until crepes are hot and coated with butter, turning them as necessary. Add the liqueur and set aflame. When flames subside, lift crepes to serving plates. Pour over them the sauce in which they've been cooked.

## MANDARIN OMELET WITH CURAÇAO
### (Serves 2)

> 1 10-oz. jar mandarin-orange segments
> 6 eggs
> 4 tablespoons granulated sugar
> ½ teaspoon vanilla
> Salt
> 2 tablespoons cold water
> 2 tablespoons butter
> ¼ cup curaçao
> Confectioners' sugar

For each omelet, beat 3 eggs well. Add 2 tablespoons granulated sugar, ¼ teaspoon vanilla, a dash of salt and 1 tablespoon cold water. Pour onto 1 tablespoon sputtering butter in the omelet pan. Immediately add half the orange segments—well drained—and stir well.

Wait a few seconds until the omelet begins to set on the bottom; then lift with spatula and tilt pan to permit uncooked egg to flow to the bottom, repeating several times if necessary. Keep flame low to permit omelet to cook through but not to burn. When it has become soft yet cohesive on top, slide the omelet to the far edge of the pan. Fold it in half or thirds and turn onto warm serving dish or platter. Repeat procedure for second omelet. Heat the curaçao in a small pan almost up to the boiling point. Light it and spoon over the omelets, letting it blaze until the flames die out. Sprinkle with confectioners' sugar and serve.

## FRESH PEACH MOUSSE
(Serves 4)

Frozen desserts made in freezer trays are often filled with indelibly sharp ice crystals. The mousse that follows is an exquisite exception.

> 3 cups sliced ripe peaches
> ¾ cup sugar
> 2 tablespoons kirsch
> 6 egg yolks
> ½ teaspoon almond extract
> 1½ cups heavy cream

Puree 1 cup of sliced peaches in an electric blender. Combine the remaining 2 cups with ¼ cup sugar and the kirsch. Chill until serving time. Beat egg yolks and remaining sugar in mixer at high speed until the yolks are fluffy—for about 3 to 4 minutes—and add almond extract. In a separate bowl, whip the cream. Fold whipped cream and peach puree into the egg-yolk mixture. Turn the mixture into ice tray and freeze until semihard. Then cover with waxed paper and complete freezing. To serve, scoop mousse onto serving dishes, spoon sliced peaches on top.

## BAVARIAN CREAM
(Serves 4)

> ½ cup whiskey
> 1 tablespoon unflavored gelatin

2 *eggs*
½ *cup sugar*
⅛ *teaspoon salt*
1 *cup milk*
½ *teaspoon vanilla*
⅛ *teaspoon freshly grated nutmeg*
½ *cup heavy cream*

(In this pudding, the whiskey flavor emerges just as it would in a julep or a highball. Use anything from straight old rye or fine 100-proof bourbon to a light blended whiskey to suit your own individual preference.)

Combine the gelatin and whiskey. Stir to soften the gelatin. Separate whites from yolks of the eggs and beat yolks well in the top part of a double boiler. Add sugar, salt and milk, mixing well. Cook over simmering water (the water should not touch the top section), stirring constantly, especially around circumference of pan, until mixture begins to thicken to the consistency of a thin cream soup. Remove from the fire. Add vanilla, whiskey-and-gelatin mixture and the nutmeg and stir until the gelatin dissolves. Pour into a wide mixing bowl and chill in the refrigerator until the mixture begins to thicken around the edges and is syrupy-looking in the center. Beat the egg whites until stiff. Fold into the gelatin mixture. Beat the heavy cream until whipped and fold into the gelatin mixture. Turn the mixture into a 1-quart gelatin mold previously rinsed in cold water and not wiped dry. Chill in the refrigerator until firm. To unmold: Run a knife around edge of mold. Dip bottom into hot water for several seconds and overturn onto serving platter. If a large mold isn't available, the cream may be spooned into champagne or sherbet glasses before it is jelled and served without unmolding.

# Creme de la Creme

Nero would probably have relished the succulence—
and certainly the spectacle—of a baked Alaska lapped
by flaming brandy, but this erratic emperor had to
pique his sweet tooth with simpler pleasures: Buckets
of snow from the distant Alps were borne to Rome
by the swiftest runners, then drenched in the rarest
fruit syrups and rushed to the festal board for the
approval of his surfeited palate. Just about a millen-
nium later, the first iced delights joined boar haunch
and blood pudding on the banquet tables of Britain's
lionhearted (and iron-stomached) sovereign, Richard
I, who returned from the Crusades with a dandy
recipe for orange ice presented to him by Saladin, the
gourmet-warrior sultan of Egypt and Syria. Enjoying
13th Century hospitality in Cathay, Marco Polo tasted
a frozen dessert made of milk and brought the strange
recipe back to Italy. But it remained for the French
to stir cream into what came to be known—and sometimes worshiped—as *glace*. Charles I became so enamored of this delicacy that he employed the services of
a full-time *glace* chef, who pledged himself to keep
the king's exclusive formulas top secret. When the
recipe was leaked, Charles properly put the ice-cream
man to death.

Happily, however, French *glace* recipes were soon
brought from France to America by our earliest and
most eminent epicure, Thomas Jefferson, who probably
had no idea what an avalanche of sweetness he was
setting in motion. In thousands of colonial kitchens,
Charles's favorite dessert—now quite accurately called

"ice cream" and cranked laboriously by hand in wooden tubs—began to supplement, and even pre-empt, such immemorial American standards as bread pudding and pumpkin pie. It wasn't long before entrepreneurs discovered that bigger tubs produced even more of the creamy stuff. Ice cream became a business. By 1867 it was being mass-manufactured and sweet fanciers from coast to coast were sitting on wire-backed chairs stowing it away amidst the candy-jar-and-ceiling-fan decor of cool urban oases called ice-cream parlors. The flavors were basic—vanilla, chocolate, strawberry and, for an exotic treat, burnt almond; even so, people couldn't get enough of it. With each generation, their numbers became legion, their tastes more sophisticated, until today Americans gobble up more than two billion quarts of ice cream a year in a cornucopian variety of flavors ranging from licorice to lingonberry. Even such frozen bacchanalia as Nesselrode pudding and cherries jubilee—long among the aristocracy of *haute cuisine*— have become familiar fare to burgeoning multitudes of ice-cream *cognoscenti*.

For the knowledgeable bachelor chef, there could be no more fitting finale to a cool terrace tiffin than such a chilled treat—perhaps one of those marron-dolloped hippodromes of oven-browned egg white and French vanilla ice cream known as a *meringue glacée* or a frappé-glassful of that velvety mixture of heavy cream, chilled liqueur and pureed fruit the French call a mousse. Before venturing to serve up such silken savories, however, any dessert*meister* worth his ice-cream scoop must comprehend some pointers on the art of frigid feasting.

The first fact to file away: *French* doesn't necessarily connote quality in ice cream. French ice cream in this country is made with egg yolks; although they do enrich the flavor, it is butterfat that imparts irresistible smoothness to the true French product—the more butterfat, the creamier the ice cream. Most American manufacturers use 12 to 14 percent butterfat. Connoisseurs, consequently, will seek out those few companies which raise the content to a buttery 20 percent.

French or American, *glace* gourmets steer clear of ice cream that's coarse or icy, gummy or frothy; there's no pleasure in eating—or paying for—an insubstantial product with air whipped into it during the freezing process. Lift the package; it must be hefty. The best plan is to buy ice cream freshly scooped out of five-gallon canisters at the local fountain. Bulk or brick, look above all for vivid flavors. The chocolate must be overpoweringly rich, the vanilla mature and refined; the coffee must call forth the aroma of freshly roasted beans; the strawberry must be bursting with juicy red flesh.

In the summer season, commercial ice creams emerge from these standard molds and appear in such far-out forms and flavors as plum and ginger, persimmon and peanut brittle. Some are inspired innovations, others merely bizarre; for the adventurous, all are worth a try. If even these exotica don't appeal, however, it's simplicity itself to ad-lib frosty fancies in answer to one's mood, using rich, pristine vanilla as a base and embellishing it with improvisations. Buttered-almond buffs have but to buy a three-ounce package of slivered almonds, bake them in a moderate oven with a few tablespoons of butter until light brown, salt them generously, soften a quart of vanilla in the refrigerator (not the freezer) until easily scoopable, then quickly stir in the almonds, secrete the mixture in the freezer for hardening and, just before serving, cover the collage with orgeat or almond syrup. *Voilà*—an almond ice cream to eclipse any frozen facsimile west of Rumpelmayer's.

For those game enough to attempt spellbinders, we suggest an exploration of the toothsome world of preserved fruits. Such sweets as brandied dates or Nesselrode, rum or brandy sauce, bottled guavas, mangoes or papayas can transform prosaic vanilla into the most dulcet extravagance in the dessert kingdom. Merely drain them, dice them and then perform the same easy ritual as with the toasted almonds. For a final fillip to such fruit-based creams, cap with canned coconut in heavy syrup.

The French *coupe*—not a car style but another realm of chilled summer delight—is simply an American sundae with no holds barred. Those with a well-developed ice-cream sense can whip up a million variations: Begin with any ice cream (from apricot to anisette) as a base, heap on any fresh fruit (from peach to pineapple), top with any liqueur (from crème de menthe to curaçao), any nuts (from cashews to filberts) and any fancied amount of sugared whipped cream—but, please, no corny maraschino crown. Or perhaps a parfait would be preferred. Years ago a *pièce de résistance* requiring hours of preparation, the parfait today is nothing more than a *coupe* that doesn't know when to stop—mountains of ice cream and compatible condiments are succulently stratified in a tall Pilsner glass.

Just remember that any ice-cream invention will conjure up more delight if it's scooped out and spooned up when it's just beginning to lounge on the soft side. If it's to be kept for any length of time, of course, it should be stored in the freezer. Simply transfer it to the main chamber of the refrigerator about half an hour before bestowing. And when the time comes, don't downgrade the delicacy by serving it in a glass-footed sherbet dish; use either a mammoth frappé or Pilsner glass or one of those oversize dessert dishes called nappies. Ladle out melba sauce, marrons and brandied fruits with a lavish hand. In all the recipes given here, serve up the portions in prodigal proportions, supply each man and maid with a great soup spoon, tuck napkins under collars—and dig in without further ceremony.

## BAKED ALASKA
### (Serves 4)

½ cup strawberry jam
1 small loaf sponge cake
4 egg whites
⅛ teaspoon salt
½ cup sugar
1 teaspoon vanilla
4 large scoopfuls ice cream, any flavor
12 brandied cherries
Confectioners' sugar

Spread half the jam on the bottom of a shallow 12-inch oval casserole. Cover with slices of sponge cake ½ inch thick. Spread balance of jam on top of the slices.

Beat egg whites and salt in mixer at high speed until soft peaks are formed. Slowly add the sugar and continue to beat until a stiff meringue is achieved. Add vanilla. Place ice cream in an oval mound in the center of the cake and cover completely with the meringue, shaping it evenly with a spatula. Arrange the cherries on the meringue. Sprinkle lightly with confectioners' sugar. Place in preheated 475° oven for 3 to 4 minutes or until the meringue is lightly browned, turning casserole, if necessary, to brown evenly. Cut crosswise into portions.

## CREPES SIR HOLDEN
(Serves 4)

> 1 10-oz. pkg. frozen strawberries
> 2 6-oz. jars crepes suzette
> 2 jiggers cognac
> 2 jiggers maraschino liqueur
> ½ cup heavy sweet cream
> 3 tablespoons confectioners' sugar
> 4 large scoopfuls vanilla ice cream
> 2 tablespoons toasted slivered almonds

(We have adapted this extravaganza from a *spécialité* at Horcher's renowned bistro in Madrid.) Thaw strawberries. Roll crepes and place in a saucepan or chafing dish. Inundate with liquid from the jars and heat until sizzling. Add cognac and maraschino liqueur and reheat. Set ablaze and let flame for a minute or so. Whip cream. Add sugar and whip a moment more. Spoon the crepes alongside ice cream on serving dishes. Spoon on the liqueurs and strawberries and crown with generous helpings of whipped cream. Sprinkle with almonds.

## APRICOT LIQUEUR CAKE A LA MODE
(Serves 4)

> 2 ozs. sliced almonds
> 1 tablespoon melted butter
> Salt
> Apricot liqueur

1 No. 2 can whole peeled apricots
¼ cup sugar
¼ teaspoon vanilla extract
½ cup heavy cream
2 tablespoons confectioners' sugar
4 slices loaf sponge cake, ½ inch thick
1 pint vanilla ice cream

Mix almonds and butter in a shallow pan and bake in oven preheated to 375° for about 10 minutes or until almonds are toasted light brown. Avoid scorching. Sprinkle almonds with salt. Sprinkle each slice of cake generously with apricot liqueur; use enough liqueur to moisten the cake without making it soggy. Drain apricots well. Remove seeds and put apricots into the well of an electric blender. Blend until pureed. Pour puree into a small saucepan. Add ¼ cup sugar and simmer over a low flame 5 minutes. Remove from fire and stir in vanilla extract. Chill apricot puree. Whip cream until stiff and fold in confectioners' sugar. Place cake on dessert plates and place a scoopful of ice cream on each piece of cake. Spoon apricot puree over ice cream. Top with whipped cream and sprinkle with toasted almonds.

## STUFFED JAMAICAN BANANAS
(Serves 4)

4 large ripe bananas
2 tablespoons frozen concentrated lime juice
2 tablespoons Jamaican rum
8 canned pineapple spears
1½ pints coffee ice cream
¼ cup coffee syrup

Cut about ¼ inch off both ends of each banana. Slit each skin lengthwise. Without tearing skin, cut the meat of each banana crosswise into chunks about 1 inch thick. Remove and mix with lime juice and rum. Place 2 pineapple spears on each banana skin. Top with small scoops of ice cream. Arrange banana chunks around them and flood with lime-juice mixture and coffee syrup.

## CHERRIES JUBILEE
### (Serves 4)

*1 20-oz. can pitted black cherries in heavy syrup*
*1 tablespoon cornstarch*
*2 tablespoons sugar*
*2 teaspoons sweet butter*
*2 jiggers light rum*
*4 large scoopfuls vanilla ice cream*
*2 jiggers curaçao*

Drain the cherries well, putting ¼ cup of the syrup (save the balance) into a small bowl with cornstarch and sugar. Mix well until there are no lumps and sugar is dissolved. Bring the balance of the juice to a boil over a low flame. Gradually add cornstarch mixture, stirring constantly. Simmer for about 2 minutes. Add butter and 1 jigger of the rum. Remove from heat and set aside. When ready to serve the dessert, scoop the ice cream into dessert dishes at the table and crown with hot cherry sauce. Heat cherries, curaçao and remaining jigger of rum in a chafing dish over a direct flame until hot but not boiling. Set ablaze and let flames flicker a minute or so; then spoon over ice cream.

# Cafe Ole!

For 600 years, professional bamboozlers have been
warning people about the evil effects of coffee. Centuries ago, men were told it would make them sterile.
Women were cautioned to avoid the wicked shot of
caffeine unless they wanted to be barren. But above
all, the dark-brown brew would fill one's nights
with shivery shakes and forever ruin one's sleep. Yet
consider the refreshing mood that inspired Milton to
write about coffee in *Comus:*

> " . . . *one sip of this*
> *Will bathe the drooping spirits in delight*
> *Beyond the bliss of dreams.*"

Some people will try to tell you that coffee's notorious stay-awake qualities are all in the mind. Students at the University of Chicago were once divided
into two test groups; one was given coffee, the other
milk. The coffee drinkers later slept badly; the milk
drinkers snoozed like logs. The only hitch was that
the milk had been secretly spiked with more caffeine
than coffee contains.

The very fact that coffee *can* keep some people
awake is what makes it such a magnificent drink.
What is proclaimed as its fault turns out to be its
virtue. Anyone from the pilot in his cockpit to the
author at his desk will agree that though the night
may have been intended for sleeping, the daytime
was planned for wakefulness.

The very first coffee ever brewed was discovered
by an abbot in an Arabian monastery. A goatherd

249

from the hills had brought to the abbot's attention some wild berries which his goats had eaten and which caused them to be unusually playful. The berries were the green seeds of the plant which we now know as *Coffea arabica*. The abbot was a venturesome fellow. He boiled the strange beans in water and concocted a novel and extremely pleasing beverage. The monks who were served the festive drink were wowed off their wooden seats.

As coffee drinking spread from Arabia to Turkey to Venice to France and finally to the New World, it enjoyed a checkered career, being alternately welcomed as man's most hospitable drink and damned because it was liquid joy and therefore a moral danger. In Turkey, for instance, during the 16th Century, coffeehouses were opened on every street corner. But the authorities soon discovered that Turks not only drank coffee in these coffeehouses but also played the tambourine and generally had a good time. So coffeehouses and coffee making in Turkey were prohibited, only to give rise to a swarm of coffee speak-easies where the outlawed brew again flowed in large volume. Like a later prohibition in a more advanced state, the Turkish edict eventually had to be rescinded. Coffeehouses returned by the thousands and travelers to Turkey told how the Turks, now on a grand national coffee jag, spent more money on their coffee than Parisians spent on their wine. The average Turk drank 20 cups of coffee a day.

Coffee historians describe a battle in Sweden between those who loved coffee and those who thought it was an evil and a threat to health. King Gustavus III settled the fracas in truly objective scientific fashion. Identical twins had been sentenced to death for murder. Gustavus ordered their sentences commuted to life imprisonment if the men would agree to a scientific test. One was to be given large doses of coffee and the other of tea. The twins and the Swedes waited and waited. Finally, at the tender age of 83, the tea drinker died. The Swedes now enjoy one of the highest per-capita consumptions of coffee in the world.

Frederick the Great of Prussia tried to eliminate coffee drinking because of the large amount of money that went to foreign exporters. "My people must drink beer," Frederick stormed in one of his manifestoes. Among those who disagreed vehemently with Frederick and the anticoffee crowd was a musician who had been invited to Frederick's court, Johann Sebastian Bach. The great composer was so riled by the stories claiming that coffee would make one sterile that he wrote his *Coffee Cantata*, published in Leipzig in 1732. In this composition, Bach tells the story of a slovenly father who threatens to break off his daughter's marriage unless the girl gives up her habit of coffee drinking. The girl agrees to renounce coffee, only to change her mind at the last minute when her mother and grandmother reveal that they have always been inveterate coffee drinkers, and who can, therefore, blame the daughter? Johann Sebastian Bach was the father of 20 children.

One need not question how the French people, the most civilized sensualists in the world, reacted to coffee. The greatest French satirist, Voltaire, limited himself to 70 cups a day. When Maria Theresa married into the French royal family in the 17th Century, she counted coffee beans as part of her dowry. Among the earliest of the chain coffee drinkers were two famous mistresses of Louis XV. Portraits in oil of Louis's playmates, Mmes. de Pompadour and Du Barry, show both of these girls sipping java from demitasse cups.

Coffee lovers have long since ceased to think about good and evil in the magic brown bean. They do know, however, that their daily drink is an excitant that revives their tired muscles, warms their hearts and livens their brains.

Knowing playboys have discovered that a good cup of coffee doesn't necessarily depend on the price but much more on freshness. Professional coffee tasters, for instance, ask when coffee was roasted, when it was ground and when it was brewed. For after each of these steps, the volatile magic which is the coffee flavor slowly disappears into the air.

Years ago, fresh coffee was delivered to restaurants and hotels each day just like bread or milk. When the coffeeboy brought his bags of coffee into the storeroom, the chef ran to feel the bags to make sure they were still warm to the touch, indicating that the coffee had been roasted only a half hour or so earlier.

The coffee was rushed to the waiting pantryman, who opened the bags and smelled the heavenly fragrance for which no words were adequate. When you open a pound of vacuum-packed coffee these days, it has the same original freshness the moment you take off the lid. But after you've used it once or twice and the pound of coffee has been exposed to the air, oxidation does its dirty work. If you could use the whole pound of coffee at one time, you'd enjoy all the original coffee goodness. For most bachelors, this is obviously impractical.

The average fellow keeping his own apartment doesn't want to burden his kitchen drawer with such utensils as rotary eggbeaters, needles for sewing poultry, basting syringes and other furnishings. But if he invested a few dollars in a small hand coffee grinder, and if he bought his coffee beans whole, and if he ground the coffee while his playmate waited in the living room, he would always be able to produce the kind of magnificent nightcap that both soothes and stimulates at the same time.

Any child can brew coffee, and we offer no primer on how to do it. But there are certain things to remember and certain things to avoid. As far as coffee makers are concerned, we find that the glass utensils are best. Aluminum and stainless steel are all right if they are kept scrupulously clean by burnishing, but the metals are frequently the source of unpleasant flavor, whereas glass tends to have little interaction with coffee.

It is extremely important to rinse out the coffee maker with scalding-hot water just before making coffee. If you smell the drip pot or percolator that has been used repeatedly, even though the utensil has been cleaned regularly, you will often detect a stale coffee odor. Fill it half-full with boiling water or very hot water from the faucet. Swish the water around to eliminate this off-odor before making coffee. After each use, the coffeepot should be washed well with warm soapy water. Use a stiff brush or scouring pad. After repeated uses, say every two or three weeks, the coffeepot should be cleaned with baking-soda water. (Fill the pot with water. Add one teaspoon baking soda for each quart of water and boil for five minutes. Rinse out well before making coffee.)

The old-fashioned coffeepot is seldom used these days, because it produces a thick, cloudy liquid that most people dislike. The percolator is an easy apparatus to handle, but you cannot always regulate the brewing time accurately and the coffee will not be of consistent strength at all times. Far superior is the automatic electric percolator that regulates the brewing time and keeps the coffee warm until it is served. The drip pot is especially recommended for its simplicity. One type of drip pot uses filter papers rather than the wire-mesh basket and produces a particularly clear strong coffee. The vacuum pots with top and bottom sections can produce a delicious brew, but they are sometimes troublesome because the top section may not separate from the bottom. An electric vacuum coffee maker does not cause this trouble readily and also keeps the coffee hot until served.

For any coffee maker, however, it is important to use the proper grind of coffee. One of the expensive vacuum-packed coffees now on the market is designed for all types of coffee makers. All other coffee brands indicate percolator, drip or vacuum type. If you grind your own coffee, you can regulate the grinder for the type of coffee you need for your own coffee maker.

It is vital to use enough coffee so that the brew is really deep, dark brown and not an insipid straw-colored fluid. For the average taste, allow two level measuring tablespoons per cup. There are special measuring spoons which are a perfect guide. In many percolators and drip pots, measurements are indicated for the amount of coffee necessary. When in doubt, use more coffee rather than less. For the man who loves coffee enough to experiment with some of the variations on the classical coffee theme, we offer the following beverages:

## TURKISH COFFEE
### (4 cups)

This is the thick, frothy brew served in Turkish cups, which are somewhat smaller than demitasse cups. The drink is a combination dessert and beverage, to be consumed like a fine liqueur. Place 3 tablespoons very finely pulverized coffee into a Turkish coffee maker (a long pot, tapering toward the top, without a lid). Add 4 teaspoons powdered sugar and 4 cups water, using the Turkish cup as the measuring unit. Bring to a boil. Remove the pot from the flame. Tap the side of the pot to settle the coffee and again bring to a boil. Remove from the flame again and tap sides. Repeat the process a third time and then serve the coffee at once, pouring so that the froth is equally divided among the four cups.

## CAFFÉ ESPRESSO
### (4 cups)

This delightful after-dinner coffee is a rich, dark brew served with lemon peel, brandy or anise. In large restaurants, it is sometimes made in special urns that steam rather than boil the coffee. In your apartment, you can use an espresso coffee maker, which is really a drip pot constructed so that you merely turn the pot upside down when the water boils and the boiling water flows over the coffee. Buy the French or Italian roasted coffee—roasted until the color is shiny black rather than the normal deep brown. Into the basket of the coffee maker, put 4 level measuring tablespoons of the finely ground coffee. Pour 2 cups boiling water over the coffee. As soon as some of the coffee has poured through, set the pot over the smallest possible flame to keep hot. Into each cup, put a piece of twisted lemon peel, ½ jigger cognac or ½ jigger anise liqueur. Pour the coffee into four demitasse cups and sweeten to taste.

## CAFÉ BRULOT

This is the glamorous show-off coffee prepared in a chafing dish. A special coffee maker designed for the brew is called the *brûlot* dish, but it is rarely used for this exotically spiced brew laced with cognac. Into the heated chafing dish, put 4 lumps sugar, 4 whole cloves, 2 pieces twisted lemon peel, 2 pieces twisted orange peel about 2 inches long, 2 sticks cinnamon about 1 inch long and 2 jiggers cognac. Let the cognac heat until it is quite warm. Stir gently. Hold a match to the cognac until it turns into a little lake of blue flames. Let it burn for 30 seconds; then add 4 demitasse cups fresh strong black coffee. Stir well and ladle into demitasse cups.

## CAFE AU LAIT

The French version of coffee with milk is made as follows: Allow 3 tablespoons coffee per cup instead of the usual 2. While the coffee is being made, heat milk up to the scalding point, that is, until the bubbles appear around the edge of the pot. Pour coffee and milk from separate pots into the coffee cups, using approximately half coffee and half milk.

## VIENNESE COFFEE
### (Serves 4)

*½ cup heavy cream*
*2 tablespoons sugar*
*4 teaspoons Dutch cocoa*
*8 teaspoons sugar*
*4 tablespoons heavy cream*
*4 cups fresh strong coffee*
*Cinnamon*

Whip the ½ cup heavy cream. Fold in 2 tablespoons sugar and keep chilled until needed. In each of the four cups, mix well 1 teaspoon cocoa and 2 teaspoons sugar. To each of the cups, add 1 tablespoon heavy cream, stirring well until a smooth paste is formed. Slowly fill each cup with hot coffee. Top with a generous mound of whipped cream and sprinkle lightly with cinnamon.

## ESPRESSO MILANO
### (Serves 4)

*4 demitasse cups espresso coffee*
*4 ozs. Liquore Galliano*
*Sugar*
*4 pieces lemon peel*

Prepare coffee in a high-speed espresso machine at table. If this equipment is not available, the Italian *macchinetta da caffè*, a drip coffee maker that allows the coffee to be poured twice over the grounds, may be substituted. Be sure to use the dark French or Italian roast coffee. Pour coffee into four demitasse cups and add to each 1 oz. Liquore Galliano. Sweeten with sugar if desired. Twist the lemon peel over the coffee and drop it into cup.

## COFFEE ZABAGLIONE
(Serves 4)

> 4 egg yolks
> 4 tablespoons sugar
> ⅛ teaspoon salt
> 2 tablespoons Marsala wine
> ¾ cup cold strong coffee

Beat egg yolks, sugar, salt and Marsala wine in a mixing bowl. Slowly stir the coffee into the mixture. Pour into the top part of a double boiler over simmering water and beat with a wire whip or rotary eggbeater until the mixture is thick and light. (Do not mistake the foam, which appears at first, for thickness.) When done, the zabaglione should look like a light cake batter and should be about four times its original volume. Pour into goblets or parfait glasses and eat with a spoon.

## COFFEE WITH CARDAMOM
(4 demitasse cups)

> 4 cardamom pods
> ¼ cup cognac
> 2 tablespoons curaçao
> 4 lumps sugar
> 2 cups (regular coffee-cup size) strong coffee

Crack the cardamom pods and remove the dark inner seeds. Put the cardamom seeds, cognac, curaçao and sugar into a chafing dish. Heat gently and, when the liquor is hot, set it aflame. Let it blaze for about 10 seconds. Pour the coffee over the liquor and stir well. Bring the coffee up to the boiling point, but do not boil. Pour into demitasse cups. Sip. Savor.

# Index

Aïoli with Horseradish, 58
Allspice, 204
Almonds
  Baked Crab with, Samoan Style, 77
  Rainbow Trout with, 55
  Shad Roe with, 59
Alsatian Pork Chops, 118
Anchovy
  Salad Dressing, 225
  Sour Cream and, Dip, 10
  Toast, with Scrambled Eggs, 36
Aniseed, 204
Appetizers, see Hors d'Oeuvres
Apricot Liqueur Cake à la Mode, 246
Asparagus Polonaise, Fried Egg, 214
Avocado
  Guacamole with Bacon, 9
  Shrimp and, Cocktail, 83

Bacon, Guacamole with, 9
Baked Alaska, 245
Baked Clams with Oregano, 91
Baked Crab with Almonds, Samoan Style, 77
Baked Deviled Crabs, 78
Baked Oysters Rockefeller, 98
Baked Scalloped Oysters, 100
Baked Veal Chops, 143
Baked Veal Cutlets with Vermouth, 146
Bananas, Stuffed Jamaican, 247
Barbecued Baby Turkey, 180
Barbecued Ham Steak, 154
Barbecued Hamburgers, 165
Barbecued Oysters, 97
Basil, 205
Bass, Boiled Whole Striped, 64
Bavarian Cream, 240
Bay Leaf, 205
Béarnaise Sauce, 202
Béarnaise Mint Sauce, 114

Béchamel Sauce, 198
Beef see also Hamburger, Roast Beef, Steak, Stew
  and Tomato Salad, 227
  Corned, Salad, 229
  Goulash, 172
  Polpetti in Brodo, 24
  Short Ribs of, Burgundy, 111
  Stew with Vegetables, 171
  Stroganoff, 172
Beignets
  Corn, 216
  Ham, Chive Dip, 16
Bigarade Sauce, 198
Birds see Game
Black-Bean Soup, 22
Black-Cherry Rum Fritters, 237
Blanquette of Veal, 145
Blender Hollandaise Sauce, 201
Blueberry Griddlecakes, 50
Bluefish with Tomatoes au Gratin, 61
Boiled Lobsters, 67
Boiled Whole Striped Bass, 64
Brandied Cheddar Spread, 9
Bread Sauce, 186
Breaded Lamb Chops Italienne, 120
Breakfast
  Coffee, 249–256
  Eggs, 31–44
Breast of Mallard Duck, 189
Broccoli Mornay with Ham, 215
Broiled Deviled Mackerel, 54
Broiled Lobsters, 69
Broiled Marinated Shrimps, 84
Broiled Oysters with Ham, 16
Broiling Steaks, 125–126

Cabbage, Burgundy, with Ham, 112
Caesar Salad, 227
Café see Coffee
Canapés see Hors d'Oeuvres
Cannelloni with Crab Meat, 49

257

Caper Butter, 137
Caraway Seeds, 205
Cardamon Seeds, 205
Carving
  Roast Beef, 108–109
  Turkey, 176–177
Cayenne Pepper, 205
Chasseur Sauce, 197
Cheese
  Brandied Cheddar Spread, 9
  Crepes with Roquefort, 48
  Liederkranz Spread, 15
  Omelet with Provolone, 44
  Roquefort Hamburgers, 167
  Roquefort Salad Dressing, 225
  Scrambled Eggs with Roquefort, 36
  Spinach Omelet Parmesan, 43
  Swiss Cheese and Kirsch Spread, 15
Cheeseburgers, 165
Cherries Jubilee, 248
Chervil, 205
Chestnuts Espagnole, 191
Chicken
  and Clams Valencia, 92
  Mulligatawny Soup, 26
  Tartlets, Hot, 12
Chicken Livers, Curried,
  Omelet with, 42
Chili Powder, 205
Chive
  Dip, with Ham Beignets, 16
  Sauce with Oysters Sauté, 101
Chops, 115–121
  Purchase, Preparation, 115–117
  Recipes
    Alsatian Pork, 118
    Lamb, Breaded, Italienne, 120
    Lamb, Fritto Misto, 119
    Pork, with Pepper Stuffing, 118
    Veal, Baked, 143
    Veal, with Ham and Truffles, 121
    Venison, Chestnuts Espagnole, 191
    Venison, Cumberland Sauce, 121
Chowder see Soup
Clams
  Varieties, 87–89
  Recipes
    Chicken and, Valencia, 92
    Baked, with Oregano, 91
    Balls, 91
    Chowder, Manhattan, 22
    Chowder, New England, 23
    on the Half Shell, 89
    Steamed Soft, 90
Coconut Cream, Pineapple Flambé, 235
Coffee
  History, 249–251
  Preparation, 251–253
  Utensils, 252–253

  Recipes
    Café au Lait, 255
    Café Brulot, 254
    Caffè Espresso, 254
    Espresso Milano, 255
    Turkish, 253
    Viennese, 255
    with Cardamom, 256
    Zabaglione, 256
Cold Dishes
  Corn Vichyssoise Soup, 27
  Salmon, Tartar Sauce, 56
  Shrimps, Mustard Dressing, 85
  Stuffed Lobster, 69
Coriander, 205
Corn
  Beignets, 216
  Freshness of, 212
  Vichyssoise Soup, 27
Corned Beef Salad, 229
Cornmeal Cakes, with Turkey and Sausage, 181
Coupe with Bananas Flambé, 236
Crab Meat
  Purchase, Preparation, 75–76
  Types, 75
  Recipes
    Baked Deviled, 78
    Baked, with Almonds, Samoan Style, 77
    Cakes, 77
    Cannelloni with, 49
    Cocktail, 76
    Foo Yong, 34
    Lobster Stuffed with, 71
    Salad, 76
Cream Gravy, 153
Crepes see also Pancakes
  Preparation, Utensils, 45–47
  Recipes
    Basic Batter, 47
    Sir Holden, 246
    Suzette with Brandy-Benedictine Liqueur, 238
    with Curaçao, 48
    with Roquefort, 48
Crostini of Ham, 157
Cumberland Sauce, 121
Cumin, 206
Curaçao
  Crepes with, 48
  Mandarin Omelet with, 239
Curry
  Butter, 10
  Omelet with Curried Chicken Livers, 42

Desserts see also Ice Cream
  Liquors for, 233–234
  Preparation, 234
  Recipes
    Bavarian Cream, 240

Black-Cherry Rum Fritters, 237
Coupe with Bananas Flambé, 236
Crepes Suzette with Brandy-
    Benedictine Liqueur, 238
Crepes with Curaçao, 48
Fresh Peach Mousse, 240
Mandarin Omelet with Curaçao,
    239
Pineapple Flambé, Coconut
    Cream, 235
Strawberries Smetana, 236
Zabaglione, 235
Devil Sauce, 198
Deviled Crabs, Baked, 78
Deviled Eggs, Stuffed, 13
Deviled Ham and Egg Spread, 14
Deviled Hamburgers, 165
Dill Sauce, 63
Dillseed, 206
Dips see Hors d'Oeuvres
Dressings see also under Salads
    Mustard, 85
    Oyster and Chestnut, 179
Duck
    Breast of Mallard, 189
    Roast Pressed, 190

Eggplant Parmigiana, 213
Eggs see also Omelets
    Purchase, Preparation, 31–33
    Recipes
        Asparagus Polonaise with, 214
        Crab-Meat Foo Yong, 34
        Finnan Haddie with, 60
        Poached, Benedict, 33
        Salmon, Hash-Browned with, 56
        Scrambled
            Indienne, 37
            with Anchovy Toast, 36
            with Chili and Tomatoes, 35
            with Roquefort Cheese, 36
            with Smoked Oysters, 37
        Shirred, with Shad Roe, 35
        Stuffed Deviled, 13
Espagnole Sauce, 196
Espresso, Caffè, 254
Espresso Milano, 255

Fennel Seed, 206
Filet Mignon, Mushroom Canapé, 128
Fillet of Sole, Fried, 57
Finnan Haddie with Egg, 60
Fish
    Purchase, Preparation, 52–54
    Recipes
        Bass, Boiled Whole Striped, 64
        Bluefish with Tomatoes au
            Gratin, 64
        Finnan Haddie with Egg, 60
        Fish Balls, Norwegian, 62
        Flounder, Mandarin Style, 61
        Halibut, Poached, Fondue, 59

Mackerel, Broiled Deviled, 54
Salmon, Cold, Tartar Sauce, 56
Salmon, Hash-Browned with
    Egg, 56
Salmon, Scotch, 55
Sardines, Grilled, White-Wine
    Butter, 17
Shad Roe with Almonds, 59
Shad Roe with Shirred Eggs, 35
Sole, Fried Fillet of, 57
Sole, Stuffed, with Mussels, 58
Trout, Rainbow, with Almonds,
    55
Florentine Minestrone, 29
Flounder, Mandarin Style, 61
Fondue see also Rabbit
    Poached Halibut, 59
French Dressing, 224
French-Fried Potatoes, 127
French Ice Cream, 242
French Omelet, 40
Fresh Ham, Roast, Burgundy
    Cabbage, 112
Fresh Peach Mousse, 240
Fried Fillet of Sole, 57
Fried Oysters, 97
Fried Shrimps, 82
Fried Smithfield Ham, Cream
    Gravy, 153
Fritters see also Beignets
    Black-Cherry Rum, 237
Frozen Vegetables, 213

Game
    Aging, 184–185
    Drawing
        Birds, 183
        Venison, 183–184
    Judging Age, 185
    Methods of Preparation, 185–186
    Recipes
        Duck, Breast of Mallard, 189
        Pheasant, Roast Dressed, 187
        Pheasant, Roast, with Bread
            Sauce, 186
        Quail, Roast, with Grapes, 188
        Venison Chops, Chestnuts
            Espagnole, 191
        Venison Chops, Cumberland
            Sauce, 121
        Venison, Roast, 191
Garlic, 206
Garlic French Dressing, Playboy's,
    225
Garlic Olives, 12
Giblet Gravy, 179
Ginger, 206
Glazed Ham Steak with Bourbon,
    153
Goulash, Beef, 172
Gravy
    Cream, 153

Giblet, 179
Roast Beef, 108
Griddlecakes see Pancakes
Grilled Sardines, White-Wine Butter, 17
Guacamole with Bacon, 9

Halibut, Poached, Fondue, 59
Ham
  Baking, 152
  Types, 150–152
  Recipes
    and Leeks au Gratin, 156
    and Mushroom Canapés, 10
    Beignets, Chive Dip, 16
    Broccoli Mornay with, 215
    Broiled Oysters with, 16
    Cornucopias, 154
    Crostjni of, 157
    Deviled, and Egg Spread, 14
    Fried Smithfield, Cream Gravy, 153
    Hash, Country Style, 157
    Roast Fresh, Burgundy Cabbage, 112
    Salad à la Playboy, 226
    Sauté with Grapes Madeira, 155
    Steak, Barbecued, 154
    Steak, Glazed, with Bourbon, 153
    Steak, with Crushed Pepper, 155
    Veal Scallopini with, 142
    Veal Chops with, and Truffles, 121
Hamburger
  Preparation, 162–163
  Purchasing beef for, 161–162
  Recipes
    Barbecued, 165
    Cheeseburgers, 165
    Deviled, 165
    Madrid, 166
    Ordinaire, 164
    Piquante, 165
    Roquefort, 167
    Steak, 163
    Steaks, Claret, 164
    Steaks, Hawaiian, 164
    Steak, Salisbury, 166
    Tempura, 165
Hash
  Ham, Country Style, 157
  Salmon, Browned with Egg, 56
Hawaiian Hamburger Steaks, 164
Herb Butter, 13
Hollandaise Sauce, 201
Hors d'Oeuvres
  Preparation, Serving, 6–8
  Recipes
    Brandied Cheddar Spread, 9
    Broiled Oysters with Ham, 16
    Crab-Meat Cocktail, 76

    Deviled Ham and Egg Spread, 14
    Garlic Olives, 12
    Grilled Sardines, White-Wine Butter, 17
    Guacamole with Bacon, 9
    Ham and Mushroom Canapés, 10
    Ham Beignets, Chive Dip, 16
    Herb Butter, 13
    Hot Chicken Tartlets, 12
    Hot Shrimps, Mustard Butter, 16
    Liederkranz Spread, 15
    Lobster Pâté, 8
    Oyster Pâté, 14
    Scallop Canapés, Horseradish Butter, 11
    Shrimp and Avocado Cocktail, 83
    Shrimp and Fennel Spread, 14
    Shrimp Canapés, Curry Butter, 10
    Sour Cream and Anchovy Dip, 10
    Stuffed Deviled Eggs, 13
    Swiss Cheese and Kirsch Spread, 15
Horseradish and Tabasco Sauce, 96
Horseradish Butter, 11
Horseradish Sauce, 200
Hot Chicken Tartlets, 12
Hot Shrimps, Mustard Butter, 16

Ice Cream
  Coupes, 244–245
  French, 243
  History, 242–243
  Meringue Glacée, 243
  Parfaits, 245
  Preserved Fruit Toppings, 244
  Purchase, 243–244
  Recipes
    Apricot Liqueur Cake à la Mode, 246
    Baked Alaska, 245
    Cherries Jubilee, 248
    Coupe with Bananas Flambé, 236
    Crepes Sir Holden, 246
    Stuffed Jamaican Bananas, 247
Irish Lamb Stew, 174
Italian Cuisine
  Aïoli with Horseradish, 58
  Cannelloni with Crab Meat, 49
  Clams, Baked, with Oregano, 91
  Eggplant Parmigiana, 213
  Lobster Fra Diavolo, 70
  Minestrone, Florentine, 29
  Mixed Salad, 229
  Polpetti in Brodo, 24
  Shrimp Marinara, 82
  Veal Cutlets Parmigiana, 144
  Veal Scallopini Marsala, 142

Veal Scallopini with Ham, 142
Veal Scallopini with Mushrooms, 143

Lamb
  Chops, Breaded, Italienne, 120
  Chops, Fritto Misto, 119
  Leg of, Roast, 110
  Saddle, Roast, Béarnaise Mint Sauce, 114
  Stew, Irish, 174
  Stew with Beans, 173
Liederkranz Spread, 15
Lobster
  Purchase, 66–67
  Types, 66
  Recipes
    Boiled, 67
    Broiled, 69
    Cold Stuffed, 69
    Fra Diavolo, 70
    Newburg, 71
    Omelet with Sherried, 43
    Pâté, 8
    Rolls, 72
    Stew à la Playboy, 73
    Stuffed with Crab Meat, 71

Mace, 206
Mackerel, Broiled Deviled, 54
Maître d'Hotel Butter, 126
Mandarin Omelet with Curaçao, 239
Mandarin Shrimp Salad, 230
Manhattan Clam Chowder, 22
Marinara, Shrimp, 82
Marjoram, 206
Marrow Butter, 127
Marrow Sauce, Red-Wine, 198
Mayonnaise, 221
Minestrone, Florentine, 29
Minute Steak, Caper Butter, 137
Minute Steak Stanley, 137
Mornay Sauce, 199
Mousse, Fresh Peach, 240
Mulligatawny Soup, 26
Mushrooms
  Canapé, 128
  Ham and, Canapés, 10
  Omelet with, in Sour Cream, 43
  Puree of Pea Soup with, 28
  Sauce, 113
  Stuffed, Rockefeller, 214
  Stuffed, with Porterhouse Steak, 138
  Veal Scallopini with, 143
Mussels, Stuffed Sole with, 58
Mustard Butter, 16
Mustard Dressing, 85

New England Clam Chowder, 23
Norwegian Fish Balls, 62

Olives, Garlic, 12
Omelets see also Eggs
  History, 38
  Purchase and Preparation, 39–40
  Recipes
    French, 40
    Mandarin, with Curaçao, 239
    Spinach, Parmesan, 43
    with Curried Chicken Livers, 42
    with Mushrooms in Sour Cream, 43
    with Provolone, 44
    with Sherried Lobster, 43
Onions, 222
  Pie, 216
  Soup, 24
Oregano, 206
Oysters
  Preparation, 96
  Types, 96
  Recipes
    and Chestnut Stuffing, 179
    Baked, Rockefeller, 98
    Baked Scalloped, 100
    Barbecued, 97
    Broiled, with Ham, 16
    Fried, 97
    Newburg with Truffles, 100
    Pâté, 14
    Sauté, Chive Sauce, 101
    Scrambled Eggs with Smoked, 37
    Sherried, 99
    Steamed, 97
    Stew, 98

Pancakes see also Crepes
  Preparation, Utensils, 45–47
  Recipes
    Cannelloni with Crab Meat, 49
    Griddlecakes, Blueberry, 50
    Griddlecakes, Maple Pecan Syrup, 49
Paprika, 206
Pâté
  Lobster, 8
  Oyster, 14
Pea Soup, Puree of, with Mushrooms, 28
Peach Mousse, Fresh, 240
Pepper Stuffing, 118
Petite Marmite, 20
Pheasant, Roast Dressed, 187
Pheasant, Roast, with Bread Sauce, 186
Philadelphia Pepper Pot Soup, 28
Pineapple Flambé, Coconut Cream, 235
Playboy's Garlic French Dressing, 225
Poached Eggs Benedict, 33
Poached Halibut Fondue, 59
Polpetti in Brodo, 24

Pork see also Ham, Bacon, Sausage
Chops, Alsatian, 118
Chops with Pepper Stuffing, 118
Porterhouse Steak, Stuffed Mushrooms, 138
Potatoes, French-Fried, 127
Provolone Cheese, Omelet with, 44
Puree of Pea Soup with Mushrooms, 28

Quail, Roast, with Grapes, 188

Rabbit see also Fondue
Shrimp, 82
Rainbow Trout with Almonds, 55
Rarebit see Rabbit
Red-Wine Marrow Sauce, 198
Red-Wine Steak Butter, 126
Remoulade Sauce, 202
Roasts see also Game
Beef
Aged, 104
Buying, 103–106
Carving, 108–109
Cooking, 107–108
Grades, 103–104
Gravy, 108
Dressed Pheasant, 187
Fresh Ham, Burgundy Cabbage, 112
Lamb Saddle, Béarnaise Mint Sauce, 114
Leg of Lamb, 110
Pheasant with Bread Sauce, 186
Pressed Duck, 190
Quail with Grapes, 188
Short Ribs of Beef Burgundy, 111
Turkey, 178
Veal Loin, Fresh Mushroom Sauce, 113
Venison, 191
Roquefort see Cheese
Rosemary, 207
Round Steak, Rustic Style, 138
Rum Sauce, 200

Saffron, 207
Sage, 207
Salads
Bowls, 219
Dressings
Anchovy, 225
French, 224
Mayonnaise, 221
Playboy's Garlic French, 225
Roquefort, 225
Sour-Cream, 225
Ingredients, 220–223
Mixing, 223–224
Recipes
Beef and Tomato, 227
Caesar, 227

Corned Beef, 229
Crab-Meat, 76
Ham, à la Playboy, 226
Italian Mixed, 229
Mandarin Shrimp, 230
Scallop, 231
Seashore, à la Playboy, 228
Tossed Green, 226
Salisbury Steak, 166
Salmon
Cold, Tartar Sauce, 56
Hash-Browned with Egg, 56
Scotch, 55
Sardines, Grilled, White-Wine Butter, 17
Sauces
Preparation, 193–196
Prepared, 195
Recipes
Aïoli with Horseradish, 58
Béarnaise, 202
Béarnaise Mint, 114
Béchamel, 198
Bigarade, 198
Bread, 186
Chasseur, 197
Chive, 101
Cumberland, 121
Devil, 198
Dill, 63
Espagnole, 196
for Egg Foo Yong, 34
Hollandaise, 201
Horseradish, 200
Horseradish and Tabasco, 96
Mornay, 199
Mushroom, 113
Red-Wine Marrow, 198
Remoulade, 202
Rum, 200
Sweet-and-Sour, 202
Tartar, 56
Tuna, 147
Velouté, 199
Vodka Fruit, 200
Sausage, Turkey and Cornmeal Cakes with, 181
Scallopini see Italian Cuisine
Scallops
Canapés, Horseradish Butter, 11
Salad, 231
Scotch Salmon, 55
Scrambled Eggs see Eggs
Seashore Salad à la Playboy, 228
Shad Roe
Shirred Eggs with, 35
with Almonds, 59
Sherry, Cooking with
Omelet with Lobster, 43
Sherried Oysters, 99
Shirred Eggs with Shad Roe, 35
Short Ribs of Beef Burgundy, 111

Shrimp
  Cleaning, 80–81
  Preparation, 81
  Purchase, 80
  Recipes
    and Avocado Cocktail, 83
    and Fennel Spread, 14
    Broiled Marinated, 84
    Canapés, Curry Butter, 10
    Cold, Mustard Dressing, 85
    Fried, 82
    Hot, Mustard Butter, 16
    Marinara, 82
    Pan Roast, 85
    Rabbit, 82
    Salad, Mandarin, 230
    Shrimpburgers, 84
Smithfield Ham, Fried, Cream Gravy, 153
Sole
  Fried Fillet of, 57
  Stuffed with Mussels, 58
Soup
  Preparation, 18–20
  Recipes
    Black-Bean, 22
    Chicken Mulligatawny, 26
    Corn Vichyssoise, 27
    Florentine Minestrone, 29
    Manhattan Clam Chowder, 22
    New England Clam Chowder, 23
    Onion, 24
    Petite Marmite, 20
    Philadelphia Pepper Pot, 28
    Polpetti in Brodo, 24
    Puree of Pea Soup with Mushrooms, 28
Sour Cream
  and Anchovy Dip, 10
  Omelet with Mushrooms in, 43
  Salad Dressing, 225
Spices
  Preparation, Purchase, 203–204
  Storage, 204
  Uses, General, 207–209
  Uses, Specific, 204–207
Spinach Omelet Parmesan, 43
Spreads see Hors d'Oeuvres
Steak see also Ham, Hamburger
  Broiling, 125–126
  Cuts, 123–124
  Purchase, 123–124
  Recipes
    Filet Mignon, Mushroom Canapé, 128
    Minute, Caper Butter, 137
    Minute, Stanley, 137
    Porterhouse, Stuffed Mushrooms, 138
    Round, Rustic Style, 138
Steamed Oysters, 97
Steamed Soft Clams, 90

Stew
  Purchase and Preparation, 169–170
  Recipes
    Beef Goulash, 172
    Beef Stroganoff, 172
    Beef, with Vegetables, 171
    Irish Lamb, 174
    Lamb, with Beans, 173
    Lobster, à la Playboy, 73
    Oyster, 98
Strawberries Smetana, 236
Stuffed Deviled Eggs, 13
Stuffed Jamaican Bananas, 247
Stuffed Lobster, Cold, 69
Stuffed Lobster with Crab Meat, 71
Stuffed Mushrooms Rockefeller, 214
Stuffed Mushrooms, with Porterhouse Steak, 138
Stuffed Sole with Mussels, 58
Stuffing, Oyster and Chestnut, 179
Stuffing, Pepper, 118
Sweet-and-Sour Sauce, 202
Swiss Cheese and Kirsch Spread, 15

Tarragon, 207
Tartar Sauce, 56
Thyme, 207
Tomato
  Beef and, Salad, 227
  Bluefish with, au Gratin, 61
Tossed Green Salad, 226
Trout, Rainbow, with Almonds, 55
Truffles
  Oysters Newburg with, 100
  Veal Chops with Ham and, 121
Turkey
  Carving, 176–177
  Purchase, 178
  Recipes
    and Cornmeal Cakes with Sausage, 181
    Barbecued Baby Turkey, 180
    Cutlets, Cranberries and Cointreau, 179
    Roast, 178
Tuna Sauce, 147
Turkish Coffee, 253
Turmeric, 207

Utensils, Culinary, see also Carving
  for Coffee, 252–253
  for Roasts, 105
  for Salads, 219

Veal
  Blanquette of, 145
  Cakes with White Wine, 147
  Chops, Baked, 143
  Chops with Ham and Truffles, 121
  Cutlets, Baked, with Vermouth, 146
  Cutlets Parmigiana, 144
  Cutlets, Tuna Sauce, 147

Loin, Roast, Fresh Mushroom
Sauce, 113
Scallopini Marsala, 142
Scallopini with Ham, 142
Scallopini with Mushrooms, 143
Wiener Schnitzel à la Holstein,
143
Vegetables
Corn, 212
Frozen, 213
Onions, 211–212
Purchase, 212
Recipes
Asparagus Polonaise, Fried Egg,
214
Broccoli Mornay with Ham, 215
Burgundy Cabbage, with Roast
Fresh Ham, 112
Corn Beignets, 216
Eggplant Parmigiana, 213

Onion Pie, 216
Stuffed Mushrooms Rockefeller,
214
Velouté Sauce, 199
Venison Chops, Chestnuts Espa-
gnole, 191
Venison Chops, Cumberland Sauce,
121
Venison, Roast, 191
Viennese Coffee, 255
Vodka Fruit Sauces, 200

White-Wine Butter, 17
Wiener Schnitzel à la Holstein, 143

Yorkshire Pudding, 109

Zabaglione
Coffee, 256
Hot, for dessert, 235